100 HIKERS
100 HIKES

100 HIKERS 100 HIKES

From TOBERMORY to KILIMANJARO

Andrew Camani

cam*trek* books

Dedicated to my three daughters,

Carys, Jesse and Katherine,

"The Blessings in my life".

ACKNOWLEDGMENTS

I would like to acknowledge all of the hikers who have given me inspiration and in particular the other 99 authors who were willing to share their most memorable hikes with me.

Finally, I wish to thank Shirley Caspin, our covergirl, for being such a great sport. It must have taken a hundred different poses before attaining the one that finally captured the underlying essence of the book.

SHUTTERSTOCK photos appear courtesy of the authors as credited on pages:
10, 15, 21, 28, 43, 51, 60, 62, 75, 92, 93, 96, 122, 140, 143, 155, 158, 162, 168, 172, 180, 187, 194, 211, 216, 218, 221

PLEASE NOTE: The choice of whether to use imperial or metric measurements in the following essays was left to the individual contributors.

Published by
CAMTREK BOOKS
c/o Andrew Camani
52 Kipling Road
Hamilton, Ontario
L8S 3X5
905-523-9152

Copyright © 2011 Andrew Camani

Library and Archives Canada Cataloguing in Publication

Camani, Andrew, 1951-
   100 hikers 100 hikes : from Tobermory to Kilimanjaro / Andrew Camani.

ISBN 978-0-9868209-0-8

1. Hiking. 2. Trails. I. Title. II. Title: One hundred hikers one hundred hikes.

GV199.5.C36 2011   796.51   C2011-900429-1

Printed in China

Contents

Water, water everywhere and plenty of drops to drink! — Photograph by Andrew Camani

Introduction

ANDREW CAMANI

Ever since I can remember, I have been passionate about sports and the great outdoors. In 1998, I became a member of the Bruce Trail Organization, which has proven to be a major inspiration in the creation of this book. The Bruce Trail is continuously evolving. It is currently an approximately 900-kilometre patchwork of landscapes along the Niagara Escarpment from Niagara to Tobermory. This wonderful trail system has been designated a UNESCO World Biosphere Reserve and is ranked among the Top 10 hiking trails in the world. It is hard to believe that it is maintained solely by a group of generous and hard-working volunteers.

Several years of participating in numerous organized hikes have afforded me excellent opportunities to both explore many of the gorgeous landscapes of southern Ontario and to meet interesting fellow hikers who wear a multitude of different hats and who view the world through a multitude of different lenses.

Gathering these 100 stories from 100 different people who have experienced 100 different local and international hikes in their own unique, personal ways, has been an amazing experience.

Each story retraces the hiker's footsteps and personal thoughts. In short, by reading each story you will experience the hike through the eyes of the individual who made the journey. After reading each passage, all you have to do is close your eyes and imagine yourself being part of the hike.

I hope that by the time you finish reading this book, you will be inspired to hike one or more of these trails.

DeCew Falls, St. Catharines, Ontario. Captain John DeCou (later spelled DeCew) purchased 40 hectares, including the falls, from a Native, in exchange for an ox and a blanket.

— Photograph by Sergei A. Tkachenko

The Niagara Section in One Day

ANDREW CAMANI

As the 2007 fall hiking season came to an end, I needed a goal for the coming year, something to get me through the cold Canadian winter. After kicking ideas around for nearly a week, I decided that my goal would be to attempt to hike the entire Niagara section of the Bruce Trail in one day. I marked Saturday, April 5, 2008, on my calendar. I would start at midnight and try to finish the entire section before nightfall.

Over the winter, I gradually created a hike plan. Since I was going to begin in the dark, I would need a headlamp. But would a headlamp cast enough light? What if the light stopped working halfway through the night? I decided to purchase a hand-held floodlight.

My second concern was footwear. I had a pair of winter hiking boots, but they were heavy. I knew my running shoes would be a poor choice for that time of year because I anticipated the trail would be wet and muddy. In addition, there were streams that would have to be crossed. I decided I would begin the hike in my boots, then change into my running shoes when my feet became sore.

The next problem I had to solve was how much food and drink to carry. I calculated that I could get by with two bananas, a can of potato chips, a bag of licorice allsorts, pretzels, and six bottles of Gatorade.

From my several backpacks, I chose the one that I considered perfect for the job. A hiking stick was a must. It would be beneficial for balance when crossing streams and would help me up and down in difficult terrain. Last but not least, I packed a camera to capture all those magical moments.

During the week leading up to the hike, I made it a point to watch the evening news for its five-day weather forecast. Saturday was looking pretty good: sunny, a high of 13 degrees Celsius. However, Friday's forecast called for showers all day.

When I finished work on Friday, I hurried home, ate a medium pizza, and tried to get some pre-departure sleep. At five to eleven my clock radio woke me up. I had arranged to meet my ride to Queenston at Lion's Pool Park in Grimsby, where I would leave my car a short walk from the official end of the Niagara section. When I arrived at Lion's Pool Park, my ride was waiting.

We made it to Queenston shortly after midnight. Before I set off on my adventure, I had my picture taken beside the stone cairn that marks the official start of the Bruce Trail as well as the beginning of its Niagara section.

I had no sooner begun my hike than I heard the honking of a truck. I turned to look and heard the driver yell, "Good luck! I hope you make it!" It was at this point that I realized there was no turning back. I was truly alone. My car was 84 kilometres away, and the only way I was going to get to it was by walking. It was a good thing that I had purchased the floodlight, as the headlamp was not as strong as I anticipated it would be, and I initially had difficulty seeing the white markers on the trees. However, I finally located the trail before it entered the woods.

After spending an uneventful time in the woods, I approached the "Screaming Tunnel." Legend has it that if you light a wooden match while standing in the middle of the tunnel, you will hear a chilling scream and your match will blow out. According to the legend, someone once met their untimely death in the middle of this cold, strange tunnel.

Hiking at night with a floodlight is like walking in an illuminated bubble. Beyond that bubble, darkness surrounds you completely. I quickened my step as I entered the tunnel. I felt the beating of my heart get stronger as I increased my pace. I glanced behind me periodically, just to make sure no ghost was following me. It is funny how these things affect you when you are hiking alone and in the dark.

Short Hills Provincial Park confirmed that I had made the right decision by wearing hiking boots. The trail was very muddy. In addition, I got my first exposure to ice and slippery conditions that I had not taken into account when planning my hike.

The landscape in the Short Hills area is quite unlike anywhere else in Niagara. It was molded into a jumble of small-but-steep hills and valleys by glaciers during the last ice age. As the sun began to rise, I saw the first and only deer on my hike. Up to this point, I had seen a lot of rabbits racing across the trail and a small snake.

Beyond Rockway Community Centre, a sudden loud gunshot nearly made me jump out of my skin. Be warned that the trail skirts a rifle range at this point.

Thank goodness it happened in the daylight, otherwise I do not know how I would have reacted.

After passing several vineyards, I re-entered the bush to reach Louth Conservation Area. This part of the Niagara section of the Bruce Trail proved to be the muddiest and wettest part of the hike. Once again my boots saved the day. Even though my feet were beginning to hurt, they were at least dry.

When I reached Twenty Mile Creek, the path was pretty much ice-covered. In places, I had to hold onto young trees as my feet slipped off the path towards the embankment. Finally, I made my way to the stairs leading up to Ball's Falls Conservation Area. In the park, I found a picnic table. After having a nutrition break, I swapped my hiking boots for my running shoes. Oh, what a feeling. It was like welcoming home an old friend.

Leaving the park, the trail takes you through a mature stand of beech and maple trees before climbing the escarpment's long, gradual slope. After the icy conditions I faced at Twenty Mile Creek, I thought the worst was over. However, this slope up the escarpment was the worst I have ever encountered. They could have used it as a Winter Olympics bobsleigh run. I literally had to get down on all fours to make it up the incline. More than once I lost my footing.

Eventually, I made it to the top. Here, I paused a few minutes to take in the beautiful views of the vineyards and Cave Springs. There are some intriguing legends associated with Cave Springs, including stories of a lost cave that contains untold riches in Native artifacts.

At Thirty Road, still 7 kilometres from my car, I realized darkness was approaching. I got out my floodlight, put on my headlamp and jacket, and consumed the last of my snacks.

The final stages of my hike took me over rough terrain. It was not until I reached the top of the escarpment, near Mountain Road, that I began to relax. I had only about a kilometre to go. The descent to Gibson Street proved a bit tricky, but no real problem.

I crossed the pedestrian bridge over Forty Mile Creek and officially reached the end of the Niagara section of the Bruce Trail. I had done it. I had achieved my winter's goal of hiking the entire section in a single day.

An Eventful Hike

PETER LEENEY

SATURDAY, JUNE 7th — FELKER'S FALLS — 12 KILOMETRES

Meet at 10:00 AM at Battlefield Park, Stoney Creek. See Maps 6-7. From QEW take Centennial Parkway (Hwy 20) south 3 kilometres to King Street. Turn left, then immediately look for park entrance on your right. We will move some cars to Gage Park, then walk back along the escarpment edge through Felker's Falls Conservation Area. Explore Devil's Punchbowl if time permits. The hike is rated medium – 4.

The weather was warm and sunny. I was looking forward to a nice, simple hike. The first inkling of trouble was the sign we noticed by the side of Highway 20 in Stoney Creek: "Shuttle bus to battle." The clincher was the row of orange safety cones across the entrance to Battlefield Park. June 7-8 was the weekend scheduled for the re-enactment of the War of 1812's Battle of Stoney Creek.

There was no place to park at Battlefield Park unless you had the foresight to wear a costume from the early 1800s. Hiking boots and quick-dry shirts did not qualify. The Lions Club of Stoney Creek volunteer who was controlling access was quite helpful. He suggested we might be able to park at a school further down Highway 20.

We never did locate the school, but in the Golden Horseshoe map book we were able to find a public swimming pool with a small parking area two blocks away. As we drove down a side street we noticed two or three people setting up garage sales, no doubt hoping to take advantage of the local events.

I walked back to Battlefield Park and stood at the entrance with my pack on, trying to look as much like a hike leader as possible. As hikers arrived looking for a place to park, I directed them to the pool parking lot, where my wife, Judy, was waiting to organize everyone. Eventually, 20 hikers gathered at the swimming pool, and we set off on the car shuttle to Gage Park and the start of the hike.

The few garage sales had now become a full-fledged street sale, with vans and pickup trucks parked all over the place, but we managed to thread our way through the obstacle course and finally arrived at Gage Park.

By this time, everyone was ready to hike. Up the Gage side trail we went. At the train tracks, we stopped to let a freight train go by. The train stopped. We waited. It went forward a little and stopped. It backed up and stopped. We waited. Finally, we decided to walk around the train. Ten minutes and a kilometre later, we made our way around the train and began our climb up the escarpment on the side trail. The train eventually rolled away to the west.

A bit further along we met a woman walking her dog — two dogs in fact, and a parrot perched on her shoulder. Her large, excitable Doberman Pinscher obviously did not care for hikers using his piece of the trail. He jumped and twisted and growled but fortunately remained tethered on his short leash. Dog number two, a tiny Chihuahua, ran around barking with great enthusiasm and attempted to

Devil's Punchbowl, Stoney Creek.
Other physical features along the Niagara Escarpment that include the Devil's name are Devil's Pulpit (Caledon Hills), Devil's Glen (Blue Mountain), and Devil's Monument (Peninsula).
— Photograph by SF photo

chase us down the trail. "Charlotte" (the Chihuahua) was less than 4 inches tall, so we all ignored her. The parrot took it all in and did not say a word.

We hiked into the Devil's Punchbowl before returning along the trail to Battlefield Park, where we were just in time to see the final stages of the re-enactment of the Battle of Stoney Creek. We asked what the score was but did not get a sensible answer. It was interesting to see the different coloured uniforms and hear the bands. The muskets sounded like firecrackers. When the battle ended, the casualties got up and walked around. It all seemed very civilized.

As we walked back down the street to the swimming pool parking lot, a woman tidying up her garage sale said, "Going hiking?"

"Just finishing," I said. "We started at Gage Park about 10:30."

"Gage Park!" she said. "I don't believe it!"

I am not sure I believe it either, especially the part with the parrot.

Fire and Ice on Mount Nemo

LES BABBAGE

Like many early summer days in southern Ontario, June 22, the first day of summer 2008, begins with high humidity and turns up the steam as the day progresses.

Four intrepid hikers gather at the Great Falls parking lot on Grindstone Creek, just south of Waterdown. Gert, Linda, Marilyn and I have all been overtaken by that magnificent obsession, the Bruce Trail end-to-end. Our paths crossed at various hiking events, and we formed the Fellowship with the mission of completing the Niagara, Iroquoia and Toronto sections of the trail.

Today, we plan to advance our cause by 25 kilometres, to the intersection of Bind Line and Britannia Road, a route that features fields and woodlands, with occasional panoramic views, followed by a major stretch of "road work" before reaching the sanctuary of Mount Nemo Conservation Area.

Hikers are philosophical about road sections. They are the "bits in between" that allow us to experience the highlight reel of hiking. In some instances, when the road is little travelled and the roadside undeveloped, such sections can be quiet walks through the woods.

Unfortunately, this is not the case with Walkers Line. On a busy weekend, this 2-kilometre stretch features constant traffic, which, paired with the rising humidity, lulls the weary hiker into a trance-like state that is broken only upon sight of the blaze indicating where the road turns.

Entering Mount Nemo Conservation Area is like suddenly being transported to another world. The dull roar of SUVs recedes and the peace of a northern rainforest settles over us. Mature trees and a rich variety of undergrowth surround us. Ahead, the trail winds its way impossibly up the northeast face of the Ontario version of a mountain. Picking our way through crevices and giant boulders, we climb slowly to the crest.

As we pull ourselves wearily onto the plateau that forms the "peak" of Mount Nemo, we are greeted by rumbles of thunder from the west — the direction we must follow in order to complete the day's mission. The drumbeat is soon accompanied by dramatic flashes of lightning. We ignore our bodies' pleas for a rest break and accelerate our pace.

On this day we do not pause to enjoy the wonders of Mount Nemo. We walk as fast a pace as we can maintain, glancing only briefly at the views to north and east, the lightning now putting on an impressive light show.

Finally, we reach the park road and follow the trail across Guelph Line onto Colling Road. A recent reroute has moved the trail off the road and over a stile to a narrow strip of land between the fence and what proves to be a massive gravel pit. Unfortunately, a wet spring has nourished a dense crop of grasses and weeds that few other hikers have ventured through. The going is as heavy as climbing the side of Mount Nemo!

We emerge back onto the road with only a 2-kilometre stretch of Blind Line between us and the relative safety of our car. The storm is directly overhead, and the rolls of thunder have become a near continuous roar accompanied by a major fireworks display across the heavens. If we can increase our pace just a little more, we might make it.

But we are not to escape the fury of this intense storm. A fusillade of hailstones bursts onto our heads. Regretting that I did not wear a hat, I shelter my head with my arms, only to withdraw them as the stinging of icy projectiles on my bare arms proves worse than the pain of "using my head." We speed up to a jog, hoping to outrun the onslaught, but hailstones the size of moth balls are piling up on the road, creating a surface like marbles, which makes every step a treacherous adventure. Finally, within a kilometre of our refuge, we disobey all the rules for dealing safely with a lightning storm and take shelter under a large tree that at least slows the bombardment of ice.

The hail is soon replaced by torrential rain, and we watch as nearby driveways are washed onto the road. Time to make a break for it! We soon reach our end-of-hike car and set out on the return trip to Waterdown and our start car. Rain is falling so heavily that I cannot reliably see the road, so we drive at a crawl all the way. We reach the Waterdown parking lot, but the downpour persists, and there is no way anyone is about to make the 5-foot run to the other car that will take them home.

Instead we sit in my car and laugh at how soaked we are, how crazy hikers have to be to venture out on the trail in all weather conditions, and how no-one will ever believe our story of a major ice storm on the first day of summer.

Where Is the Car?

BILL FULTON

It was the spring of 1997 and Elizabeth Beckett was in the process of fulfilling a dream. She was going to complete the entire Bruce Trail as a celebration of her 50th birthday. Friends were to take turns accompanying her, and on this day it was my turn. I was sure she had said to meet her at the Tim Horton's at Aberdeen and Locke in Hamilton at 7:30 in the morning. There I was, on time and patiently waiting for her.

Forty-five minutes passed and no Elizabeth. I finally phoned her husband, Gordon, who said that she had left some time ago, and that he knew that if the two of us got out there on the trail we would be lost forever! It turned out that Elizabeth was waiting several blocks away, at the Tim Horton's in the Fortinos Plaza on Dundurn Street. After expounding on our good fortune at finding each other, we set off, an hour late, for Terra Cotta, in the Toronto section of the trail. But this failure to rendezvous at the initial meeting place and time was a bad omen!

Terra Cotta was the projected end-point of our hike, so we parked our return car near a prominent, well-maintained stile along a well-travelled road and proceeded to our starting point in the other automobile. It was well into the morning when we began our hike. The weather was ideal for hiking. The wildflowers were abundant. We saw a fox. The conversation was great. We ate lunch sitting on a log while enjoying the scenery. We walked and we walked and did not tire.

Finally I said to Elizabeth, "Do you think that we should have arrived at the car by now?" She agreed that, since it was after five in the afternoon, we probably should have. We noticed a large family picnic nearby and asked the picnickers if they knew where the highway was. They indicated that it was 5 miles back. We could not believe it. We had overshot our goal by 5 whole miles!

Being rational people, we initially considered taking a taxi, but there are no taxis on this part of the Bruce Trail! We finally decided that our only solution was to walk back. With heads hung low and shoulders bowed from the weight of our packs, we started our extra hike. Then a light went on in Elizabeth's head. There was a man cutting his lawn, and she announced that she was going to ask him for a ride to the car. I was pretty tentative about this imposition on the man's possible good nature but went along with the idea. She approached him with her proposal, but he said no! Well, this was the final straw for Elizabeth. He had a nice rock garden, and she said, "I am going to kick his rocks!" I said that those were not the rocks that she really wanted to kick. We again set off on our long walk.

However, goodness prevailed, and the gentleman soon pulled up beside us in his car. He told us that he had hiked a lot in his day and was willing to give us a ride. We climbed happily into his car and were where we wanted to be in no time. Before he left, he helpfully pointed out that we had left our vehicle at a side trail prominently marked with a blue blaze.

Keeping It Natural

CYNTHIA EMILI

Hiking the Bruce Trail under nebulous skies; the forest floor glistens with an early morning blessing from the rain gods. Flora reborn as the terra descends, our beginner boots seep into muck with no end. A welcoming wooden bridge made just for us to pass over marshes and tall grass. We stop to take it in, this flowering wilderness, how it has blossomed since last weekend. An amber bottle floats still beneath us, trapped by a tall, watery prison speckled in algae. It is so out of place. How long has it been there?

We continue on our adventure through ups and downs, washing our hands with dewy leaves. Deer prints appear. There are others who share our path. What do they think of what we leave behind?

Reaching into my backpack, I pull out a clear bag and begin to collect the manmade objects. Another wooden bridge appears. The first step is unnerving. It floats and bobs over water, with elegant swans cozy in their cove.

When we head back, the amber bottle is waiting patiently for us. Lying flat on the bridge, I reach for it. "I have got it!" I smile while emptying its contents and gently place it in my bag.

Ascending the forest with foreign objects in hand and mud on our shoes was all that remained of our adventure on the Bruce.

The Gourmet Hiker

SHARON KERR

The Bruce Trail has a mysterious gourmet hiker. He comes out with many delicacies, and I have the pleasure of trying a few: shrimp with garlic, crepe suzette and, the best, cherries jubilee.

Who would ever think that lunch on the Bruce Trail would feature such a decadent dessert as cherries jubilee?

The gourmet hiker carried all his gear for the day — cutlery, bowls, cherries, and some rum. A friend of his carried the ice cream, packed in several ice packs to prevent it from melting.

After lunch, the gourmet hiker asked if anyone would like dessert. No one refused. It was amazing to see a dollop of ice cream drop into a bowl and remain solid on this very, very hot day. The gourmet hiker then added the warm cherries on top of the ice cream, topped it off with a dash of rum and served it to all who wished to have a taste.

Once lunch was over, we were all very content, and as we continued to hike through the woods, there was an aroma of rum wafting in the air.

The Saga of the Soggy Seven

GORDON PROUDFOOT

In 2001 and 2002 Phill and Anne Armstrong led a group of hearty souls on the Bruce Trail "End-to-End in Quarters," the goal being that we would hike from Niagara to Tobermory in two years, hiking only spring and fall each year. Eighteen of us reached the cairn in Tobermory on November 3, 2002. Not all of the 18 were with us for the whole way; some used the opportunity to hike the portions of the trail they needed to complete an end-to-end. There was a "core" group of 14 or 15 that stuck it out together for the whole distance. Phill and Anne were probably the only ones who knew all the participants individually. Many of us came together as complete strangers. We became a wonderful, happy family and

Early morning near Tobermory. — Photograph by Gareth Leung

forged strong bonds as we journeyed the Niagara Escarpment. Many of us are very close friends to this day. The camaraderie forged on a challenge such as an end-to-end has to be felt to be believed.

We had an extremely dedicated record keeper to keep a log of our hikes. Tom made up a detailed summary of all the hikes and invited us to compile reports of each hike. With such a large number of hikers, it is inevitable that not all walkers can be present for all the scheduled hikes on the set dates. Hence, the need for small groups to make up hikes they have missed or will miss. Tom made great job of keeping all this straight.

Seven of us completed hike number 20 of the end-to-end, from Caledon Trail (32.3) to Centreville Creek Road (49.1) on Sunday, August 19, 2001. The overall plan of the End-to-End in Quarters was to hike south to north, Niagara to Tobermory. For this hike, however, we decided to hike north to south, from 49.1 to 32.3. This led to a major discussion among the seven of us, since we were not sure if Tom's database could handle a "reverse" hike. Would the distance show up as a negative? Would Tom accept this backward direction? It was suggested by Carol that we could say that we walked backward so that, even if we were travelling in the wrong direction, we were facing the right way. However, although a little exaggeration may be permissible in the log, we must stay reasonably close to the truth.

Peter, Pat, Paul, Marlene, Al, Carol and Gordon all arrived at the meeting place at the Caledon Municipal Building at around 8:30, and after completing our traditional period of milling and "the map ritual," we drove to kilometre 49.3, our starting point. We set off at 9:06 (noted for Tom's log) in a gentle rain, optimistic that the weather forecast for gentle showers would hold true. The first half of the hike was through some very attractive evergreen forests with open spaces and clearings. The ground undulates gently, no major climbs or descents, and no rocks. In spite of our optimism, the rain continued — sometimes bordering on a downpour — for more than the first part of the hike.

Once we emerged from the wooded area onto Duffy's Lane, a look at the map was called for: the dreaded "map ritual." Our map-reader swung her belt pack to the fore, removed map and spectacles and made an assessment. With seven people, we had eight opinions as to where we were and where we had to go.

After a kilometre on Duffy's Lane, a short, sharp ascent was made onto the trestle of the Caledon Trail, and we had another quick look at the map. Just a moment! Where were the map-reader's spectacles? Three intrepid souls backtracked Duffy's Lane, while four stood around or wandered up and down the lane. One even took the advantage of the delay to eat a soggy sandwich lunch. The intrepid search-and-rescue souls eventually arrived, mission successfully accomplished. The spectacles were found, though an extra 2 kilometres had been added to their hike. (Does that count in the log, Tom?)

By about 11:45, the rain had almost stopped, and we made the easy hike of 8.5 kilometres to arrive back in Caledon East at 1:02 PM, as noted in Tom's log.

Those who were wise had brought a change of clothing and shoes, the rest of us complained a little. After a short stop at a local delicatessen, the vehicle located at the start of the hike was retrieved. The slightly dryer seven of us then moved on to the Caledon Inn for some light refreshment, to moisten the insides of our bodies and thence our second spectacle: One hiker could not understand why his one eye could see better than the other. He reached up to touch his lens and nearly poked out his eye! Fortunately, the wayward lens was found behind his chair. Somehow the waitress had not stepped on it in her coming and going.

Our memorable hike had come to an end, another hike to strengthen the bonds of one hiker to another.

A Memorable Hike!
or a Memorable Hike?

JIM VANDERLIP

When I was asked to write a description of a memorable hike, my first reaction was to think that this would be incredibly easy. All I would have to do was to search my memory and come up with one hike on which a lot of things had happened to make it memorable. What could be easier?

Well, it wasn't easy.

I did think of a memorable hike. After all, I have been a hike leader for almost 15 years, and I have been on a number of hikes that have stuck in my memory. But what made them memorable varied from hike to hike, and what made them memorable to me may not be what would make them memorable to somebody else.

When I took the hike leaders' training course, we experienced what was referred to as "an eventful hike." This was a hike on which prearranged crises were staged with frightening frequency in order to test the skills of the fledgling hike leaders. After almost an hour of non-stop heart attacks, strokes, broken limbs and difficult hikers, we were somewhat shell-shocked. We consoled ourselves with the thought that this could not possibly happen in the "real" world.

Don't kid yourself. It can and it did.

One spring day in the Hockley Valley, everything happened. The night before the hike had been cold and frosty, and the morning dawned clear and cool. People coming to the hike wore the appropriate early spring clothing. All had jackets and some had mitts.

By 10:00, the temperature was 25 degrees Celsius and climbing. The sky was clear and there was no shade canopy. Hikers began to shed clothing desperately, some experiencing the first signs of heat exhaustion. One lady borrowed a knife and cut away her long pants to create instant shorts. This was only the beginning.

By the end of the hike, one lady had dropped into a ditch with an injured ankle, another had suffered violent stomach cramps from the heat, a group of rebellious hikers had bolted into a local stream, and another group, for some reason, still wanted to continue the hike, even when their fellow hikers were falling like flies. Fortunately, it all worked out and we did not lose anyone that day.

What made this hike memorable for me was the incredible challenge to my hike-leader training. What also made it memorable was the group effort that took place to overcome these obstacles. Everybody remembers those hikes that test their skills and challenges them as individuals. They also remember those hikes that bring us together to work through adverse circumstances.

I remember the day that someone fell into an incredibly cold stream in the late fall and was soaked in icy cold water. The wind that day was biting, and there was a light spray of sleet in the air. Everyone searched their backpacks, and a pair of socks, a wind jacket and T-shirt were produced. Everyone pitched in and helped.

But other, quieter things can make a hike memorable: the peace that a person feels walking through a beautiful woodlot, those moments when you catch sight of the natural world after having been in a city all week, and the fleeting glimpses of deer or a rare porcupine sighting.

A hike can also be memorable for less quiet reasons, such as walking through the woods as a group and engaging in robust, animated conversations about politics, religion, travel, books, movies — almost anything is grist for the hikers' conversational mill. I have learned more while hiking than in many hours listening to the radio or watching television.

I have also been exposed to some of the most memorable and screwy points of view in the same forum. As somebody once said, "I am entitled to my point of view and everyone else is welcome to it." Or as someone else wisely remarked to a particularly opinionated hiker one day, "Did you process that through your brain before it came out of your mouth?"

Ultimately, what makes a hike memorable varies from person to person. Those moments of quiet contemplation on the beauties of nature; those funny, witty moments with the group; the times when difficulties are experienced and people pull together to overcome challenges experienced along the way; or those post-hike trips to the pub, when a cold pint of beer gives comradely closure to the day.

And hiking, of all activities, is certainly one that continues to provide both individual and group memories.

Noisy River Hike Survivor

Have you ever noticed the large variety of badges some hikers have stitched to their daypacks? Most common on the Bruce Trail are the Bruce Trail diamond and the various sectional end-to-end badges. However, one of the rarest is a plain white rectangular badge stating NOISY RIVER HIKE SURVIVOR, APRIL 4, 2009. There are just ten of these and, as yet, not all have been sewn onto packs. These badges relate to the first hike of a series I led that summer, from Lavender to Owen Sound. In promoting the hikes, I had used "summer" as an adjective and justified it on the grounds that summer is just an attitude of mind. Without doubt, that offended the weather gods on the Bruce.

All seemed fine that morning as I drove north from Waterloo. However, from Shelburne northward, high winds and blowing snow closed in. Snowplows and sand trucks worked on the roads, and when I arrived at the Lavender cemetery, it looked like a driving blizzard out there. I was not the first to arrive, and I was told by several early arrivals that their drives had included close encounters with ditches. Subsequently, three more of the intended hikers arrived. Shaking and showing signs of Post Traumatic Stress Disorder, they decided to go straight home again. Only ten brave souls remained undeterred, and at the appointed hour we proceeded to carpool to the starting point at kilometre 20.9 in the Blue Mountain section.

We eventually began at a small parking spot in the Nottawasaga Bluffs Conservation Area, in driving snow, with a blustery northwest wind and the thermometer reading -2 C. For 2 kilometres, we passed through a cedar woods, with many downed trees to clamber over and few visible blazes — most were covered by the snow that plastered the trunks of the cedars.

Even though at least four of us were familiar with this section and pink plastic ribbons were attached to some of the trees, we still took several detours off trail. On numerous occasions, we plunged waist-deep through snowdrifts adjacent to fallen trees or snow-filled gullies. Given the very real risk of injury, and the fact that we had taken more than an hour to cover this short distance, for the first time in my life as a hike leader, I started to give serious consideration to abandoning the hike.

ONTARIO — NIAGARA ESCARPMENT / BRUCE TRAIL   25

We eventually emerged, almost exhausted, from Nottawasaga Conservation Area onto a road allowance, which gave us some respite. Further relief came as we turned east and followed an old logging road, where cedars gave shelter. Soon, though, we were edging open fields on hilltops, where the wind was particularly fierce but fortunately behind or beside us on our rear quarter. The pastoral vistas — if we could have raised our heads to see them — were shrouded by the blizzard.

At noon, when we would normally stop for lunch, our location was open and inhospitable, so we pressed on in our search for shelter. In one of the worst such places, one of our numbers reached a state of near collapse, so the decision was made for me. We stopped for lunch. We hunkered down behind a few rocks and a small coppice of scrappy trees as the gale continued to blow. This was possibly the worst place for a lunch stop I have ever experienced in all my years of hiking, so we kept it short.

Soon we crossed 12/13 SR, scattering a flock of wild turkeys as we went. Some of us questioned who the real turkeys were! More windy fields followed, then 9/10 SR and more fields, entered and exited by stiles. Then several boardwalks, one continuous and one sectional, and a fairly new bridge got us over very active streams.

Onward we went. As we walked through the Noisy River Conservation Area, we encountered a very surprised porcupine sitting in the middle of the trail. It took several seconds for him to adjust to the shock of finding hikers on the trail in such conditions and to head for cover. Eventually we emerged onto Baseline and stayed on it as we headed back to our cars. A slight diminishing of the winds, snow on the road turning to slush, and a bluebird observed flitting from tree to tree gave us hope that spring was a possibility.

Goodbyes were, of necessity, brief before we headed home or back to the shuttle point. Exhausted as we were, we could not help but notice a significant improvement in the weather as we headed back south. Waterloo was calm, with intermittent sunshine. One hiker arrived home in Cambridge to find that a family member had spent the day motorcycling in the warmth of the spring sunshine.

Were lessons learned? Definitely! Do not presume that the weather gods allow spring and summer to arrive as early near Georgian Bay as they do on the southern sections of the Bruce Trail.

But where do the badges come in, you might ask? Well, the whole event proved so memorable to some that it was suggested that a special badge be commissioned to commemorate the event. The rest is history.

Close to Nature, Close to Home

EARL COWAN

The slogan of the Bruce Trail Conservancy says it all: "Close to nature, close to home." Our hikers climb Mount Kilimanjaro in the dark and chase yurts across Outer Mongolia, but our lives are lived at home, and home is a place that is close.

If you live in the Greater Toronto Area the Dufferin Hi-Land Section is one-and-a-half-hour drive from Markham, downtown Toronto, Hamilton and Kitchener — an easy drive for a day hike or far enough to justify an overnighter at a nice rural B&B and a dinner at a hot country pub.

The farms on the dead-end rural roads that were broken by the Niagara Escarpment were the first to be abandoned during the migration to the cities in the 1940s, and they have been reclaimed by nature. Areas of the Mulmur Hills are now wild forest. The current trend is for big money to build big estate houses in the forests, but the Bruce Trail has managed to find another way, and you can walk, free of charge, through long stretches of wilderness.

In Dufferin, the cliffs of the escarpment are often buried under the gravel and clay soils of glacial moraines, so the hills are rounded, and you will find smooth, compact single-file treadways and long, steady climbs through deep valleys. The trails have been carefully designed for hikers from ages 8 to 80.

Dufferin is not spectacular — you will not see the peaks of the Himalayas or the pristine waters of Lake Louise, there are no tigers or tiger sharks — but there is space to stretch your muscles, air to breathe, solitude for your soul, and you can come here every day.

The Dufferin Trail is in the high country, 1,000 feet above Toronto. In winter, there is always snow for snowshoeing and skiing, and in summer, fresher air than that found in the cities.

Check our website at www.dufferinbrucetrailclub.org for our Moonlight Snowshoe Hikes, our 20-Kilometre Challenge Hike and free hikes guided by our experienced hike leaders.

Come and explore Dufferin with us, and add a forest to your life.

Hogg's Falls is named for William Hogg, a son of the illustrious Hogg family of 19th-century York. He settled in the area in the 1870s, but today only faint traces remain of his mill. The site is now protected as a forest reserve, and the clean waters abound with speckled trout. — Photograph by igor kisselev

Hike the Falling Water Trail

JACK MORGAN

This is a brief description of my favourite hike, the Falling Water Trail in the Beaver Valley section of Ontario's famous Bruce Trail. It is a 30.4-kilometre loop and can be accessed from a number of starting points. Because the terrain is rugged in places and because of frequent changes in altitude, it is a strenuous hike requiring six to ten hours, depending on the pace. It also requires fitness, proper equipment, food, water, emergency preparedness and boon companions. For hikers who find 30.4 kilometres too long, it can be broken into two or more smaller segments.

The best way to visualize the hike is to purchase a copy of the *Bruce Trail Conservancy's Bruce Trail Reference* guide or the Beaver Valley Bruce Trail Club's "Day Hike" map kit. Both publications contain maps of the Falling Water Trail (on Map 26 in the former and Map 3 in the latter).

This section of the Bruce Trail is called the Falling Water Trail because trail-builders and early hikers noticed that the steep upper Beaver Valley fastness was graced generously with moving water — gentle seeps, trickling rivulets, karst resurgences, small but spectacular cascading waterfalls pitched over the western scarp face, the two signature waterfalls of the upper Beaver Valley, Hogg's Falls and Eugenia Falls, and of course the rivers themselves, the Boyne and the Beaver, the confluence of which lies cradled between the eastern and western arms of the Falling Water Trail. One is never far from the sight or sound of falling water.

Perhaps the best-known feature on the Falling Water Trail is Eugenia Falls, so that is where we will start the hike. We gain access to 30-metre-high Eugenia Falls on the Grey Sauble Conservation Authority property, in the village of Eugenia, on Grey County Road 13. We park in the Authority parking lot and walk down the paved trail to the falls' lookout and the Bruce Trail. Because the hike is a loop, we could set off in either direction from here, but we will go clockwise, heading south. We will follow the white blazes of the main Bruce Trail almost the whole way, using the blue blazes of Valley Crossover side trail just once.

From the falls, we hike south along the ridge high above the Beaver River before descending gradually through thick cedar cover, eventually crossing an old cart track before climbing again to a singular 360-degree lookout that affords breathtaking views up and down the upper Beaver Valley.

The trail crosses the Lower Valley Road and soon intersects with the Hogg's Falls lower side trail. At that point our hike takes us south, following the white blazes along the Boyne River upstream to the East Back Line. However, before we do that, we take a short detour to see beautiful Hogg's Falls, Grey County's best-kept secret. Then we turn right at the intersection and follow the blue blazes north to the falls, where the Boyne River cascades 7 metres over a dolostone shelf.

Now we retrace our steps back to the main trail and on to the East Back Line. We walk west and cross the Boyne via the road bridge.

Reaching busy Grey Road 30 at the bottom of Bowles Hill, our trail turns upslope (west) and then almost immediately right (north) across a stile and onto a hydro corridor.

We follow the hydro line across another stile and enter the property of the Beaver Valley Ski Club. Here we proceed across an open field, down the lower slope of the "Beaver South" ski run, past the lower terminus of the south chairlift, and along a utility road before descending to the bottom of "Boomer" ski run. Now we have the challenge of hiking up the left side of the run to intersect the Valley Crossover Side Trail.

At this point, our hike turns east and follows the blue blazes of the Valley Crossover Side Trail for 2.6 kilometres down the valley, across Grey Road 30, and then up the other side, in effect crossing the neck of the upper valley.

At the top, on the east side, we follow Grey Road 13 south for a short distance to a stile on the west side. We go over the stile, across a field and into the woods.

The trail follows the scarp edge to Ontario Power Generation property, where we have to make a steep climb beside the penstocks that carry the water from Lake Eugenia to the turbines in the generating plant far below in the valley.

The trail eventually descends steeply to the north side of Eugenia Falls. In this section, the trail passes close to two stone arches, one at each end of the climb to the lookout, which mark the ends of a tunnel downstream to the lookout over the falls, our starting point and so the end of the hike.

Unlocking the Future at the Keyholes

BRIAN FOLEY

I arrived at 8:30 AM and feelings of nervous excitement set in as I stood with my back to the information board for Nottawasaga Conservation Area. I had put my foot in my mouth back in September 2001 on the Dufferin Hi-Land's 2-Day E2E when I asked president and hike director Kristen Farrier what sort of winter program they had. Answer: not much. By spring, I was the new hike director. I had little hiking experience and knew nothing about the Dufferin Hi-Land section of the Bruce Trail, but I had put my foot in it and put my foot on the path of my first led hike and my future.

As I waited, I was thankful the weather had co-operated: clear skies, 26 degrees. Cars began to arrive, and I greeted my hikers nervously. The last car to arrive was a green Toyota Corolla containing a woman driver and a male passenger. I noted that he was in his late fifties and that she was petite, blonde, attractive, athletic-looking and wore glasses, a green sleeveless blouse, cream-coloured shorts, brown socks and hiking boots.

I had hiked the route the previous weekend with my friend Tom. The plan was to hike the main trail to the Keyhole Side Trail through the keyhole. Now, here was my first problem as a hike leader: a hiker had brought his two dogs with him, one of which was too big to fit through the entrance to the narrow rock cut. The dog owner volunteered to follow the upper route and reconnect with us on the other side, but this did not happen. Half an hour into my first hike, I had already lost one hiker and two dogs.

We then bumped into two women in their twenties — reasonably fit and wearing running shoes, but greener-looking than me. They were searching for someone named Bryan. The others assured me that the guy with the dogs was prone to disappearing, so we carried on to Freedom Rock, where we took pictures, had a snack break, and I pondered the relationship between the guy and the blonde. A couple? Friends?

As we headed east toward Best Caves, I chatted with Carol, the woman from the Corolla. I did my best to make the impression that I was quite the experienced outdoorsman — hiking, cycling, canoeing, snowshoeing — dropping the hook to see if I could get a nibble and find out who this guy was that she was with.

At the bottom of the hill, we connected with the beginning of the Ganaraska Trail, which led us into Glen Huron, where we hooked up with Mad River Side Trail. I called for a lunch stop at the cabin alongside the river. I had all but forgotten about the other hikers and had long forgotten the guy I had lost and his two dogs. By this point, Carol's male friend had pretty much clued in that I rather fancied Carol. He volunteered the fact that he was very much married to a non-hiker and that he and Carol were just hiking friends.

After lunch, we packed up and continued our hike to the base of the ski hill at Devil's Glen, another rookie mistake! Do not plan your hike so that your group must climb one of the steepest hills on the trail when the air temperature is 30 degrees. I suppose I was somewhat redeemed when the hiker and his two dogs, lost three hours earlier, appeared from behind a chalet. Reconnected, we proceeded straight up the ski hill, with the two 20 year olds climbing barefoot, their running shoes having proven ineffective.

The group was either too polite to complain or had come to the conclusion that I was the worst leader they had ever met. The rest of the hike was fairly uneventful, and we all parted at the end.

Somehow I managed to attract people out for subsequent hikes and spent the next six years as hike director. I must say thanks to the hundreds of hikers who supported the Dufferin Hi-Land Club and the events — the two-day E2E, the one-day E2E, and all the hikes we shared, often in hot, merciless weather. They were among the most wonderful and wonder-filled six years of my life.

Peter, Carol's "other man," tore up the trail. He was often the first to sign up for the E2Es, and with his easygoing nature and hearty laugh, always one of the first to reach the finish.

Glynnis, the Welsh woman, remains very involved in the Dufferin Hi-Lands Club as social director, hike leader, trail captain, and one of the founding members of the Tuesday hike group.

And then there is Earl and his dog Sarah. Who does not know Sarah? Earl is trail director extraordinaire. The Dufferin section has never looked better and continues, under his direction, to grow in size and reputation.

Carol and I celebrated our fifth wedding anniversary on June 19, 2009. She had called me a couple weeks after that first hike in 2002, inquiring about upcoming hikes, and our hiking boots have been parked next to each other's ever since.

Following the White Markers

CARYS CAMANI

I was 17, and I was going backpacking for the first time with my friend from school, Megan. Quite frankly, I was surprised my mother had agreed to the trip. Maybe it was because Megan had been backpacking before, or maybe my mother was just excited to have a weekend alone. Whichever it was, she agreed to the idea and agreed to drop us off at our starting place, Battlefield Park in Stoney Creek.

We unloaded our packs from the back of the car and, in true teenaged fashion, wandered off into the woods with barely a wave goodbye.

I had taken my friend Megan's advice and packed only the necessities, but I was still surprised at how heavy the pack was. I had no idea how I would last five days with all that weight on my back.

"You know, Carys, I am so glad I invited you along. The last time I went backpacking with someone who had never been before, they needed to take a break every few minutes because they were so intolerant of the pack. You seem to be holding up okay."

Not wanting to let my friend down, I trudged on. We had started much later than we had originally planned, and it would soon be dark.

"You are sure you know where you are going, right?" I asked Megan as she reached into the pack to pull out her map and flashlight.

"Sure, we just need to follow these white markers." She pointed to the tree that had a small white stripe painted on it.

It seemed easy, just follow the white markers. Eventually, we came across a beautiful waterfall. We stopped for a bite to eat and sat at the top of it, mesmerized by the water flowing over the edge and hitting the rocks below. Not wanting to get caught setting up camp too late, we moved on.

After hiking quite a distance further, we came to a stop. "We should have reached the camp by now!" Megan said, looking around at the dense trees on every side of us.

"Well, we have been following the white markers, right? We have to be heading the right way!"

Then we came across a beautiful waterfall. Funny, it looked a lot like the other waterfall. Megan pulled out her flashlight and shone it at the marker. Blue! "I think we must have taken a side path. Maybe we should set up our tent here and try again in the daylight."

"Here? Where?" I asked.

"Do you have any better ideas?" she replied.

So, by flashlight, we set our tent near the top of that waterfall. We fell asleep to the sound of water rushing over the cliff and into the stream below.

We woke up early the next morning and realized we had camped smack dab in the middle of the trail. In the light of day, the markers were clear to see. We would not make that mistake again.

The next three days of the trip were rather uneventful. We marched on, spending our days talking about our crushes, our fears about trying to decide what to do with the rest of our lives, what universities to apply to, what courses to take. We snacked on granola bars and cooked Kraft dinner, without the milk, over a small stove that we lighted with rubbing alcohol. When we came to our destination on day three, we were both starving.

"Do you smell that?"

"Smells like barbecue. Oh, what I wouldn't give for a hamburger right now!"

We climbed the hill to the campground that was supposed to be our next stop. When we entered the clearing, we saw hundreds upon hundreds of people. There was a large tent with people barbecuing under it. Picnic tables were pulled together and covered with tablecloths. There were plates of fruit, chips, brownies, cookies — anything you could imagine.

"Is this where we are supposed to be camping?" I asked.

Megan looked at the map.

"Well, on the map it looks like it is supposed to be a campsite. I am sure they will all be gone soon."

"Oh, that smells so good!"

"Do you think they would notice two more?"

We stashed our bags in the woods and casually joined the party. We played Frisbee with some other teens, ate a lot of food, joined a baseball game, and ate more food. Then everyone was brought together under the tent. Not wanting to stand out, we figured we should follow the rest of the group. When we got there, the group began singing Christian hymns and handing out bibles. We graciously accepted them and sat down with the group as they read passages and discussed what the scriptures meant in their everyday lives. It was clear to us that we had been lured by the food into some kind of religious retreat. Not knowing how to make a graceful exit, and not wanting to get caught for eating a lot of food that was clearly not meant for us, we tried our best to sound like we knew a thing or two about Jesus. We blindly found passages in the Bible that we thought illustrated our weak tales of enlightenment.

At the first moment we could, we snuck off back into the woods and laid down in the brush until the group loaded themselves onto buses and drove off into the night.

"Well, that was certainly different," Megan said as she hung our bag of food in the tree so that it wouldn't attract bears.

"At least we got some good food out of it."

We set up our tent in the dark and, bellies full, we went to sleep. In the morning, I woke up to hear Megan swearing outside the tent.

"What happened?"

"Our food is all gone!"

Sure enough, the bag with all of the food in it had disappeared. No sign of it anywhere. God has a strange sense of humour.

We had two days left in the woods and no food. We wondered how we would keep going for the rest of the trip. Then a man pulled his car into the parking lot.

"You girls okay?"

"Yeah, we're fine."

"Do you need help?"

"No, not really, someone stole our food, so we are just figuring out what to do next."

"Would you like a ride into town? I can take you and then drive you back if you would like?"

He did not look creepy. Still, every school assembly about "strange danger" came flooding back to me. "Never get into a car with a stranger!"

Megan and I looked at one another and silently weighed our chances with this man in his car.

"Sure, we will take the ride."

Megan and I climbed into the back seat of the car together. We figured it would be safest if no one actually sat beside him. I noticed that Megan had brought along her Swiss army knife just in case.

We both kept our eyes firmly on the driver during our 15-minute ride.

When we got into town, we ran into the store, grabbed some supplies to sustain us for the duration of the trip, and then hopped back into the car. True to his word, the man brought us back to the spot where he had picked us up and let us out of the car without incident.

"You girls be careful out there."

We packed up our camp and travelled on. The remainder of our trip went off without a hitch. We got to our pickup point on day five to find Megan's mom waiting for us in the van as planned. We threw our packs into the back and climbed in, exhausted.

I do not remember what part of the Bruce Trail we did on that trip or even very much about what we saw. What I do remember was feeling that sense of freedom for the first time. We were caught in the middle of being kids and being adults, getting lost along the way, forging our own path, trying to find ourselves, all the while making decisions that were sometimes smart, but often reckless, with a total disregard for the consequences.

If only growing up came with a map, and it was all just as simple as following the white markers.

With Tracy
on the Bruce Trail

FRANK HOLLEY

As we live within sight of the Bruce Trail, about 1.5 miles north of Jones Falls, it is not surprising that when our little Tracy, then three years old, asked to go for walks, I took her on the trail. After repeatedly walking routes along the same 20-mile stretch, we realized that there were possibilities for her doing the whole Sydenham section. Tracy completed the 65.1 miles about a month after her fifth birthday.

To any other Bruce Trailers who decide to take on a similar adventure with their little ones, I wish you all the good luck and happy times we had. Although Tracy tries our patience sometimes at home, she was the most delightful little partner on the Bruce Trail. We were out 19 times, which would make the trips about 3.5 miles on average, each one taking the whole of an afternoon. The longest stretch we did at one time was the 6.6 miles from Skinner's Bluff to Oxenden, which took us from 10 AM to 4 PM.

Tracy is the only one of our family to qualify for the Blantyre to Wiarton chevron, as the rest of us were either unable to go on certain portions or we had to be part of the transportation crew, driving around to the finishing point. I was with her most of the way and have written up a little log of her trips.

She stuck her stick in every hole between Wiarton and Blantyre. She caught pollywogs, chased butterflies, and sat down and played with the little car she usually carried. And she made me smell flowers. There was not much we missed as we toddled along — the perfect way to travel the Bruce Trail.

I was reprimanded many times for such breaches of etiquette as stepping on her stick, walking on the wrong side, not letting her "through" to go in front, and for offering to help her over stiles. It has got so that I do not want to go on the Bruce Trail without Tracy, so if you see a big 'un and a little 'un going along sticking their sticks in holes and smelling flowers, give us a wave.

The hike described here took place in 1969 and early 1970 when the Bruce Trail started at Tobermory and ended at Niagara.

The Bayview Escarpment Nature Reserve

RON SAVAGE

When the Bruce Trail was built in the 1960s, in its rush to completion, several sections of the Niagara Escarpment were not included. As research into the Ontario's landforms continued, these areas were better understood, and they were mapped in the 1980s as part of what was called the Bruce Trail's "optimum route." Most however remained a dream until an intense period of trail development beginning around 2002 brought the proposed trail closer to achievement.

In 2007, the biggest reroute in the history of the Bruce Trail moved the footpath to the Bayview Extension, opening up to hikers some beautiful escarpment country. At 69 kilometres in length, it was longer than the entire trail in several of the Bruce Trail clubs.

The newsletter of the Sydenham Bruce Trail Club celebrated this achievement: "Stand up and congratulate your selves, Sydenham. It has taken five years and thousands of hours of hard work by hundreds of volunteers from both near and far away. We have built hundreds of feet of boardwalks, built 1,800 feet of fencing, trimmed and cleared 55 kilometres of bush, built stairs and ramps up and down the escarpment, and painted thousand of blazes." Trail director Chris Walker, who died an untimely death a week before the opening, wrote: "You must be wonderfully proud of your volunteers and their accomplishments."

There are many sections of the Bayview Extension that provide beautiful hiking opportunities, but a favourite is the Bayview Escarpment Nature Reserve. Here you choose one of two loops.

For the shorter loop, from the parking area, take the blue-blazed side trail on a logging track. It leads you northeast through a largely reforested area until it reaches the white blazes of the main Bruce Trail. If you turn left, it will lead you past some spectacular lookouts over the Meaford Land Base (formerly known as the Tank Range). These are especially interesting if the base is on maneuvers.

For the longer loop, from the parking area, follow the white blazes. The trail follows the escarpment edge and then the fence line of the military base east to reach, again, the escarpment cliffs. Continuing on, you will enjoy wonderful views out over Georgian Bay. Then, after crossing a logging road, keep a close watch for the blue-blazed and signed River Kwai side trail on your right. Follow it back to the townline road about a kilometre south of your car.

Jack Morgan, a past president of the Beaver Valley Trail Club and a resident of Meaford, has written about the Bayview Escarpment Nature Reserve:

"What kind of park is a Nature Reserve? Since no individual provincial park can be all things to all people, the province established six classes of park, of which Nature Reserve was one. Underlying the decision to do so was the recognition that the Ontario parks system must fulfill two basic needs: environmental protection and outdoor recreation needs. The Nature Reserve 'park' would be attached to the environmental protection end of that range.

"The Bayview Escarpment Nature Reserve is an extensive dolostone-capped escarpment promontory with almost eight kilometres of environmentally sensitive slopes and cliffs — some of them over 25 metres in height. Close to the edge of the escarpment are deep moss-filled crevices and dramatic outlier rock formations.

"The vegetation in the Nature Reserve matches in interest the landforms it inhabits. For instance, there are at least 20 fern varieties whose names enhance their beauty — among them green spleenwort fern, Christmas fern, ostrich fern, rattlesnake fern, the lovely maiden hair fern, and the provincially rare hart's tongue fern.

"Perhaps the most interesting aspect of the Nature Reserve vegetation is its tree cover. The top of the escarpment is covered with a bedrock hardwood forest, which is mostly sugar maple. Along the rim of the escarpment, in the talus slopes below it and on the face of the scarp itself is a strip of white cedar forest mixed in places with white birch.

"It is this tree cover and the fact that the Nature Reserve has been relatively untouched by humans that has attracted scientific researchers to the area. It was at this site, among others, that Cliff Ecology Research Group based at the University of Guelph identified what amounted to an ancient forest of eastern white cedar, a complete, undisturbed biological community. It was determined to be the oldest intact forest in eastern North America. On this specific site the Group found three significant trees with ages of 681, 591 and 507 years.

"Hikers and all others who appreciate the wonders of nature are fortunate to have this Nature Reserve accessible."

It Is Just Bruce

MICHELLE MADDERSON

"**S**hould not you stay another day?" asked the concerned campground host. It was a reasonable request, considering that the skies had darkened early that morning. A light drizzle dampened my face, but not my spirit, for I was a Bruce Trail thru-hiker with several hundred kilometres behind me and many more steps to take. Thanking the man, I heaved my 40-pound pack over stiff shoulders and climbed into the darkness. I was on my own again and eager to keep moving. The path led me along a ridge overlooking Hope Bay, where the slippery ancient seabed held my attention, perhaps a little too long, as a faint rumble was already calling in the distance. "It will clear, just keep moving," I argued aloud. Unfortunately, nature had other plans for this hiker. At approximately 5 PM, on July 31, 2005, I inadvertently found myself centre stage during one of the worst deluges ever to hit the peninsula. The woods now appeared darker than before, but alive with movement, as the wind effortlessly rocked full-grown pines back and forth. The once-familiar white trail blazes faded, and the rumbling crept closer. An unyielding streak zipped across the inky skyline, and for a moment I could clearly see the immensity of the approaching storm.

Waves of sound, similar to cannon fire, barreled across the escarpment, over the water, and then back again. Swirling curtains of rain threatened to block my viewpoint, but with every thunderous burst of illumination, an overhang in the rock revealed itself. The demands of the trail had rendered my inexpensive rain suit useless long ago, and now a large piece of thin green plastic, extending from my shoulder to wrist, was flapping furiously. Crouching under that overhang, with my thoughts wandering and hypothermia already in motion, I shuffled for my pack. Almost robotically, my eyes scanned the terrain for a suitable platform. Only one small, slanted piece of earth was found. I dashed forward, as if competing with an imaginary opponent, to set up the tiny two-man refuge. Off came my wet clothing and out came a sleeping bag in record time. Oh, the simple pleasures of warmth and shelter! Just seconds later, while shifting my weight away from an underlying tree root, another volley of fire erupted. *Craaaaack!* Terrified into stillness, there I sat, wide-eyed, wishing for daylight. But no relief would come. A long, sleepless, humbling night lay ahead on the Bruce.

McKay's Harbour

PETER NICHOLL

I recently celebrated my 70th birthday and cannot really understand where all those years have gone — a common complaint in my age group. You can tell the passage of time by trees. Consider those tree plantings along the trail. At the time that work was completed, any casual passerby would not have known any trees were there. Now that empty meadow is becoming a forest right before our eyes.

My first memories of the Bruce Trail go back 40 years. At that time, as a newcomer to Canada looking for exercise and company, I had joined the Caledon Hills Bruce Trail Club. I went on several hikes with an enthusiastic and energetic gentleman by the name of Tom East. Soon after that, I found myself exploring other trails and learning many wonders along the way from that great student of nature Ray Lowes. I still have the *Bruce Trail Handbook* purchased at that time, a 1968 edition with all the maps in basic black and white.

Soon, other paths took me away from the trails. My career, marriage and a hobby farm led me in other directions. Those regular domestic chores and catching up on sleep never left much time at weekends, and my happy hours on the Bruce Trail became increasingly distant memories.

Our closest friends, J and A, had a farm at that time. When my wife, Amy, and I moved to the country nearby, we were frequent visitors; perhaps it had something to do with A being such a good cook. We met their friends D and Db, and we three couples would get together quite often. We never missed a celebration with these fine friends together around Christmastime. J and A had a family, with three girls. Much later, D and Db had two boys. For Amy and me, parenting was limited to a dog and numerous cats.

As 1995 approached, my 55th year, I was feeling somewhat disillusioned with the corporate rat race. Increasingly, it seemed like I was running on a treadmill with no stop button. I wanted to explore other things in life. Material belongings assumed less importance. I felt a spiritual regeneration whenever I walked outside in the fields and woods. Though it was challenging financially, I was ready to retire.

By now, our friends had more time, too. Pleasant memories of the Bruce Peninsula beckoned, and one warm, sunny afternoon, six of us found ourselves in

Lion's Head. We all knew the Bruce Trail travelled south from Lion's Head around Gun Point to Barrow's Bay. D had the idea that it would be a nice easy walk if we dropped a car at Barrow's Bay and started hiking from Lion's Head. We had no concerns at all about completing 10 or 11 kilometres on foot before sunset. We explored a glacial pothole with an entrance at the bottom and wondered how it could have formed. Soon, the trail became increasingly rugged. Climbing up, we came to an incredible lookout, a little off the main trail, with great views off to the north of Lion's Head and beyond. Progressing ever more slowly, we continued to enjoy the many cliffs and views of Georgian Bay.

The trail eventually took us down a steep slope under an overhang to a pebble beach. This we learned was McKay's Harbour. Littered along the shoreline was the most extraordinary collection of boulders. These large boulders were not composed of limestone like the escarpment rock we had been hiking over. Glaciers must have transported them from all over Ontario. We spent an hour or two marveling at the variety of colours and compositions of these rocks. Some were a glistening black, some pink or green, others striped and layered. Such a variety of forms in one place! When were these rocks formed? What cataclysmic event dropped them all here? The boulders have an interesting story to tell!

At this point, a look at the map made us realize how far it was to Barrow's Bay. With the sun sinking lower and lower, we finally realized this was not such a short walk after all. Chastened, we made our way back to Lion's Head along the Inland Side Trail. This trail was quite a contrast to the escarpment edge — quieter, with moss-covered rocks like cushions. Our little hike to McKay's Harbour ended with all of us pleasantly tired and amazed at the wonderful views and sights along the trail. This, we decided, was a hike worth repeating.

Amy will never hike again now, and J was later diagnosed with lymphoma and sadly is no longer with us, but the memories of that day are treasured still. For me, it rekindled my passion for hiking and all the wonders the Niagara Escarpment holds. It brought me back to the Bruce Trail that I first trod 40 years ago. I have stopped counting how many times I have completed the whole trail. It may be six or seven. At some point, I joined a hardy group that hikes most of the peninsula every year. We usually stop briefly at McKay's Harbour for a drink and a snack. Looking at those boulders makes me want to linger. That part of the trail will always hold a special place in my heart.

A Tale Worth Telling

JACK BOULDER

It is nice to be able to write about a series of events that have a happy ending. A happy "tail" ending, that is! So let us get wagging it right now.

This story starts during a series of Bruce Trail end-to-end hikes that took place around the beginning of this century — 2000, that is. We were hiking on the spectacular Lion's Head escarpment in the Peninsula Section.

I was with three hiking companions at the time, a couple of friends from my section of Caledon and a younger fellow fairly new to the hiking fraternity. While having a well-deserved break overlooking Georgian Bay at McKay's Harbour, our new hiking friend decided to venture down to the beach and do a bit of exploring. The rest of us were just happy to relax from the challenging 18-kilometre hike. When he finished his exploring on the rock beach, we continued our hike.

We had been hiking for just under an hour when our new friend started to complain of his aching shoulders. "What's the problem?" we enquired. "Oh, nothing much," he replied. "It is just that this rock in my backpack is heavier than I thought."

"What!" we enquired. "Did you take a rock from the beach? That is not permitted these days, you know. In order to preserve the beauty and integrity of the peninsula for all to enjoy, rocks must not be removed."

Our "young" friend was a new hiking enthusiast at the time and was most disturbed that he had, in all probability, broken a rule or even a law.

Oh well, we thought, it was just this once and in all innocence, so let us just continue. We certainly did not want to return 3 kilometres and back again, especially after considering the safety aspects. We debated placing the rock beside the trail. Finally, we said, "Take it home and enjoy it."

All of us have interests and hobbies and it turned out that our new friend happened to be an avid rock collector as well as a hiker. I have seen his collection and it is quite excellent and most beautiful.

Several years later, I dropped by to see my old friend.

"You might be interested in some photos that I took while hiking with my son on the Lion's Head peninsula last month," he said.

In one photograph, there he is, on McKay's Harbour beach, replacing that most heavy and beautiful rock in the original location from which it was taken so many years earlier.

Cliffs along the shores of Georgian Bay, Bruce Peninsula National Park.
A variety of interesting geological formations and many displays of wildflowers,
rare orchids and ferns attract hikers to the park. — Photograph by Viktor Gmyria

Lost Hiker Summons Ghosts of the Past

LOIS CORFY

My life has been steeped with the memories and lore of the Bruce Trail. I can honestly say that for more than half of the years I have been alive, I have been touched almost continuously with direct and indirect experiences related to the Bruce and the natural feature that it traverses, the Niagara Escarpment. From the tender age of 12, I was made aware of its wonders. When my parents, Larry and Marion Duke, joined the organization, I accompanied them on countless hikes and camping trips. A love of nature was fostered and grew through osmosis.

There have been so many hikes, so many stories, it is hard to choose just one. But as this is meant to be an account of a particular hiking experience, there is one which stands out in my mind, as it in a sense travels through time, evoking and summoning ghosts of 30 years past, and thus bringing parts of my life full circle. The location is Lion's Head.

The story begins 30 years ago, when I was nearing completion of high school. After buying a fancy new Peugeot ten-speed bicycle (no one had heard of 18 speeds back then), I became possessed with the idea that I wanted to do a long bicycle trip. I talked two girlfriends into doing it with me, and before we knew it we were on our way to Tobermory (from Dundas), carrying all that we needed on the backs of our bicycles. At that time, it was highly unusual for girls to strike off alone on an adventure of this sort. After all, this was the era that still legally restricted women from competing in marathons. Girls were not supposed to go in for extreme sports or serious outdoor adventure. I feel fortunate to have had parents who allowed me to experience life to its fullest, unrestricted by societal expectations.

Our trip lasted two weeks, and along the way we had many adventures, but the most memorable started one day as we cycled down a back road towards Lion's Head. As dusk began to descend, a car drove by and slowed to a stop. A woman poked her head out the window and asked, "Where are you girls headed at this hour?" She could not help but notice the packs, tents and sleeping bags tied to the backs of our bicycles. We responded that we had cycled from Hamilton and were simply camping anywhere we could find a spot. She expressed shock that we would even contemplate such a thing and insisted that we really must follow her to her cottage, where she would put us up for the night.

One night turned into three nights, and it became a memorable visit. The lady (we shall call her Mrs. Kowalski) was staying there for the summer with her 12-year-old daughter while her husband remained working in Toronto. She was a distinctive character of Polish descent, a weaver who she made her own dyes from wild plants placed over a large iron cauldron suspended on a wooden tripod on the pebble beach. A giant loom filled the central room of her cottage.

Her young daughter was no less interesting, and led us on daylong meanderings along the Bruce Trail, through the woods and along the beach, which she populated with imaginary creatures and names. She showed us all her secret places, and we swam in the pristine but frigid waters of Georgian Bay. It was a magical time that left an indelible memory.

A few months later, we three friends went to Toronto to view the then popular musical *Hair*. We paid Mrs. Kowalski a visit, and she offered me a gift, a carved soapstone necklace depicting a beaver. I wear it often, as its smooth texture is soothing. When times get rough, it reminds me of the beauty and peace of nature and conjures up some wonderful memories. It reminds me how lucky I am.

Now to the second part of my story, 30 years later. I am still fortunate and still exploring the Bruce Trail, this time with a somewhat older group of hiking friends, united in our effort to complete the Peninsula section.

We have been hiking all day, many kilometres, and decide to take a break before doing a 6-kilometre section of road that heads north and ends at Richardson Access. When we continue our walk, we spread out and break into smaller groups, talking along the way. Eventually, we all end back at the parking lot at Richardson Access — all of us except one. We are puzzled, as our missing friend was well at the front, having sped on ahead of the others. We are also worried because he comes from far away and does not know the area. As time passes, we become increasingly concerned. We realize that he must have missed the turnoff for the access trail that would have taken him to the parking lot. He must have kept going, unaware that 12 kilometres will pass before he reaches another road.

The hour is getting late, so a search begins. Two hikers head out in the direction we think he must have gone, calling his name, but he does not answer. A kindly woman, however, does answer and expresses concern over a lost hiker as darkness draws closer. She mentions the cliffs and the possible dangers. Eventually, without success, the searchers return to the parking lot. The kindly woman returns shortly later in her van, bearing sandwiches, hot coffee and a cell phone to call the police. As darkness falls, the police take charge.

While we wait anxiously in the parking lot, I engage in conversation with the kindly woman and mention my memories of the bicycle trip taken so long ago. Those memories are very foggy. I have never been able to recall exactly where the cottage was, not even that it was near Lion's Head, and I long ago lost all contact with the fascinating Polish lady who so hospitably welcomed us. I begin to relate the story, and to my surprise, she declares that my description matches that of her elderly neighbour who owns a cottage nearby. She tells me that Mrs. Kowalski is doing very well, and still comes up to her cottage every summer, as she has done for so many years, and that she is still a weaver.

A shiver runs up my spine as I think of the passage of time and the many memories in those intervening years, yet the Peninsula remains through it all, preserved in its natural beauty, connecting the threads of time as the threads on Mrs. Kowalski's loom.

As we stand talking, and the day closes in on 11 o'clock, car lights appear in the darkness of Richardson Access parking lot. It is the police with our friend, safe and sound. It signals the end of a dramatic day. The day has held drama for members our hiking group and our lost friend, but for me the drama has been heightened by the conjuring of ghosts from my past, connected to the present by this beautiful landscape.

Shake, Rattle, and Roll

DAN WELSH

Hi! My name is Dan Welsh and I have agreed to write this article in order to set the record straight.

During the summer of 2005, a group of us, 11 to be exact, decided to hike from Dyer's Bay to Richardson Access Trail parking lot. We set off from Dyer's Bay shortly after 8 AM and hoped to hike 32 kilometres by suppertime.

It was approximately 5 kilometres into the hike that the rattlesnake's path crossed ours. I was leading the hike when the person behind me said, "There is a dead snake on the trail." I stopped and turned around to observe it with my own eye. The snake could not have been more than 3 inches long. I bent over and picked him up by the tail. He slowly moved. Seeing he was alive, I gently placed him back on the trail. I then realized that if I left the snake on the trail someone might step on him. In order to prevent this, I proceeded to pick him up again with the intent of moving him off the trail. As soon as I picked him up, he nailed me with one fang. I quickly released him. I then bent over to examine the little guy who had just bit me. He was shaking his tail even though his rattle had not developed. Noticing blood on my finger, I put my hand behind my back.

"He got you!" someone in the group commented. If the snake had got me with both fangs, I do not know whether I would be telling this story.

At this point, the other hikers wanted me to leave the trail. There were a few cottages close by. I felt good and I wanted to keep hiking. However, the other hikers convinced me to go up a driveway and talk to a couple who were having breakfast on their balcony. I told them that a rattlesnake had bitten me. They asked whether I was sure it was a rattlesnake. They insisted that it was probably a hog-nosed snake. In short, this couple did not seem willing to interrupt their breakfast in order to give me a ride to Lion's Head.

Finally, I told the group that I wanted to continue to hike, and if I felt bad I would bail out.

After approximately two hours, my hand had doubled in size. My knuckles had virtually disappeared. The swelling extended to my elbow. My arm looked more like Popeye the Sailor's arm — and that was without eating any spinach. I informed the group not to worry because if I were going to die, I would have been dead by now. I insisted that we stop wasting time and get moving.

When we finally reached Lion's Head, we stopped at the hospital. I explained to the receptionist that I had been bitten by a rattlesnake, five hours before. She asked me how it managed to bite me on the hand. I informed her that I had picked it up.

She yelled, "You picked it up!"

"Yes," I said.

"You know," she said, "women do not get bitten by rattlesnakes."

"How is that?" I asked.

"Because they do not pick them up!" she replied.

Finally, I got to see the doctor. He examined my hand.

"It must have been a little rattler. They are the stupid ones; they inject right away."

"Well, Doc, I do not know. He was sunning himself on a rock, I picked him up, and I am the one here. Who is the stupid one?"

"OK," he replied, "this is how it works. We will take a blood sample. If it measures 10 on the scale, we will keep you overnight. A reading between 5 and 9, we will give you an antidote. Between 1 and 4, we will send you home and tell you what symptoms to look for."

Since there was no lab in Lion's Head, the blood sample needed to be sent to Wiarton. I asked whether I could go home while we awaited the results.

"Yes," he replied, "on the condition you look for the following. If the puncture turns black, you get back here as soon as possible. Blackness means the wound is infected."

"What about the swelling?" I inquired. "How long will it take to go down?"

He did not know. As it turned out, the swelling lasted about two weeks.

MONTY JONES FOOTNOTE: To this day, hikers still tell the story of the man who got bit by a rattlesnake and survived to tell the tale. If you are ever hiking the Bruce Trail near Dyer's Bay, you might come across an image of a hiker carved into the escarpment's face rock. Look very closely and you will notice a rattlesnake attached to his hand. And now you know the rest of the story.

Dyer's Bay

ELAINE WASSERMANN

This lovely hike takes you along the Niagara Escarpment overlooking Georgian Bay, as well as inland, and can be done over a weekend, approximately 7 kilometres each day. The area's three B&Bs — the most convenient being Cape Chin Country Inn — allow for a leisurely exploration of this portion of the Bruce Trail.

Travelling north of Wiarton on Highway 6, turn right (east) on Lindsay Road 5 to the East Road, where you turn left (north). This will take you past the lovely St. Margaret's chapel, a heritage site built in the late 1920s. Turn right (east) onto Cape Chin North Road, follow that winding road until a fork opens, with Borchardt Road on the left. Follow the white blazes of the main Bruce Trail along Borchardt Road to the parking area at the end.

To begin your hike, backtrack approximately 50 metres south to where the main trail turns east and takes you along the escarpment, with vistas of Georgian Bay. This section is mixed forest — cedar, spruce, fir, maple, beech, birch, ironwood, ash, the occasional hemlock, and red pine — and hosts a wide assortment of birds, including downy, hairy, and piliated woodpeckers, red-eyed vireos, black-throated green warblers and chickadees.

Once you reach the main lookout point, the sea stack known as Devil's Monument, a side trail marked by blue blazes descends the escarpment below a cascading spring to the rocky shore of Georgian Bay, a welcome picnic spot and swim opportunity on a hot day. If you would prefer a break on the return leg, the Minhinnick side trail branches off to Devil's Monument. In spring, lilies and apple blossoms, as well as the original cedar-rail fencing, acknowledges pioneering homesteads. Up to this point, the main trail is rated moderate difficulty.

Continuing north, it becomes more strenuous in places, but spectacular. Turkey vultures are a common sight along the escarpment. Soaring red-shouldered and red-tailed hawks, as well as bald eagles, grace the cliffs, while loons patrol the bay.

When the trail turns inland, beware of occasional patches of poison ivy. On the south side of this stretch, watch for the Glacial Pothole and, further on, the Lillie side trail, where another, much larger pothole can be seen.

Soon you will come to Britain Lake Road. Continue north to the parking lot and the entrance to the Cottrill Lake side trail. An easy trail through mixed forest leads to this small lake, where you will see signs of beaver activity. This is also ideal habitat for the grey flying squirrel.

You soon rejoin the main trail. At this point, you may either follow the main trail south, looping back to where you entered the Cottrill Lake side trail, or follow the main trail north, leading to caves along the escarpment, which are worth the extra couple of kilometres.

Although the main trail continues north along the escarpment, once you have experienced the caves, simply double back, remaining on the main trail to return to the point where you entered the Cottrill Lake side trail.

You now are on the return loop, retracing a short distance on Britain Lake Road, this time passing the main trail and taking the Minhinnick side trail, an easy walk through beautiful open forest, which returns you to the parking lot at the end of Borchardt Road. If you walk this part of the Bruce Trail in spring, you will be treated to white and red trillium, trout lilies, various violets and wild leeks. The Massasauga rattlesnake enjoys the sunny areas along here. This completes the first loop, approximately 8-10 kilometres.

In order to get to the second loop, drive back to where you turned off onto Borchardt Road and turn left onto Cape Chin North Road. You can park near the community mailboxes. From Cape Chin North Road, take the main Bruce Trail north to where you cross Borchardt Road and enter the Otter Lake side trail.

This hike offers a mixed bag of farm pasture and wooded areas. In the spring, it's a wonderland of migrating birds, ducks and nesting sandhill cranes. In summer, Otter Lake is resplendent with both yellow and white water lilies. Near the end of this side trail, you will spot a stand of milkweed where monarch butterflies find shelter.

The side trail ends on Cape Chin North Road, which you cross to enter the main Bruce Trail. Initially a sparsely wooded area, the trail opens onto a pasture. Look carefully to the left, and you will see where the main trail re-enters mixed woods. Bypass the Bard side trail, staying on the main Bruce Trail, which makes its way to the escarpment. There you begin your return loop north. Again, you will experience wonderful vistas overlooking Georgian Bay as you return to the parking area on Cape Chin North Road. This loop is 6 kilometres.

One Hiker, One Story

DONNA BAKER

The Bruce Trail beckoned me to move to Ontario's Bruce Peninsula, the 100-kilometre length of land separating Lake Huron from Georgian Bay, in 1999. It is a starkly beautiful, sparsely populated area with friendly people who enjoy a wide range of environmental interests.

One of my favourite walks, although not on the Bruce Trail, is at Singing Sands, so named because of the sounds made by the wind as it whistles through the dunes. This wonderful little park is part of the Bruce Peninsula National Park and is located at Dorcas Bay on Lake Huron, just a few kilometres south of Tobermory. It is well known for its rare species of flora, such as the pitcher plant, lakeside daisy and dwarf iris.

One beautiful sunny day in summer, a few years ago, my husband and I were walking along a trail at the edge of the heavily treed area on the north side of the bay when we heard a rattling sound. We stopped, and there, under the cover of a cedar tree, a few feet away, was a Massasauga rattlesnake. It was a beautiful specimen, perhaps 70 centimetres in length, enjoying its lunch. That day, it had happened upon a red squirrel, which apparently had ventured close enough (probably 20-30 cm) for the snake to strike.

Cypress Lake by dawn's early light. — Photograph by Chris Hill

Most people who visit the peninsula never see a rattlesnake. They are shy and harmless to humans unless threatened by invasion of their space. Massasaugas rattle to warn of their presence. The rattle sounds more like a buzz. Massasaugas are active from April to November, depending on temperatures. For the rest of the year, they hibernate in cavities and crevices below the frost line.

Well, that was one of the most exciting walks I have had on the Bruce. It is always a thrill to see wildlife on or near the trails. Most animals are shy and may be spotted at a distance but rarely close, unless they are unaware of your presence. Birds are plentiful, especially during spring and fall migration, and throughout the summer. Chickadees, blue jays, cardinals, finches and juncos are common winter birds. Snowy owls sometimes hunt on the Ferndale flats in winter if food is scarce farther north. One summer I spotted two garter snakes entwined in a small tree beside the trail — but that is another story!

No matter the season, hiking Bruce Peninsula trails can be invigorating, educational and fun. Keep your eyes and ears open!

That Day on the Bruce Peninsula

ELDON SPURRELL

Almost all of my hikes on the Bruce Trail have been with a group and have been since I retired. Therefore, all of my hiking partners are retirees with a passion for the activity of hiking and are dauntless in its practice. In the final stages of my first end-to-end, a group of ten of us were in Tobermory for three days at the end of October.

Being mature individuals, we usually limit our hikes to about 15 kilometres per day. This day, however, after consultation and agreement, we decided to not only hike from Crane Lake Road to Halfway Dump side trail, but to push on to Mar Lake side trail, making our hike approximately 20 kilometres. Now, I know there are many people who hike a lot more than 20 kilometres in a day, but none of us were those people. As well, none of us had hiked any of this territory before, so we really did not know what to expect. We were also gambling with the time of the year. The end of October is not the worst time up there, but the weather can be very uncertain, and we were about to encounter some of that uncertainty.

After parking a vehicle at the end-of-trail at Cypress Lake and doing the long car shuttle to Crane Lake Road, we set off. The weather was overcast, with a threat of rain, and the temperature was about 10 degrees Celsius. Our group consisted of three men and seven ladies, one of whom was almost 80 years old.

If we had been smart we would have A) done the hike from north to south, and B) turned back after the first hour. We were not smart, however. We did not know that north to south was downhill and that the easy part therefore would have been at the end. Also, we felt we could not turn back because to do so would have postponed our end-to-end completion till the next spring.

Half an hour into the hike it started to rain; at first gently, but then in ever increasing ferocity. By the time we got to the escarpment, around High Dump, the rain was almost torrential and a gale-force wind was coming off the bay.

We trudged on through the wind and the rain, but, as if being wind-blown and soaking wet were not enough, the temperature started to fall and the sky darkened to where it was difficult to see our feet.

Most of us were wearing, as rain gear, simple plastic rain capes, and these were being ripped to shreds by the wind. Fatigue started to set in, and frequent stops became a necessity and were taking longer and longer.

Bearing in mind that none of us had done this stretch before, we could not anticipate where we were, and each time we came to a road or a side trail, we were crushed to find that we still had further to go.

The mind can play funny games with you when you are in distress, and, as the leader, mine started imagining horror scenarios. We usually hike at about 4 kilometres per hour, and after five hours I started to worry about why we were not there yet. It was virtually impossible to have missed our cut-off at Mar Lake, but my mind kept wondering whether we had. Unfortunately, our pace had slowed to a crawl due to fatigue, wetness and slippery conditions and all our reckonings were off.

Real dark was descending when, after seven and a half hours, we reached our vehicle and were flooded with relief. We still had the car shuttle to do and to get back to our motel, but the worst was over.

Later that night, after showers, drinks and dinner, we realized we had been careless and could have gotten into real trouble, but a funny thing started to happen. Each of us started to smile about it and began to refer to our "hike from hell" as an adventure. We started to feel we had accomplished something powerful.

We celebrated with toasts to everything and everyone and created a bunch of comical awards for each other.

The next day, we headed home to Oakville, happy and grinning about our victory over the elements.

That was in 2003. All ten of those hikers completed their end-to-end. Some of us have done that same hike many times since, but never again have we encountered those conditions.

Today, whenever two or more of those ten hikers are together, the conversation invariably turns to hikes we have done, and, also invariably, that day on the Bruce Peninsula is remembered as everyone's most memorable hike.

A Neophyte on the Peninsula

MARILYN MacKELLAR

I have had many memorable hikes, both in Canada and in other countries, but my first backpacking trip is still one I remember vividly. It influenced my feeling about hiking and, as a result, my later treks.

When I saw it listed as a July 1 weekend hike on the Bruce Trail Peninsula Section, I was tempted, but there were obstacles. I was a relatively new hiker, I had never backpacked, and I did not have a car. Luckily, I had a friend, Diana, who did have a car, had also never backpacked, and who was interested. We decided to tackle this new experience together.

Nervous about whether we could do this, we pared down the contents of our packs to a minimum: one tube of toothpaste to share (but two toothbrushes), one bottle of sunscreen, and so on. We shopped for freeze-dried gourmet items (though almost nonexistent then). I went to Hercules and bought a backpack. I sawed off the top extensions on the pack, since they were bashing my ears. We did trial runs with full packs to see if we could walk distances with a load. We camped overnight (it snowed).

It was immediately evident, as we assembled at a motel near Cyprus Lake, that we were the only inexperienced backpackers. But off we went toward the Bruce Trail, past Cyprus Lake and then east on the trail along the coast. I neglected to mention that these were early days for the Bruce Trail, and it was not as accessible as it is now. One of the first surprises was a rock face with a rope hanging down to help with the ascent — a challenge in any case, but even more so with a full pack. We were happy we had weeded out our nonessentials. We were also happy to have people who could advise us on the ascent of rock faces by rope.

Along the trail there were new plants to look at (and people who recognized oyster mushrooms and twin-flowers). There were the amazing views. There were logs that could trip you (and did). And places where areas of rock surface with a few scrubby trees seemed to have no trail markings at all. The two of us stuck together, but the hike was often spread out with no other help than our maps and our sense of direction. There was much searching back and forth for markers.

At Halfway Dump we lost our leader. His son, young and even less experienced than we were, was unable to go on, and so a terrific man named Bill Thompson took over as our leader. He and several of the others had recently been to Scandinavia on a backpacking holiday, and they co-managed the rest of the hike.

We continued to High Dump, where the two of us straggled in after most of the rest. At that time we were allowed to camp on the beach, and we arrived to find a hive of tent-raising activity. We looked at each other, dropped our packs, and lit our camp stove to make tea with a slice of lemon and a tiny bit of brandy (two of our "luxuries"). We shared this with another hiker, John — a smart investment, as in return he helped with our tent and gave us cups of red wine. To our great surprise, out came bottles of wine, steaks, potatoes, and other heavy things. Campfires, stories and songs followed. We indulged in freeze-dried stew and then slept deeply to the music of the waves.

The next day, after a breakfast of instant porridge and instant coffee, we climbed back up to the trail and continued east along the coast. Around midafternoon we left the Bruce Trail on an old logging road that Bill knew. It was in the midst of a particularly remote boggy area that I saw my first Massasauga rattlesnake (I have only ever seen two on the Bruce), a rather sleepy individual who was not interested in us.

That night, back at the motel, where we camped for the night, when everyone else was eating freeze-dried food, we brought out *our* cooler with our steaks and potatoes and wine.

The next day, we hiked west from Cyprus Lake with day packs, admired the Grotto, jumped into the water (and out almost as fast), and finished off a weekend that has given me friends and acquaintances for decades, a lasting love of hiking, and a host of memories of my first time.

As the Crow Flys

JESSE CAMANI

"Life is not measured by the breaths you take, but by the moments that take your breath away!"

In August 2002, my father had planned to hike the Peninsula Section of the Bruce Trail over nine days. He invited me to join him for the final three days of his hike.

At first I was a little reluctant to go because neither my dad nor I had ever done any overnight camping. To make matters worst, we would have to spend two nights in the Bruce Peninsula National Park. The park is pretty remote. Cell phones do not always work. In addition, the area is home to black bears and Massasauga rattlesnakes, all of which made me a little nervous.

After weighing all the pros and cons, I decided to go.

On Wednesday, August 14, I met my father at Cape Chin Connection. While having breakfast at the inn, I learnt that Cape Chin is the centre of what locals call "cutting cedar." Truckloads of cedar and balsam are still shipped from the Cape Chin area to southern markets, where they are used in floral arrangements for the Christmas season.

After packing our freshly made lunches in our backpacks, we exchanged goodbyes with our hosts, the Bards, and headed out for the trail.

The Bruce Trail circles the Bards' property as it makes its way to the escarpment brow. After passing several beautiful lookouts, we arrived at Devil's Monument, the largest flowerpot formation on the Bruce Peninsula. A steel staircase strategically placed by a former owner of the property descends the escarpment to the base of the flowerpot formation.

Approximately 3 kilometres further along the trail, we discovered another interesting physical feature. Named after the landowners who discovered this formation, the Lillie side trail leads you to a 4-metre-diameter by 4-metre-deep glacial pothole. This feature reminded my dad of an old washing machine tub.

After walking over some rocky ground, we soon reached Britain Lake Road. As we travelled along the dirt road, I noticed something far in the distance. As we drew nearer, the object appeared to move. With each step, I tried to figure out what it was. "Dad," I said, "Is that a cow?"

"Well, Jesse, I think it is a bull!" he replied. "Just stay close to me." He continued on as he reached for his bear spray.

In the field close to the road, I could now make out several cows. The fence had been pushed over, permitting the bull to make his way onto the road. The bull stood still as we slowly approached. When we were roughly beside the bull, my dad raised his hiking stick and poked the bull in the hindquarters while he yelled, "Get!" Much to my relief, the bull obeyed his command and trotted back into the field to join his herd. I asked my dad how he knew what to do. He replied that he didn't. He admitted however that he had regularly watched the TV series *Rawhide* when he was a kid. The bear spray was going to be his last resort in case the bull decided to charge us. After several minutes, the beating of my heart returned to its normal rate.

At Gilles Lake Road, we turned left and passed Larkwistle, a colourful jewel of a garden in the midst of the peninsula wilderness.

When we reached Crane Lake Road, we turned right and headed north. The road crossed a large marsh. The trail continued north on Crane Lake Road, gradually deteriorating into a track. Up to this point, I was feeling okay. However, when I saw the sign welcoming us to the Bruce Peninsula National Park, I started to be concerned.

The sun was starting to set and we still had not reached our destination, High Dump. I later learned a "dump" was an area where logs were stored and dropped off the escarpment into log booms on Georgian Bay.

As we hiked and the sun continued to set, I kept saying, "Maybe we are not going to make it." My dad kept assuring me that we were nearly there.

Finally, the trail wandered off to what was just a rope. By way of the rope, we descended down a cliff, passing the remains of a dry log flume. We had reached our destination. There were nine tenting platforms, none of them occupied. This wilderness site was advertised as being sold out. Where were the other hikers?

After locating our campsite, we tried to set up our two tents. The tents overlapped the platform, and I hardly slept a wink that night because I was afraid of rolling off the platform, tent and all. In addition, every strange noise was amplified by the stillness of the night. I was happy to see the sunrise. It meant I had survived the night. I was alive, tired but alive.

The second day of our adventure was to be a short hike. According to the map, the distance between High Dump and Cyprus Lake was only approximately 11 kilometres. My dad assured me it would take no more than five to six hours.

Well, I do not know what happened, but it took us a lot longer. I think they must have calculated the distance on the map based on the direct flight of a bird. It could not have been the actual hiking trail. The trail consisted of a lot of ups and downs. I whined the whole time. To make matters worst, we had made the decision to carry all our water. My backpack was becoming heavier and heavier as the day progressed.

Along the way, we met another father-and-daughter team camping beside the trail. Their destination had also been High Dump. They had left Cyprus Lake the day before and, like us, figured the distance between the two points would take them only six hours. However, when darkness came, they decided to make camp.

A few kilometres further along the trail, we came across a father and son who also had miscalculated the time it would take them to reach High Dump. They too had decided to make camp before dark.

At last, I had the answer to why we were the only campers at High Dump.

The next section of the Bruce Trail we were about to hike, between Halfway Dump and Storm Haven, is considered to be the most rugged and challenging of the entire trail. However, there were many scenic lookouts along the shoreline towards Halfway Rock Point that proved to be great rest areas.

After crossing a beautiful boulder beach, we made our way to Cyprus Lake Campground. Our second day had come to a successful end.

Early the next morning, my dad and I decided to leave all our camping equipment at Cyprus Lake for our final hike to Tobermory. Our family was going to meet us in town, so it would be a lot easier to drive back and pick up our hiking gear. Without a backpack, my legs felt like I had a pair of springs attached to the bottom of my shoes.

The final day was great. We passed by several popular caves, including the Natural Arch and the Grotto, before following another boulder beach, which separates Marr Lake from Georgian Bay.

My dad was in front of me when he came to a sudden stop near Overhanging Point. "Don't move!" he shouted. "A rattlesnake is near. I heard its rattle!"

He lifted back some vegetation with his hiking stick. Sure enough, there it was, curled and ready to strike. We took a few steps backwards. Dad then took out his camera and snapped a few pictures. We continued to view the snake for a few minutes before carefully taking a large detour around him.

For the final part of the day, we enjoyed breathtaking views of the bay from atop the high cliffs.

Finally, we reached and touched the cairn perched beside Tobermory's storybook harbour.

After three days of hiking, a hot shower felt great. We ended the day by celebrating our accomplishment with the rest of our family at a local restaurant called The Crowsnest.

Overall, the hike proved to be a good learning experience. I learned a lot about my dad, and I learned a lot about myself, including the fact that I could do a long, difficult hike once I put my mind to it. I ended up having a great time, and I will always remember the time spent with my dad.

Wonders of the Bruce Peninsula

NORA DOBELL

Visiting the beautiful Bruce Peninsula had been a dream of ours, and an article in the fall 2009 Bruce Trail *Magazine* gave us the impetus to cut short our time at the cottage and head to the peninsula in September of that year for three days of hiking and sightseeing.

Fortunately, the B&B we had selected turned out to be great. Located on Main Street in Lion's Head, it is only a five-minute walk from the Bruce Trail. The three bedrooms, each with their own bathroom, were very comfortable. There were restaurants within walking distance and a couple more in Ferndale, only another five-minute drive away.

On Friday, our first day of hiking, the morning weather was dark and gloomy, with strong winds, but it cleared by about 9:30 AM and we decided to proceed. The route we had picked, with Larry Haigh's recommendation, took us north along the main trail past the giant cauldron, potholes, Lion's Head Point, numerous spectacular lookouts, MacKay's Harbour and back on the side trail.

Our lunch spot overlooking MacKay's Harbour was gorgeous. Winds were high and the bay was rough, with large waves crashing over the immense rocks that had fallen from the escarpment. It was simply awesome!

As a photographer, Ramesh had a field day. We were on the trail for six hours but hiked only 12 kilometres.

On Saturday, after a delicious, hearty breakfast, we headed to Tobermory

Flowerpot Island, the ultimate cruise destination from Tobermory.
— Photograph by Viktor Gmyria

to take the ferry to Flowerpot Island. First, we stopped at the Visitors' Centre in the Bruce Peninsula National Park, just east of Highway 6. The staff's helpful suggestions shaped our next two days.

A beautiful, calm day made our visit to the geological wonder of Flowerpot Island fascinating. We hiked the Flowerpot Route trail, about 5 kilometres, and enjoyed the sights — caves, cobbled beaches leading to the flowerpots, and Georgian Bay's ever-changing blue and green waters. We took the last ferry at 4:30 PM to Big Tub Harbour in Tobermory, where we grabbed a meal in the Coffee Shop, one of the few eateries open at that time of year.

On Sunday, we had another great start, with a warm farewell from our hosts and fair weather. We returned to Tobermory to hike the Burnt Loop side trail, starting from the Visitors' Centre. Lunch at Dunk's Point allowed us to soak in the beautiful scenery of Georgian Bay.

Around 2:00 PM we reluctantly started our trip back to Toronto. We returned relaxed and fulfilled, looking forward to another visit to the Bruce Peninsula.

The Scroll Hike

IAN REID

The Bruce Trail was completed as a continuous footpath from Tobermory to Niagara in 1967. The northern cairn overlooking Tobermory harbour was constructed by Ivan Lamkee of Barrow Bay. In those days, the Peninsula Club was only 41 miles, from Tobermory to Wiarton. The Lion's Head Club (30 miles) and the Lower Bruce Club (also 30 miles) later merged with the Peninsula Club for a combined distance of just over 100 miles. (All distances in the early guidebook were measured in miles, from north to south.)

In 1970 it was decided that, in celebration of the completion of the trail, a scroll should be carried from north to south through the terrain stewarded by 11 clubs. The greetings to the municipalities en route would give some publicity to the Bruce Trail and its objectives. A timetable was set up to allow each club a week to ten days to publicize the Bruce Trail and make contacts with local politicians.

It was my responsibility to ensure that the scroll was moved from north to south in time to arrive at Queenston Heights by September 19, 1970, the date of the Bruce Trail clubs' annual meeting. All went well, and the Hon. Rene Brunelle was present to unveil the new cairn at the south end of the Bruce Trail on September 20, 1970.

My only active participation in carrying the scroll was on the first day, when, with Don Johnston, son of Jack Johnston, Reeve of St. Edmunds Township, I carried the scroll from Tobermory to Halfway Rock Point. I was the only person who managed to keep up with him on this 21-mile hike — just a week before my 50th birthday. I remain a Bruce Trail life member, Iroquoia, 1965 to present.

Fall colours in all their glory. — Photograph by Petoo

The Elgin Trail Story

ELENI STOPP

Our mission was to complete Hike #2 of a two-hike end-to-end, about 21 kilometres, from the St. Thomas trestle bridge to the Elgin Trail terminus at the beach on Lake Erie at Port Stanley. The Elgin Trail is approximately 41 kilometres in total. We had completed the first 20 kilometres or so on Saturday, May 10, 2008, a year and a half earlier. The trail that day was pleasant and well blazed, excellent for a spring outing.

On Hike #2, my friend and I ventured forth in good faith after a summer of record rainfall, completely unaware of the lack of trail maintenance we would encounter. Quite possibly, no one had applied their feet to this section of trail in the past couple of years.

We drove in one car, parked at the Port Stanley terminus, and had a taxi driver drive us back to the start of our hike in St. Thomas. She entertained us with snippets of local legends and folklore, and shared her excitement about spending her next vacation, in February 2010, at the Olympic Games in Vancouver. All was arranged and paid for, right down to great seats at the men's final gold medal hockey game!

Mother Nature was at her gleaming, golden best this day. The access into the forest looked promising, beautiful and primeval. We were happy.

Gradually, it became evident that a lot of trees and branches had fallen across the trail. We climbed over; we crawled under. A chainsaw would have been more useful than hiking poles, however. Some of these trunks and branches were huge.

Eventually, brambles joined the mess. Brambles crisscrossed the trail repeatedly, their enormous thorns gouging holes and scratching into all available body parts, even through our clothes. The brambles also kept snatching away our hiking poles.

Doesn't anyone here have a machete or loppers? A team of energetic trail workers would have made us very happy. Oh, for the weed-whackers and choppers to eliminate the enormous goldenrods standing in our way, so ripe with pollen that they coated us mercilessly, getting into our eyes, ears, noses, mouths and under our clothing. The yellow stuff was everywhere, all over everything.

On we trudged, carefully trying to avoid thorns and pollen etcetera.

Some of the etcetera included spiders and their webs, laden with sticky insect corpses. As we passed, we released a deluge of skittering spiders and a flurry of bugs and flies, which created an even more chaotic mess upon contact with the yellow marigold pollen — which I half expected to sprout on our sweating skin and soggy clothing.

The brambles and vines and long, crazy grasses must have spent a long time laying in wait for an opportunity to toss around a pair of unsuspecting tourists. It remains a mystery how my safety goggles vanished right off my face somewhere in that jungle. It may have been fun for them, but not for us.

Still, we were determined to hike on and so the plodding continued. Bridges were not where they should have been. We would spot them elsewhere, washed away, turned over or lying sideways in the gullies, deposited recklessly, out of our reach. Consequently, it became our mission to negotiate up and down rocky, muddy, slippery banks, in and out of riverbeds. At one spot, a huge tree had fallen across the river from one side to the other. With no bridge, this fallen tree was our only way across. This option was scary, but so was the thought of going back through what we had been through. Happily, our rambunctious youthful optimism prevailed, and we succeeded.

The challenges and obstacles presented by this overgrown trail were eventually behind us. Suddenly, and quite thankfully, it was over. We could stop the curses and insane giggles. "What happens on the trail must stay on the trail."

Seven and a half hours for 20 kilometres or so must be some kind of slow-going record. Had we anticipated this, we probably would not have attempted it. But then, who knows?

I suggest you do not hike the Elgin Trail unless you can take time at the end to remove those hiking boots and socks and cross the sand right into the soothing warmth of the late summer Lake Erie waters. We just stood there, in up to our thighs, watching the sun set gently while our feet gradually recovered. After such a long and crazy day, we could now anticipate a lovely, restorative and celebratory seafood dinner near the beach, in one of several inviting Port Stanley establishments.

The trail had presented conditions and situations that had potential to test any friendship. Happily, we survived the test, and our friendship, optimism and joy of hiking remain intact despite what the Elgin Trail dished up for us on September 2, 2009.

To Hell and Back

RANDY SMITH

When I answered the phone that day I did not know that the whole pattern of my life was about to change. It was my friend Wayne, and he had an idea, a plan for the next few years, and that was threatening enough to make me wary.

He had been hiking the past few years with a couple of friends, and he was proposing that he, I and another friend, Bob, begin to hike the Grand Valley Trail, a 275-kilometre walk following the Grand River.

The truth is the hiking did not interest me at all, but I always had a good time with Wayne and Bob and so agreed to try it. And so it was that on a Saturday soon thereafter I found myself leaving the house to meet them at a Tim Horton's in Dunnville, where we talked about old times and the new adventure ahead of us.

Our first challenge was to drive one car to the spot where we would end the day's hike. With three illiterates attempting to decipher the riddle of the lines on the page of our trail map, this was not going to be easy, but after some wrong turns we accomplished it.

Next stop was Rock Point Provincial Park, where we spent a couple of hours looking for the cairn at the beginning of the trail. A slow realization came upon us, a foreshadowing of what lay ahead, when we realized there was no cairn. We dipped our feet into Lake Erie and headed off.

Well, had the fun started? Was I missing something? I'd left the house for this hike at 8:00 AM. It was now 1:30 PM. I'd been getting ready to hike for five hours but had not taken one step on the trail. Already I was thinking I'd had enough. I could not help but think that this was not a good omen.

This was the first day of what should have been declared "the Walk From Hell." We got lost two or three times each hike because of missing trail markers, and we ran into unforeseen hazards such as long stretches where there was no trail and areas of very uneven terrain, with rocks and holes in the ground that we could not see because the plants were thick and often higher than our heads.

But between being lost, trying to find the next markers and breaking trail where there was none, something very odd happened! This adventure was making me happy! It was fun! We were adventurers going where no man had gone before! I know you're thinking that I had lost it, that what I was feeling was ridiculous, and I would agree with you and call my EAP to get counseling, except that my two friends were having the same experience.

We came together on that walk as we shared each other's lives and emotions. We overcame frustration and exhaustion. We celebrated victories and successes. There are no distractions when walking in a small group, and so talk cannot help but be honest and personal.

One day, while going through a section that definitely had no trail, we came upon a long expanse of a waist-high plants we had not seen before. As we pressed on, they began to slash our legs. Having no choice, we continued for the next hour until we got into trees again. Wayne started to look awfully uncomfortable, contorting his face and rubbing his legs. Bob and I started to chuckle, but our laughter soon turned into the same war dance we were witnessing. Our legs were covered with welts. We washed them with our precious water and made them feel a bit better.

We ended up at Bob's mom's trailer that night and spent an hour in front of the fire picking burrs and nettles out of our socks. At some point, to Bob's mom's protests, we tossed our $25 socks into the flames, realizing it was impossible to get all the burrs out; they could not be worn again.

We got very little sleep that night, our legs swollen, itching and burning. Wayne ended up going to the hospital in the middle of the night to be checked over. We decided we must have walked through a field of stinging nettles. It had taken us six hours that day to walk 7.5 kilometres.

The next day, the trail took us across farmland. We hesitated a moment when we saw three dogs by the house. Bob assured us that these were friendly breeds of dogs. Bob was wrong. I cannot write this in a way that will adequately convey the terror we felt. Let us just say that when I saw the look of terror on the faces of prisoners in front of the dogs at Guantanamo Bay, I understood exactly how they felt! The three dogs were protecting their territory and they let us know we were not welcome there. They stayed very close to us, sniffing, growling and baring their teeth, as we clenched our fists to protect our fingertips, while walking slowly and with no sudden movements. We didn't want to give them a reason to attack. It must have been a while since they had checked the trail. At a later date, we would discover, on a tree on the other side of the laneway, a sign saying, PRIVATE DRIVE – BEWARE LOOSE GUARD DOGS. I have to confess that we did not complete the full trail that day. Our recent memories of the dogs were still fresh in our minds, and we decided against going further down the path.

The more we hiked together, the more we came to count on the fact that when our hikes were completed, always taking hours longer that we had planned, they led inevitably to a local pub, usually an old one with lots of personality. It has been in these establishments that we have had some of our most memorable experiences.

One of these, in Paris, Ontario, had the word "New" before its name. This struck us as humorous, as the building looked like it had been bombed. There was certainly nothing "new" about it. On entering, we saw Wayne Gretsky's photo on the wall, with an inscription wishing the owner the best. There was one very loud, raucous table in the otherwise quiet pub. Across the aisle from them, a man was making gestures to let this group and everyone in the place know that he did not like them. When he spoke to the waitress, he sounded like Johnny Depp in *Pirates of the Caribbean* after consuming about ten beers. We could not understand a word.

Soon a new character entered from behind the bar wearing a huge Mexican sombrero. He danced around at the bar while everyone cheered and clapped. He danced right over to the table of revelers situated beside the Johnny Depp character, laid his hat on that floor and sat down. Mr. Depp looked at the hat, and at the neighbouring table. He reached out his arm out and knocked the ashes off his cigarette into the sombrero as he muttered something uncomplimentary. We sat in the corner, our grins turning to laughter as we took in the scene. This day only served to remind us why we frequent the pubs that many would avoid.

I could tell you about the time we leaped the fence to get away from the bull that was charging us, or maybe about the time the three of us were so exhausted we fell asleep on a church lawn for a couple of hours, or about the time we hid in a clump of thick trees even though it was lightning — a calculated risk chosen over getting soaked in the driving rain, as we had no rain gear. But I won't. I will just tell you that I do not know if I could ever find another 275 kilometres that would demand so much perseverance, sweat and blood, yet give such memories, experiences and lasting friendships in return.

The Grand Valley Trail

LOIS MAGEE

As one of the most elderly members — I was in from the get-go, when our wonderful Betty Schneider decided that we should establish a hiking trail — I have so many memorable hikes in my poor, old, deteriorating, muzzy mind that it is very hard to single out a Most Memorable hike, so this is probably going to be a hodge-podge of recollections, but hopefully it will do. And sadly, I cannot consult with dear Betty, who is still alive and kicking but suffered a severe stroke several years ago that has left her vigorous mind even more muzzy than mine.

First of all, I would like to say that the most wonderful and memorable thing I recall is the beauty of hiking in a group (a group that has mushroomed over the years, growing from the little cluster of us who set out to explore and chart what were to become the Grand Valley trails, to a membership of 400 and counting). It is the miracle that happens when you are walking beside another hiker and, however alone (sometimes through recent loss of a mate or perhaps just plain being a loner), for whatever wonderful reason, with no particular soliciting, you are just inclined to pour your heart out to a fellow hiker as you both marvel at the beauty of the woods and fields.

As is the case with people my age and beyond — our amazing Tom East is well into his nineties, still involved and probably walking much better than me — most of us have had hips and/or knees replaced and sometimes experience screaming arthritis in every joint, such that our walking, let alone real hiking, is curtailed.

But the memories are great! And not least of the happy activities on the trail are the maintenance times. Tom East's wonderful wife, Isabel, long since departed, sadly, was such a crackerjack. We never dodged a wearying but necessary clipping or clearing. And the standards are still right up there, with the likes of Nick Ebner and Co. and, oh, so many others carrying on in their quiet but very meaningful way.

So, instead of recalling in detail any specific memorable hike, I have given you my reasons for being a hiker. All hikes are memorable, and I treasure them all, especially the great people, past and present, and the young people who carry the torch, even organizing special family hikes — which is the best thing ever a child could do. Hiking brings families and people of all ages closer together.

The Humber Valley Heritage Trail

DAN O'REILLY

The longtime vision of creating a hiking trail that reaches up the Humber River at Lake Ontario to connect the Bruce Trail on the Niagara Escarpment and the Oak Ridges Moraine is steadily inching closer to reality with the ongoing development of the Humber Valley Heritage Trail in the Bolton–Kleinburg area.

Passing through an interesting array of old fields, meadows, lowland cedar groves and mature maple forests with wonderful twists and turns, it winds its way south to downtown Bolton. This hiking-only footpath begins at the headwaters of the Humber River near the scenic village of Palgrave. The official start of the approximately 18-kilometre trail is at the multi-use Caledon Trailway, just east of Humber Station Road.

When compared to long-established trails, such as the Appalachian Trail in the eastern United States or Ontario's Bruce Trail, the Humber Valley Heritage Trail is relatively new. It was first opened in 1996 after two years of planning by the volunteer Humber Valley Heritage Trail Association.

At the time the association was created, its founding members purposely included the term "heritage" in the trail's name, in recognition of the historic role that the Humber River performed in the settlement of the Bolton–Kleinburg–Woodbridge–West Toronto area. This was a prescient decision, considering the fact the Humber River was designated a Canadian Heritage River in 1999.

Establishing a new trail in virgin territory is not an easy endeavour. Apart from the actual physical construction, there were numerous logistical, planning, financial and administrative challenges the association had to overcome.

The genesis for the creation of the Humber Trail was a Toronto Region Conservation Authority concept plan unveiled in the early 1990s. As a result of the devastation caused by Hurricane Hazel in 1954, the authority had acquired several hundred acres of land for a proposed dam north of Bolton. Fortunately the dam was never built, and the idea of a hiking trail that would emphasize the area's green space and environmental features took root instead.

While the authority favoured a trail, it also had to be convinced that a responsible and viable group would build and maintain it on a long-term basis. That was the goal the original Bolton volunteers set out to achieve after scouting a potential route with conservation officials in November 1994.

To achieve that goal, those volunteers decided to organize a public meeting early in the New Year to generate public interest and support. Just before that meeting, the group appeared as a delegation to the Town of Caledon. Their purpose was to advise the town of their plans and to invite Carol Seglins, the mayor at that time, and council members to a meeting at a local high school in January.

This was strictly a public relations measure, as the town was not asked to contribute any funds. A consistent policy of the HVHTA from its birth has been to apply for environmental organization grants to finance the trail construction and to rely on membership fees and service club donations to offset administrative costs, the most onerous of which is liability insurance.

Despite it being a wet, foggy night, the idea of a walking trail in Bolton's backyard attracted an audience of 60 to 70 people. This was the level of support that the Toronto Region Conservation Authority needed to see in order to convince them to sign the required license agreement for the use of the Humber Valley for trail purposes.

Gradually, as those footbridges and boardwalks were put into place, the trail evolved from a concept into a real amenity. In tandem with that physical work was the creation of an interpretive trail guide by executive member Bill Wilson. Titled *Points of Interests Places of Power*, it includes descriptions of the environmental and historic features hikers can discover along the trail.

But a major goal had yet to be achieved. In its early years, the Humber Trail dead-ended at the north edge of Bolton because the only way into the village's downtown core was to cross the wide, sometimes turbulent Humber River.

In late 2002, however, a 6-by-110-foot prefabricated-metal span bridge was erected over the river, allowing the trail to be extended through the remnants of a 19th-century industrial village — where a commemorative pavilion has now been built — and into downtown Bolton. The installation of the bridge can rightly be described as a truly historic milestone in the history of the Humber Valley Heritage Trail.

End-to-End on the Oak Ridges Trail

HAROLD SELLERS

From April 24 to May 2, 2009, I undertook to walk the length of the Oak Ridges Trail, from Palgrave in the west to Gore's Landing in the east, a distance of 216 kilometres. There were two major reasons for this adventure. First, after a decade of walking the ORT and five years as executive director of the Oak Ridges Trail Association, I was leaving Ontario. My wife and I would be relocating to British Columbia that summer. The second reason was to raise awareness and funds for the Oak Ridges Trail.

Day 1 – We had a great send-off from the village of Palgrave, with area politicians and media present. Seventeen hikers began the trek with me. The weather was great, though windy, and as a result I got a sunburn! We saw early spring flowers. With comings and goings, nine of us finished the day. Cathy Simpson announced that she was going to hike with me every day. Great, I would not be alone and start talking to myself!

Day 2 – Cathy and I began the hike alone, but over the course of the day a couple of dozen hikers joined us. It was also the day of the naked jogger! Some of you will know that there is a nudist camp beside the trail south of Pottageville. This fellow is a frequent trail user, according to reports I have heard over the years. Less noteworthy, but perhaps more pleasant, we saw deer, turtles, a salamander, a red-bellied snake and many birds. The day finished before a storm arrived.

Day 3 – We started in Aurora and as soon as the clock struck the 9 AM it started to rain. The rain continued for an hour, but it did not dampen the spirits of the 11 who started. With the much cooler temperatures, we finished with more energy — plus I felt I was getting the hang of this! We celebrated with a pub stop in Mount Albert.

Day 4 – We passed the 100-kilometre mark as we reached Brock Road in Uxbridge Township. It was another warm day, and also a very long day. A detour around a flooded section — caused by the wet spring — added 2 kilometres to the route, bringing the day to at least 28 kilometres. But we made it and lived to hike another day. The regular Monday Trekkers linked up with us in the Second Pond area, so we had plenty of fresh conversation for the final hour.

Day 5 – This special day began in Coppin's Corners with a large group of hikers being led down Brock Road by two bagpipers for almost a kilometre until it turned into the forest. The day ended as Scugog Township Mayor Marilyn Pearce greeted us at Ocala Farm Winery.

Day 6 – Oshawa Major John Gray joined us at the start and hiked through Purple Woods Conservation Area with us. Here we saw the best display of spring flowers yet. There were even many white trilliums in bloom. Again we set a very good pace, finishing an hour or more ahead of schedule. With the sunshine and with time on our hands, we went to the general store in Enniskillen for some delicious Kawartha Dairy ice cream.

Day 7 – Soon after we began in Long Sault, we had a very special sighting on the trail. An expert checked my photographs later in the day and confirmed that we had happened upon an uncommon Blanding's turtle. Very cool! Hiking past the Wilmot Creek near the village of Leskard, we spotted several large rainbow trout trying to swim upstream to spawn.

Day 8 – On our second-to-last day, we entered the Ganaraska Forest. There was no rain and the temperatures were good. We had periods of blue sky in the afternoon.

Day 9 – The final day started with Cathy and me being joined by two other ORTA members. In the afternoon, more and more people joined us as we approached Gore's Landing. Some clouds were rolling in and the temperature dropped as a few raindrops fell, but that all passed as the day ended under clear skies. By the time we finished, there were about 30 folks on hand. Pictures were taken at the waterfront, and then about 20 of us went for dinner at Pitcher's Place Restaurant.

The walk was over. After nine days of walking, it takes a while to comprehend that the next day you do not have to put hiking boots on.

By far the best part of the experience was the time spent with so many friends: those who hiked all day; Cathy, who hiked every kilometre that I did; some who hiked a few hours; others who I had not seen for some time; mayors and members of provincial parliament; colleagues from other organizations; and the much appreciated hosts who billeted me.

This was an experience I will never forget. Thanks to everyone who helped make it possible. Now that I have done it, who wants to do it next year?

The Nanabush Trail

BEVERLEY NEVYN

Petroglyphs Provincial Park, home of "the Teaching Rocks," was established as a historic-class park in 1976. This 4,000-acre park is located 55 kilometres northeast of Peterborough, Ontario. The park has the largest collection of ancient First Nations rock carvings in Ontario. There are approximately 900 carvings of symbolic shapes and figures. The flat expanse of rock is generally believed to have been carved by the Algonquin people. The carvings are thought to be a thousand years old.

A large, windowed building was constructed in 1985 to house and protect the carvings. Inside the building, a gallery allows visitors to walk around the edge of the great, sloping mass of marble containing the mysterious glyphs. Their presence was known locally from at least the 1920s but did not become apparent to outsiders until May of 1954, when a group of prospectors chanced across them.

The rock site itself is a sacred place. To protect the spirit of the Teaching Rocks, it is respectfully requested that visitors not take pictures while at the site. It is believed that cameras steal the spirit of the rocks.

The deep crevices in the rocks are believed to lead to the spirit world. At certain times of year, the sound of underground water can be heard issuing from these crevices. Aboriginal people have interpreted these sounds to be the voices of the spirits speaking to them.

One of the markings on the rocks is a long-eared figure. It is thought to represent Nanabush, a trickster-type spirit who sometimes takes the form of a hare.

After visiting the Teaching Rocks, one can learn more about nature and Aboriginal legends by hiking the Nanabush Trail. The Nanabush Trail takes you through a mixed forest with exposed marble outcrops interspersed with low-lying wetland areas. Two boardwalks and a bridge take you across marshes and swamps. The trail loops around the northern shore of Minnow Lake. There is a steep hill near the beginning of this segment of the trail.

The Nanabush Trail is marked by red blazes and is approximately 6 kilometres in length. A trail booklet describes Native legends such as how the white birch got its black marks, why moss grows on rocks, how chipmunks helped the people, and how the Milky Way was created.

Ganaraska Wilderness Trail

ROSE MILLETT

"The terrain in the Wilderness is rugged and in places very strenuous. It should be attempted only by experienced hikers. Averaging 3 kilometres an hour is considered good going. West of Loon Lake, for about 10 kilometres, the route goes around beaver ponds, swamps, small lakes and over beaver dams with no landmarks visible, so watch the Blazes! Carry a compass and GPS, and have a good map with you. Never go into the Wilderness alone!" So it says in the *Ganaraska Hiking Trail Guidebook* – 2006 Edition.

Intimidating words, indeed…or a challenge!

The 65-kilometre section travels mostly through the Queen Elizabeth II Wildlands Provincial Park between Moore Falls and Sadowa, Ontario. It can be split into three hikes. The two outer ends can be done as day hikes, but the 37-kilometre middle section must be done in one go. Because of the rough terrain, most hikers backpack it over two days, camping overnight at the halfway point, Loon Lake.

Carrying a heavy backpack has always been a challenge for me, so it is not something I do much of. Having done the middle section twice before with a guided group, I knew how difficult it was and how easily one could get off trail and lost. I also knew how wild, beautiful and peaceful it is and yearned to go back. I did, and here is my story.

I could not go with the guided group due to a previous commitment, therefore I decided to go the following weekend with two friends, Michelle and Rob, who were brave (or foolish) enough to go with me.

We started off on the right foot — late! I misjudged the time it would take to do the shuttle from Victoria Bridge to Devil's Lake. The drive from Sadowa to Victoria Bridge is about 20 kilometres on a narrow dirt road with lots of twists and turns, and took much longer than I thought it would. Anyway, by the time we got to Devils Lake, our starting point, the rain had stopped, so it was not all bad.

Michelle and I had managed to get our packs down to about 25 pounds, but Rob, a big, strong guy, carried a much heavier pack. The access trail from Devils Lake to Petticoat Junction (the main trail) is 5 kilometres. Michelle and I found this to be the most difficult, probably because we were still adjusting to our pack weight and a bit apprehensive about what we were getting ourselves into.

The terrain of the Ganaraska wilderness is rugged, and in some sections the hiking is difficult and should only be attempted by experienced hikers. — Photograph by Derek Cripps

The trail was much better blazed and maintained than the last time I travelled it. We had very few problems finding our way. It helped that a group had gone through the week before, as the grass or ground cover was still bent from their footsteps in places. We were able to follow them when we could not find any blazes, though they sometimes led us in circles!

There are many beaver dam crossings, but the beavers seem to be slacking off. Wet feet are guaranteed! The first big dam is between Victoria and Wolf Lakes, where we saw huge piles of bear scat. We tried here, we tried there, finally realizing that the dam was under some 3 or 4 inches of water (more in places) and the willows had grown in considerably, concealing even more of the dam. We fought the willows and sloshed our way to the other side, managing to keep dry from the knees up. It was great!

We reached the camp at Wolf Lake around 4 PM, just as the skies let loose. We were under some trees, so were okay as we hastily put on our rain gear. After a rest and a snack, we decided to push on to Loon Lake, guessing it would take us about two hours at the pace we were going. The break must have helped because we picked up the pace and made it to Loon Lake by 5:30 PM. Menacing black clouds were coming our way, so we quickly set up our tents and a couple of tarps, one overhead and another sideways, for a windbreak. Our tarp setup was in a lower area with smaller trees, so we felt safe from any lightning strikes, as there was a big pine higher and in the open.

The rain poured, the wind blew, the thunder rolled and the lightning flashed for about 30 or 40 minutes. We were snug and dry under our tarp, with a litre of wine and a small bottle of Bailey's that Rob pulled out from the depths of his pack (no wonder it was so heavy!). How much better could it get? After the storm passed, we made our supper, finished the wine and packed up our food and garbage to hang. Finding just the right branch for hanging the food bag is always a challenge for me, and this time was no exception. After much searching and a few failed tries, we finally found one and safely hung our food.

The skies had cleared and a beautiful moon was shining. Right on cue, the wolves started howling, one of the highlights of the trip.

Much rested after an early night and late morning, we broke camp. For most of the second day, the trail crossed down and then up through ravines and gullies. Otherwise, the terrain was fairly flat and made for faster and easier travel. Nearer the end, there are three very deep, steep ravines that require good balance and strong legs, or a tough butt. Michelle and I chose the tough butt route more than once!

After the last ravine, the trail travels through an area in which waist-high (and higher) ferns, vines and brambles grab at your feet and legs. We were fortunate that the trail had been broken for us by the previous weekend's group, so it was not too bad — until we got to the creek.

The last water crossing is normally a small, quiet stream with a simple step-over crossing. However, today, it was a raging, deep, muddy, much wider creek. After checking it out, Michelle thought we could put some bigger branches down and cross on them. As we started to do this, the ground gave away beneath us. I was behind Michelle and was able to jump back onto firm ground. Michelle started falling and yelled to get her pack off as she was unbuckling it. We got it off and got her onto firm ground. Rob, meanwhile, had been checking out a spot. He saw what was happening but knew he could not get to us in time, so figured he would grab Michelle as floated by. He will be a long time living that down. Michelle and I briefly thought of using the broken away chunk of dirt as a stepping spot, but it was already dissolving and soon moved downstream. Then we realized that the bank we were standing on could also give way at any second, so we scrambled back up the bank. I glanced over towards Rob just as the ground gave way under him. He managed to grab onto some foliage and got safely up the bank as well. Crossing here was out of the question.

It wasn't an option downstream either, because the creek widened before it flowed into the Black River. Upstream was the only way, which meant fighting our way back through the tangled vines and brambles. We got separated a bit in the dense underbrush, but remained within earshot. Suddenly Rob yelled that he was across. He had waded across at a narrow spot, but it was waist deep for Michelle and me. We really did not want to get that wet, so we continued further upstream. I found a submerged beaver dam with small trees growing along most of its length. The overflow was about 6 or 8 inches, but that was a whole lot better than 3 feet! I had some difficulty maneuvering around a few of the trees, but I made it. Rob saw where I was and came upstream to join me. Then Michelle emerged from the bush and joined us.

Once we were all on solid ground again, and on the right side of the stream, we took a breather, and then climbed over the knoll, found the trail and continued to the end without any further excitement.

The Highland Backpacking Trail

TARA CAMANI

One of my memorable hikes was with my father, Bryan, when I was in Grade 8. He was evaluating a trail in Algonquin Park to see if it was suitable for his Grade 11 Physical Education class. The hike was to be the Outdoor Education component of the course. His reasoning was that if his 13-year-old daughter could handle the overnight trip, then it should be no problem for a group of 16-year-olds.

The Highland Backpacking Trail is located just off of the Highway 60 corridor at 29.7 kilometres. It consists of a short, mostly uphill lead-in trail that is a bit of a challenge with a backpack. You then come to a junction. At this point, you keep to the right and begin a loop. You have the choice of doing a 19-kilometre hike or 35-kilometre hike.

This was the first time that I had gone on an overnight backpacking trip, so my father carried most of my camping equipment in his regular backpack while I carried a smaller pack filled with snacks, socks and my sleeping bag.

We arrived at the start of the trail early in the morning, surrounded by a cool mist. It was decided that we would try the 19-kilometre loop. I got to set the pace for the hike. I remember it being mostly uphill in the initial stages. Our first rest stop was beside a small set of rapids. It was a beautiful setting. I took the opportunity to photograph red squirrels, chipmunks, birds and the water. It was quiet and restful. We then packed up and continued on our way. As the hours of climbing up and down the trail passed by, I began to feel tired. This led to the inevitable questions of a 13-year-old: "Dad, are we there yet? How much longer? Do you know where we are? Are we lost?" Of course my father had an up-to-date map of the trail, which you can pick up at either of the main gates.

Because it was September, there were no bugs, but the temperature began to drop as soon as daylight started to fade. We arrived at our campsite as the sun began to disappear over the horizon. This was approximately the halfway point of our trip. My father scrambled to find the best spot to put up the tent and secure the site. The temperature had dropped so quickly, I wrapped myself in my sleeping bag as we made dinner, which was some sort of freeze-dried concoction. This, with a cup of hot chocolate, made me feel a lot better.

A couple of times during dinner, the silence of the evening was disturbed by unidentified noises. The crackling of leaves and small twigs, the swaying of tree branches as the wind blew through them, and the cry of the loon were all part of these strange sounds. Despite being a city girl, I was adjusting to my new environment. This was my first camping experience in Algonquin Park, and I was actually beginning to relax.

I was sitting at the fire with a flashlight in my hand, sipping my hot chocolate, when out of the dark came this chilling howling noise. It sent a shiver down my spine. I quickly asked my father what it was.

"Wolves!" he responded.

I jumped up immediately. "Can wolves get into tents?" I asked.

"No!"

My response to that piece of knowledge was to close and zip the tent door and whisper from inside: "Good, I will eat dinner in here!"

Thankfully, he did not tell me that one normally does not eat in a tent because other animals, such as raccoons and bears, might then be interested. I did not get much sleep that night as I reacted to every small noise that nature provided. I am sure my father did not get a good night's sleep either, what with all the poking and me asking, "What is that?"

In the morning, we awakened to a bright blue sky. It was crisp, but once we got moving, it was wonderful. My father made instant oatmeal and hot drinks. Then and now, almost 20 years later, I still feel that it was one of the best breakfasts that I have ever had. There is something about hot oatmeal and the start of a day of trail hiking. Maybe it is the dirt or the pine needles that always seem to find their way into your breakfast, but it always tastes so good. The same thing at home is just a gross, glue-like mixture that has no appeal whatsoever. After breakfast, we packed up our gear and began the second half of the loop.

The walk back was brisk and challenging for me but also a lot of fun. We made numerous stops to accommodate my tiredness and so that I could take pictures and collect fallen leaves. We tried feeding the red squirrels and chipmunks, but they wanted nothing to do with our trail mix.

All in all, it was a very exciting and challenging trip for me. It allowed me to prove to myself and to my father that I could handle an overnight hike. As a result, my father took me on canoe and hiking trips with his classes into Algonquin Park on numerous occasions. This experience opened up a whole new world for me, and to this day I go up to Algonquin Park at least once a year to explore other trails and lakes. Thanks to my father.

Algonquin Provincial Park, home to abundant wildlife (both two- and four-footed).

— Photograph by Andrew Camani

Algonquin's Sasquatch

KATE ELLIS

Every year, I try to escape the urban sprawl of southern Ontario to explore the sights and sounds of Algonquin Park. Just four hours from Hamilton, Algonquin offers me a variety of activities, from the simple pleasures of sitting around a campfire by a small lake to hiking over one of its many day trails. There are 13 self-guided hiking trails, each of which illustrates a different aspect of Algonquin's nature.

On Friday, July 31, 2009, I decided to hike the Mizzy Lake Trail. This 11-kilometre trail has the reputation of offering the best wildlife viewing possibilities along Highway 60. For the best chance of seeing wildlife, it is recommended that you hike the trail early in the morning.

With that in mind, I started my hike at 8 AM. Less than a kilometre into the trail, I passed a picturesque beaver dam and kept my eye out for the expanding V wake of a swimming beaver. Beavers are more active at night, but come autumn it is possible to see them out and about almost any time of day. Apparently, all the beavers were sleeping in that day. They must have had a late night.

Mizzy Lake is approximately 2 kilometres along the trail. It was here that I saw a family of otters playing along the shore of the lake. It is well known that otters are masterfully at home in the water. They swim so fast and effortlessly that they can actually out-race fish, and they can do that while swimming right side up or upside down. After observing these playful creatures for a good ten minutes, I decided to move on. As I turned to walk, I noticed what appeared to be a footprint, but I didn't give it a second look as I continued on the path. After walking approximately 600 metres, I arrived at the abandoned roadbed of the Ottawa, Arnprior & Parry Sound Railway.

Over the next 2 kilometres, I noticed moose, deer, bear, beaver and wolf tracks pressed into the damp forest floor. Amongst these tracks, I kept seeing what appeared to be human footprints. What person would be walking these woods without any shoes? This trail was rocky and root-covered. It was not humanly possible. Maybe, I was following a wild, hairy monster — a Sasquatch!

As the trail was about to leave the old railway bed, a moose stepped out of the bush and came to a stop approximately 20 metres in front of me. I immediately froze, astounded at the size of this particular animal. Her legs were nearly as tall as me. Thank goodness it was a female moose rather than a bull moose during the mating season. All I needed at this point was to have a bull moose come up behind me with a blood-chilling roar followed by the unmistakable clatter of his antlers being thrashed violently against small trees.

The standoff seemed to last forever. Eventually, she got bored of looking at me and much to my relief walked off into the bush.

The second half of the hike was wetter than the first. There were more boardwalks, including one that crosses a lovely open beaver meadow about 2 kilometres from the end of the hike. It was here that I noticed a fresh set of the strange footprints. Was it man or beast? Breaking into a run, I was determined to find out.

Over the next kilometre, my pace quickened along with my heart rate. Suddenly cresting the hill, I noticed two other hikers. My eyes were quickly drawn to their feet. One was wearing hiking boots, the other was not. When I finally caught up to the two hikers, I started up a conversation with the purpose of finding out as much as I could about this shoeless individual.

Early in our conversation, I discovered that they were father and son. The father was the one hiking barefooted. He had started hiking that way approximately ten years ago when he noticed a pair of sandals at the side of a trail with only footprints carrying on from that point. That inspired him to take off his shoes and try walking barefooted. He enjoyed it so much that he has never laced up another pair of boots and since that day has hiked barefooted all over North America. He stated that it was the intimate feeling he experiences with the trail that keeps him coming back for more.

Upon reaching the end of the trail, we wished each other a good day and continued on our separate ways.

As I was leaving the parking lot, I could not help but think how the Mizzy Lake Trail is without question the best trail for encountering wildlife. As it turned out, I did not encounter a Sasquatch but a man named Peter who turned out to be a good substitute!

Track and Tower Trail

SUSAN CHREST

Of all the hiking trails along Highway 60 corridor in Algonquin Park, the Track & Tower Trail was one that I knew we had to hike from the initial planning stage of our camping trip. It looked challenging, but more importantly, it looked interesting. I had purchased all the trail guides ahead of time from the Friends of Algonquin website and had already read through them weeks before we left for our trip. When the time finally came to hike the trail, we were ready!

The Track & Tower Trail is a 7.7-kilometre trail that winds its way around two lakes and through some beautiful Algonquin scenery, with some interesting historical sites along the way. There is an optional trail that spans a linear distance of 5.5 kilometres.

We only had the morning to hike, so we opted to do the main loop portion. I consider myself an avid hiker and have enjoyed the pleasure of hiking many unique trails in Ontario, as well as the Bruce Trail close to home, so the length of the trail did not seem daunting.

My husband, Dave, was my hiking partner on this trail. Our plan was to wake up early, while the morning was still cool, and be the first hikers on the trail. True to plan, we arrived at the trail before 7 AM and started the hike with our trail guide in hand.

We hiked for a fair distance before the trail broke through at Cache Lake. The lake was smooth as glass that morning, with a clear blue sky and fluffy white clouds reflected on its surface. Looking across the lake, we saw the remains of two wooden train trestles from the Ottawa, Arnprior & Parry Sound Railway.

After taking in our fill of the scenery at this stop, we continued on. Along the trail, we noticed an abundance of moose tracks in the soft earth. Many of them appeared to be recent. The thought of seeing any wildlife on a hike is thrilling, but we were especially hoping to see a moose.

As we continued through the forest, the sound of rushing water grew louder. The trail exited the forest abruptly into a clearing at the Madawaska River. It is here, where the river empties from Cache Lake, that a dam has been recreated. We learned that the site of this dam is in fact the site of a former log dam and chute built sometime in the 1880s.

The next part of the trail crossed the Madawaska River on a sturdy wooden bridge then continued up a small set of stairs. The trail wound around to a pretty little waterfall on the river. After the initial climb, we came to a point where we had to decide whether to climb the trail to the former site of a fire tower and a lookout or skip this short loop trail and continue on. It was an easy decision for us; we wanted to see it all.

I found myself slightly unprepared for the next part of the trail. We climbed higher and higher until it seemed impossible that we could climb any higher. Eventually, we came to the former site of the Skymount fire tower. Not much is left, only cuts in the rock that outline the location of the pad for the tower. In 60 or so years, what was once a clearing with an 80-foot fire tower has been taken over by tall spruce trees.

After another short uphill, we finally reached the long-awaited lookout. It provided us with a beautiful place to stop and stretch and have a much-needed refreshment break. The Cache Lake parking lot can be seen in the distance and marks the areas where the Highland Inn and the old Algonquin train station were once located.

After enjoying a long rest stop at the lookout, we hit the trail again. From this point on, the trail descended until we were back at the point where the trail branched off and the climb to the fire tower and lookout began. The trail then followed the old railway bed.

A short distance down the trail, we came upon the remnants of the wooden trestle and the subsequent steel trestle that crossed the Madawaska River. Again, other than some concrete abutments, one would never know that up until the 1940s a bridge spanned the river and carried lively groups of passengers by train to their outdoor adventures in Algonquin.

We continued to follow the old railway through the forest before the trail finally turned away from the railway bed and headed back towards the trailhead. Our last stop was at Grant Lake, a sheltered little lake that can be found only by hiking the trail. At one time the lake was named Gem of the Woods.

About three hours after we first set our hiking boots on the Track & Tower Trail, we emerged from the forest into the parking lot. The hike had been an amazing experience filled with both the beauty and the history of Algonquin. We were tired after our hike, but very happy that we had taken the time and effort to hike this trail.

Hiking in Killarney

MARJ ODELL

For my 40th birthday, we decided to do something fun and special as a family. In love with the outdoors, somewhat experienced and with three boys of healthy and adventurous constitutions, we settled on Killarney as our destination of choice.

First set aside from development in 1962 as a 48,000-hectare recreational reserve, today Killarney is designated and protected as a Provincial Wilderness Park.

Thousands of years ago, nomadic tribes travelled the La Cloche Mountain Range in their hunt for mastodons and caribou. Then came the Woodland natives, ancestors of today's Ojibwa nation. They called it "Heaven's Gate," a place for spiritual healing and vision quests. Samuel de Champlain explored the area in 1615, and it became a preferred route for the voyageurs in seasons of bad weather. Killarney has long been popular with fine artists, since Franklin Carmichael first visited in 1926, joined eventually by Lismer, Jackson, and Casson, fellow members of the Group of Seven.

It took months of planning and preparation for our five-day, four-lake backcountry canoe trip, which would be highlighted by a day-hike to the tallest peak in the park.

We picked up and packed our canoes at the Bell Lake access point and set out across the water for our adventure in perfect July weather. The heart just swells from the breathtaking and seemingly untouched beauty of the water, trees, land and sky of the park. Our canoes glided on dark blue lakes surrounded by granite, sometimes pink, rising high up from the water and topped with pine trees shaped by the wind.

Portages were opportunities to hike cool trails out of the sun and sometimes to meet up with other families on the route. Smack dab in the middle of a grueling 700-metre trek — heavily populated with mosquitoes and uphill both ways — we came across a huge animal deposit that created quite an obstacle, especially for those carrying the canoes. It also brought new appreciation for the name Hungry Bear Restaurant, which we had seen at the French River Trading Post on the highway before the park road.

Killarney Provincial Park boasts spectacular quartzite rock faces and pristine waters.

— Photograph by Paul Lewis

It would be five more years before I would see a bear in Killarney, on a trip with a friend. Just east of the main George Lake park entrance, we hiked a woodsy trail to "the Crack." That day there were warnings of bear sightings in the area and alternate campsites for those planning overnights. After a cautious and intentionally noisy two-hour hike, we came to a rock climb through crevices, around boulders and onto ledges that lead to the top of the range. Climbers are rewarded with a spectacular view of the Ontario Society of Artists Lake and the rich blue waters of Georgian Bay. It was while enjoying a rest in the beauty at the top that we watched, in safety and with respect, a black bear far below us, ambling without a care, soaking in the bright afternoon sun, here and there rising on his haunches to munch happily.

What a perspective from Silver Peak! Billions of years old, bared and gouged by ice, the quartzite of the La Cloche Mountain Range is such an amazing sight.

Today, we took a brief few moments to rest and try to absorb it all, and then we made our way back on the trail in order to avoid searching for our campsite in the dark. With the sun on our backs, we clambered down over rock, through blueberry patches and into the trees, finally reaching the long path through the woods where, despite the diminished sunlight, we were comforted by the sight of clear markers and familiar trail. We arrived "home" feeling safe and snug.

Reaching the tents in good time before dinner meant time for a swim. The boys had all the confidence they needed to turn a long floating log into a kind of bobbing game. They showed no trace of the fear I would have had even touching something that had risen from the depths.

They returned their friend the log to its resting place and swam to retrieve towels warming on the rocks, the climbed up to the campfire and their dad. Looking after them, in the setting sun, across our own private if temporary little bay on the lake, I contemplated the nature of fear and courage. Suddenly, less than 2 metres from the seat where I was pondering, and crossing the path where the boys had been swimming with such carefree abandon, the largest snapping turtle I have ever seen calmly broke the smooth surface of the clear water with her head and looked at me directly as if to say, "You are welcome," after sharing so gracefully with us her part of heaven.

The Hike From Hell

CHRISTINE BLAKE

Fortunately in a hiker's life there are repeated "wow" moments when you feel so very blessed to be alive. There is the physical exhilaration of having conquered the challenge, however large or small. There is the feel of wind on your face, the rustle of leaves underfoot, the occasional scurrying of wildlife behind a rock, and the appearance of a white carpet of trilliums — surely one of nature's masterpieces.

I was living in British Columbia when my sister called to ask if I would like to join her on a club hike in July. The hike was to cover the last 100 kilometres of the Rideau Trail. The group had started in Kingston and were working on completing the entire length of the trail. It was an opportunity to visit friends and relatives and spend the first week doing my favourite thing.

The schedule called for an average 20-kilometre hike per day, ending in Ottawa at the cairn around noon on the final day, with members of the Rideau Trail welcoming our little group and handing out certificates to those who had successfully completed the entire trail.

The weather forecast was not encouraging. Temperatures promised to be in the mid-30s all week, hardly conducive to heavy-duty hiking! The first day was brutal, and 2 litres of water barely seemed adequate. The only things worse than the humidity and the searing heat were the mosquitoes. They just thrived in this steam bath.

Forewarned, we lathered ourselves in bug repellant, carried as much water as our backpacks would allow and approached the hike in various forms of "undress."

Day three gave no relief. It soon became apparent that some of the group were moving at a snail's pace to conserve energy. After about 10 kilometres, the hike leader decided to split the group in half. While I was not a fast hiker, I fancied myself capable of keeping up with the faster group. Pleasant conversation and the camaraderie of fellow hikers helped dissipate the sweat on one's brow. It was not until we suddenly found ourselves separated from the group that concern started to set in. Here we were, three ladies, about 17 to 18 kilometres into our hike, without a trail map, scrounging the last few drops of water between ourselves, when the trail blazes suddenly led us through a swamp. We doggedly followed the blazes through the swamp — one hour, two hours. While my feet felt pleasantly cooled off, the lack of water became critical. We finally reached dry ground, convinced we were still on the right path. But based on the time of day, we should have reached our cars.

It finally dawned on us that we must have missed our cutoff. We stayed on the trail and at long last heard the life-saving music of highway sounds. We tore through the woods in the direction of those noises and found ourselves on a highway. Motor traffic was sparse and we must have looked a sight. We hiked north along the highway perhaps 15 minutes when a young man in a van stopped to pick us up. He offered us each a cold drink from the cooler wedged between the seats. Soda pop never tasted so good! Our knight and saviour then transported us directly to our motel. It was nearing 7:30 PM when we pulled in to find the rest of our group in a mini-panic. They had called the police at this point to report us missing.

I awoke the following morning to a burning sensation on the bottoms of my feet, and when I tried to get out of bed, I literally fell to the floor. On the balls of my feet were two huge Easter-egg blisters, the telltale signs of poison ivy. The blisters on my feet were so severe, I was unable to walk, let alone hike, on day four. On good advice from my friends, I burst the blisters and then applied Compeed, which works like artificial skin to protect an open sore. I was bound not to miss another day of hiking, and so I accompanied our group on day five, wrapping my feet in moleskin and my now thankfully dry boots. The heat of the previous four days persisted, and for much of the hike we were without the cover of trees or shelter of any kind. Every step was one of endurance and agony.

By the time we reached Ottawa, my arms, chest, neck — every part of my body —had blisters, aches and pains. My sister drove me directly to the hospital. An antibiotic injection and anti-itch cream mercifully translated into a restful sleep.

Back in my B.C. home, about three months later, I awoke to find myself once again covered in blisters. I needed another prescription of antibiotic cream, so I made an appointment at the clinic. The doctor seemed puzzled: "Are you sure it's poison ivy? We don't have anything like that in British Columbia!"

"No! We do not get 30-plus-degree temperatures and bugs and mosquitoes in the middle of summer either. For that experience, I had to go to Ontario on a vacation I will never forget!"

Lake Superior Provincial Park

RUDI BOSSHARD

The Lake Superior Coastal Trail is 65 kilometres long and is usually hiked in five to seven days. It is a part of the Voyageur Trail and hopefully will be connected to the north and south.

Lake Superior is the largest freshwater lake in the world; it appears more an ocean, wild and unpredictable. The northern shoreline is a vast wilderness area with a rugged trail, some trail markers, cairns and, of course, the lake. I have chosen the month of August because the weather is the calmest. Blueberries are usually in season, but due to the colder climate all around, they were not so plentiful.

As with all outings, preparation for this hike started long before the event. Eight friends had committed to join me for this hike. The long drive north is an experience in itself. The landscape changes as you go north, the rocks appear, lakes, swamps and so many other changes of scenery.

The first night we car-camped at the Agawa Campground. We sat around the campfire and talked about days ahead. The following day, we carpooled to Gargantua Harbour, an abandoned fishing village, and hiked to our first campsite, just 2 kilometres. There, we pitched the tents, hung the food and hiked north to Devil's Chair.

The trail follows an old logging road. Warp Bay has many campsites and a sandy beach, so it is a popular spot. At the end of the trail is Devil's Chair, where, 300 years ago, Natives mined red ochre for their pictographs.

Day 2, daybreak was 6 AM and on the trail by 8 AM. We passed by the cars again and packed food. The trail started out flat but soon climbed steeply to a lookout. The rain had stopped and the wind was drying the rocks. We had one last view north, back to Gargantua Harbour. The trail went up and down over difficult rock formations. We were hiking south, and this northern part of the trail is the most rugged section. We moved at a speed of 1 kilometre an hour, fully concentrating on our footing. The rock is volcanic, black and on many places overgrown. The view to the southwest is of the lake with waves pounding the shore. Our camp spot was Rhyolite Cove. The rock had changed again to a reddish flaky stone. Everyone was beat from the journey, which had required a high level of concentration to avoid falling.

Day 3, on to Orphan Lake. This was another long day, with just as many obstacles along the path. The trail climbed a raised boulder beach 30 metres above the water. It was chilly under the cover of brush and hot on the shoreline. The sky was constantly changing: overcast one minute, blue sky the next. The group had stretched out a bit, and so we waited for each other at many places. Boulder beaches are not easy to master; the rocks are of all various sizes and some are loose. Hiking sticks are a great aid while carrying a pack. I do not know if there is a scale to describe the trail's difficulty, it is simply rated as very demanding. This makes the trail attractive for many who possess the physical strength and endurance.

Day 4, we left a great campsite, with its bank of small stones washed up by the water. We crossed over the Baldhead River and went a fair stretch along a sandy beach towards Baldhead Hill. At Kathryn's Cove we re-supplied with food for the next two days. This is close to the highway, an easy access and departure point. A long, sandy beach followed after lunch and tired us out. There were more boulders visible up ahead, but we were now more confident in crossing them. We met a group of people heading north, but the trail is not overly used, and many camp-sites were empty. We stopped at the pictograph site at Agawa Rock. The lake was calm, so we had the opportunity to go out on the ledge to see the paintings on the rock face. Not all the pictographs have been explained, and many have been faded by wind, water and ice. The trail from here is rated 7 kilometres and 6 hours. There were many tricky passages, including boulders as big as a house that we had to hike around. The Agawa Point campsites were empty but not inviting to stay at, so we moved on to the next sandy beach. From here, we could see across the water to our destination, Agawa Campground.

Day 5, we enjoyed the last day on the trail. It was all flat and easy going. We passed the abandoned resort and crossed the Agawa River. We were soon back on the beach, and shortly after we arrived at the campsite where we had stayed a week ago.

A great many thanks to all my friends for making this possible — enjoying such a demanding trail, seeing nature and enjoying camaraderie. August 1 to August 8, 2009 Location: 140 kilometres north of Sault St. Marie, Ontario, Canada.

WESTERN CANADA

Sheep Mountain

MANUEL SAUMON

Hiking up Sheep Mountain was one of the highlights of a nine-week trip out West that my girlfriend and I did a couple of years ago. We were in transition from Ottawa, where we had lived for six years.

Sheep Mountain is located in Kluane National Park in the Yukon and is a must-do hike if you want to see Dall sheep. (You are pretty much guaranteed to see sheep.)

The trail started off nice and easy, with gradual climbs. We saw a few other hikers, but not many. Hiking like this is paradise, I thought — easy trail, beautiful views. The trail brought us pretty well to the base of the real Sheep Mountain Trail. In trying to find the correct path, we took a couple detours up goat paths, and we ended up bushwhacking for the first half kilometre, but we finally found the right trail. We then followed it as it appeared to climb to the sky.

Dall sheep. Where do you shop for your hiking boots?
— Photograph by Chris Alcock

The main reason we had decided to do this hike was to see the white Dall sheep. More than halfway up Sheep Mountain, we still had not seen any sheep, and we were starting to wonder if we were going to see any.

Somewhere along the mountain, I discovered I was

Kluane Lake with the Saint Elias Mountains in the background.
Kluane National Park, Yukon Territory. — Photograph by Jonathan Tichon

following another goat path. I found myself on a very steep side of the mountain. When I looked down, I saw that it would be about a 500-foot drop to my death if I slipped. Wanda, who was huffing and puffing along behind me at a slower pace, saw a better line up the mountain and got us out of trouble.

After seemingly endless false peaks, we finally made it to the top. Once I reached the summit, I had to quickly step back to avoid falling off a straight vertical drop over the top. It was one of the most stunning views I have ever seen. And it was here, at the summit, that we spotted our very first Dall sheep. They were about 30 feet from us, on the edge of the mountain. They saw us but did not seem to care. Looking around the mountain, I spotted hundreds of sheep.

We spent about an hour at the top, enjoying the view and the sheep. On our descent, we came across a sheep standing directly in our path. We were not sure whether it would charge us. Eventually it walked around us and gave us a clear path. The rest of the descent went well. What a great hike!

A Hike in the Far North

CLIFF KEELING

In October of 2008, I was one of approximately 75 passengers on the *Akademic Joffe*, a Russian icebreaker chartered by Adventure Canada, on a voyage whose primary purpose was to get as far north as possible.

We started in Resolute, after a charter flight from Ottawa, visited Beechey Island, where three of Franklin's men died (a question of lead poisoning) and are buried, then east through Lancaster Sound and north up Baffin Bay between Ellesmere and Greenland.

During the fifth night, the winds picked up to 50 kilometres, straight at us, and our ship started to ice up. In order to get further north, we would have to shelter somewhere for a day or two, and we did not have enough time. The captain decided to turn around at 78 degrees north. (I will get to the hike in a moment.)

By morning, we were sailing west along the seldom-visited south shore of Devon Island when someone spotted a herd of muskox halfway up the sloping stone beach. We all got into our waterproofs and were taken ashore by the guides in the Zodiacs. We landed well to the east of the herd and out of sight.

Beautiful scenery, pebbly beach leading up to red-brown mountains dusted with snow, clear skies, our white ship anchored offshore in the sparkling blue water.

About half of us walked slowly up from the beach and gradually circled around and behind the muskox. They came into our sight as we moved, nine of them, including two big bulls.

We were thankful for our binoculars and a bird-watching telescope as we slowly moved closer. They saw us but were indifferent until quite suddenly, after telepathic communication I presume, they took off together, thundering straight toward the other half of our party, a kilometre away, near the Zodiacs — straight at them — then veered upward to the left at the last moment and away, out of sight.

It was more exiting for the shore party than for us, to be sure.

The best part of the hike came next. For some reason we decided to head straight to the water rather than angle left towards our Zodiacs. As we approached the shore, we came upon a stone circle. Eight or ten large round rocks enclosed a space the size of a tennis court, with several smaller square stone structures encircled. One in particular intrigued us. One of our guides was an archaeologist, but she had no idea what the patterns represented. Fortunately, we also had as part of our tour party an 80-year-old Inuit who had grown up in the old ways. Jamsie Mike was his name. "Oh, yeah," he explained to her, "they used to put their female dogs inside so other dogs did not eat pups as they were born."

This was possibly a 200-year-old Thule hunting site. Our archaeologist planned to return to study the area in the near future. As for us, it was a hike we will always remember.

A Perfect Hike

ANNE ARMSTRONG

Take fantastic scenery, rugged and challenging terrain, and loads of history, and you have the makings of a perfect four-day hike.

At the end of June 1995, my husband, Phill, and I set off to hike the famous Chilcoot Trail. The trail goes from Skagway, Alaska, to Bennett Lake, in the Yukon. It was used by the thousands of people who rushed to Dawson City, Yukon, in hopes of hitting it rich in the gold fields. Our quest was simple: to retrace their steps.

We were challenged every step of the way as we hiked through rich rainforests, up long, boulder-strewn hills, and over the steep talus-filled slope of the Chilcoot Pass, covered in many parts with snow and spring runoff.

It was with great relief that we reached the end of the trail and waited to be taken out by train. But what a hike and what a trail it had been! Covered with artifacts from 1898, the trail is truly a living history book. Add the company of fellow hikers from as far away as Norway and Maine, and one has a perfect hike and a remarkable, memorable experience.

Sunset and fog in the Coast Mountains. — Photograph by David P. Lewis

Hiking at Cathedral Lakes

PAULINE COPLESTON

A vid hikers often have a spouse who is less enamoured of the sport. Such has been my observation after joining our local hiking group, where many conversations may include comments about a significant other's hiking reticence. I have personal experience — husband Gunter has too many other priorities to list in his top "faves."

However, since hiking is a big favourite of mine, and I like to hike once in a while with my husband, I periodically plan short hiking getaways for the two of us.

And so we come to Cathedral Lakes in British Columbia. This gem of a hiker's paradise lies hidden in the Coast Mountains. The lodge is located in Cathedral Provincial Park, next to the United States border.

The first adventure is meeting at a base camp location near Keremeos, British Columbia, and being transported to the lodge. As the Cathedral Lakes Lodge is located at 6,800 feet above sea level, in a rugged area, there are only two ways to get there, either in an all-wheel-drive vehicle or by hiking. We opted for the relative comfort of the motorized vehicle, which required about 45 minutes of bumping up a steep grade, over rocks and obstacles, before reaching the lodge. Some might need Gravol.

Our visit was at the beginning of July, still considered early season, and in fact there was snow in several places along the trail. We were lucky with the weather for the most part. It was cold and drizzly on the day of our arrival, but the weather turned clear and sunny for the next two days, which happened to be our hiking days. The clear skies made for unsurpassed views. Then the weather turned to wet snow on the day of our departure.

Of the many trails at Cathedral Lodge, the Rim Trail is a must-do. It is one of the longer trails in the area (8-10 kilometres), and it took us the full day. Six to eight hours are recommended, and it took us the full eight hours.

We began the Rim Trail at the lodge at Quinisco Lake and passed through forested areas with minimal elevation gain before the trail began to climb through alpine meadows full of wildflowers. Our new camera got a lot of exercise here, as I learned and experimented with the macro feature. My two goals were to come up with beautiful, frameable photos, and to be able to later identify the many flowers we observed. Unfortunately, these goals were not actually met. I should have read the camera manual before we started the trip. Gunter was patient with my experimentation, and we were delighted with panoramic views of glacial lakes and high mountain ridges. Photographic efforts were more successful here, with the outstanding scenery providing an excuse to catch one's breath.

Before arriving at the highest ridges, we scrambled up rocky slopes and traversed barren hilltops. The total increase in elevation is significant. One climbs to 8,500 feet above sea level, about 1,700 feet from the base lodge. Since much of the trail is above the treeline at this point, cairns (piles of rocks) rather than blazes are used to mark the way and are easily spotted along the trail.

Upon reaching the high point of the trail, one is rewarded with 360-degree views of the surrounding mountains (North Cascade, Coast, Kootenays). Being able to see mountaintops for miles in every direction makes one realize just how infinitesimal man is in relation to natural forms. Mother Nature's unique and natural beauty is also evident in the geographic formations seen along the trail. These impressive rocky formations have been given names such as Devil's Woodpile, Stone City, Smokey the Bear, and the Giant Cleft.

The route back to the lodge follows a different path, as one descends through gradually increasing plant cover back below the treeline. Although it was early July, one of the lakes (Ladyslipper Lake) was still ice-covered, and there were significant amounts of snow along the trail. Peak season at Cathedral Lake does not begin until the middle of July.

Upon returning to the lodge, we had a scrumptious home-cooked, buffet-style dinner, along with a complimentary glass of wine. The atmosphere was one of exhilaration as Gunter and I exchanged hiking tales with the other guests. After all that exercise and fresh mountain air, a relaxing soak in the hot tub topped off the day. Then it was off to bed, so we could prepare to do it all again the next day.

Our accommodations were in one of the bungalows, with four bedrooms and two shared bathrooms. Other types of accommodation were also available, including lodge rooms and cabins. Three nights at the lodge allowed two full days of hiking, along with other smaller walks on travel days.

The whole trip was a success, and even though Gunter often needs a bit of encouragement to go out hiking, he thoroughly enjoyed himself on this couples' getaway. This became even more evident when, some years later, he was asked to name a memorable holiday. "Cathedral Lakes Lodge" was uttered with hardly a hesitation.

The Canol Heritage Trail

AL PACE

The Canol Heritage Trail stretches 230 miles from the Yukon border to Norman Wells, Northwest Territories, and traverses the spectacular Mackenzie Mountain wilderness. The original Canol Road and Trail were built by American and Canadian military engineers during the Second World War. It was to provide a secure oil pipeline from Norman Wells in the event that the Japanese cut off Alaskan oil. The pipeline was constructed over one of the most rugged, mountainous terrains in the world and became operational just as the war ended. Production was halted and all of the camps, vehicles and equipment were simply abandoned in the field. During the 1970s, much of the pipeline and some equipment were salvaged, but many artifacts remain and are slowly being reclaimed by the landscape. The Canol Heritage Trail offers experienced hikers a challenging and remote hiking adventure on a trail steeped in history and stunning beauty.

The trail is rugged and wild, so we travelled with ultra-light gear, dehydrated food and lightweight two-person tents. We also packed a first-aid kit and a satellite phone. Having flown over sections of the trail on numerous occasions on the way into rivers in the region, we were excited finally to have the opportunity to hike a significant portion of the trail. Our hike led us from Mile 222 at the Yukon border, where there is air access, down to Godlin Lakes and Ramhead Outfitters, where there is another airstrip. It is one of the most beautiful sections of the trail. The many river crossings were quite manageable, and this section drops in elevation from 2,300 feet to 1,700 feet. The seven-night, eight-day hike was well paced, and we averaged eight to ten miles per day.

Our group was made up of eleven people, five men and six women. The age range was from 19 to 70, and all the hikers had intermediate hiking skills. Our group assembled in Norman Wells, NWT, which is accessible by Canadian North Airlines through Edmonton or Yellowknife. The flight into the heart of the mountains is simply breathtaking. We actually flew through the mountains, not over them. We arrived at the trailhead at Mile 222 in a North-Wright Airways Twin Otter. The wildlife manager stationed at the trailhead greeted our gang. While at Caribou Pass, we met an Aboriginal youth group who were working with Native elders in a traditional skills camp.

The first two days of our hike, we crossed the Mackenzie Barrens on a firm trail with a gentle downhill run. Once we reached Caribou Pass, we entered a more rugged mountain landscape. We all remarked that the hike down from Caribou Pass was one of the most beautiful regions in the Far North. The trail was mostly in good condition, deteriorating only near the rivers that flowed in the valleys. The rivers did require some care in crossing. We linked arms and used walking sticks to find our way across. The rivers and creeks were not deep, but they were fast flowing. We had all brought Neoprene water shoes for these crossings and took all the time necessary to switch footgear before and after river crossings.

We saw a myriad of caribou, several bull moose, and though we saw frequent traces of bear, we never saw a single one. Bugs were not an issue at all, and while campsites are not designated and are sometimes hard to find, they were often close to a creek and on flat terrain.

We carried light fishing gear and were rewarded with several fresh trout and arctic grayling, which supplemented our dried-food menu. Fresh blueberries provided colour and flavour to our pancake breakfast. The mountain scenery was spectacular, and the skies were continually changing. The weather in these mountains is mainly dry, but we experienced intermittent rain on most days.

At the Intga River, we explored the old pumphouse station where several old buildings remain, along with a collection of old GM vehicles, dump trucks and graders. At all of the river crossings, there are remnants of the original bridge structures. A flood destroyed all of the bridges in the 1970s. The trail follows the route of an ancient Aboriginal footpath that served as a trade route through the mountains, connecting the Mountain Dene of the Mackenzie River Valley with the Kasba First Nations people of the Ross River, Yukon, area. This part of the Canol Trail has great historic and cultural importance to the Aboriginal people.

Hikers interested in completing the entire 222-mile trail should allow a minimum of three weeks. On this longer hike, several large river crossings can create serious obstacles for even the most seasoned hikers. Ramhead Outfitters can provide helicopter support for food drops or to assist with river crossings, especially at the Twitya River. The Canol Trail lies in the heart of grizzly bear country, and the bears use the trail frequently, but groups of four or more hikers can travel with relative confidence knowing their critical mass will likely cause a bear to avoid contact.

Hiking the High Country

HARRY MOERSCHNER

My first encounter with the Skyline Hikers of the Canadian Rockies was in the summer of 1983. I hiked into their camp at Baker Creek in Banff National Park as a guest of the Kananaskis Guest Ranch, but was made so welcome throughout my short stay that I decided to join the club the next year.

In the summer of 1984 I spent two weeks with the Skyline Hikers in their base camp at Allenby Pass, Banff National Park, close to the border of Assiniboine Provincial Park, British Columbia. This is one of the prime hiking areas in the Canadian Rockies, with spectacular scenery. Mount Assiniboine, called the "Matterhorn of the Canadian Rockies," is the prominent mountain and is visible for many miles from all directions.

Two friends and I shared a common goal: to climb nearby Mount Cautley in Assiniboine Provincial Park. We headed out of camp just behind another group from our camp, led by the chief guide, Stephen Klatzel. After a side trip to take pictures of a waterfall, we eventually found the Lower Assiniboine Pass trail and crossed Assiniboine Pass. While trying to find the right trail for our approach of Mount Cautley, we reached an alpine meadow that was ablaze with wildflowers and offered a spectacular view of Mount Assiniboine.

Looking up at Mount Cautley, we noticed a large cairn challenging us. Off we went, up steep grassy slope, which gave way to broken shale and then to a narrow gravel path fit only for a mountain goat. This eventually petered out and became a shallow snow-filled trench.

Upon reaching the cairn, we found a spectacular view — looking 1000 metres straight down. By now it was about 3 o'clock in the afternoon, a light rain was falling, and we still had to get back to camp. We decided to make our way back by sliding down a grassy slope. It was while searching for any signs of a trail that we realized that we were lost.

We decided to follow a game trail, and with the aid of Jack's compass and map, we re-oriented ourselves and started bushwhacking towards the Assiniboine Pass trail, which would eventually take us back to camp.

Meanwhile, back at camp, fellow hikers were getting concerned about our failure to show up for dinner. In fact, the chief guide had radioed Parks Canada to send a helicopter to look for three missing hikers before it was too dark.

After what seemed like the longest part of the whole 35-kilometre hike, we finally arrived at camp around 8 PM. The call to Parks Canada was cancelled, and after apologies all round, we ate supper and gratefully fell into our sleeping bags.

On Saturday, the group hiked back to the trailhead to meet the bus that would take them back to Banff, while another hiker and I stayed in camp. The camp was quiet and almost empty over the weekend, as if it were returning to its wilderness state.

On Sunday evening, the cowboys arrived with a string of pack ponies. They were bringing in food supplies for next week's group of hikers. As we were watching the staff unload the horses, we noticed two majestic Rocky Mountain elk (wapiti) slowly coming up the valley towards the horse corral. We felt as if we were the intruders — which in fact we were.

Monday morning, two Parks Canada wardens came by on horseback to inspect the camp and talk to the outfitter's staff. The staff reported that a bell, hung at the root cellar, had rung during the previous night, and grizzly bear tracks had been seen in the area.

Because hiker safety is of the highest concern for Parks Canada and the outfitter, as well as the Skyline Hikers organization itself, bear warning signs were posted at strategic points in the area. All camps have since installed solar-powered electric fences for the safety and security of hikers and staff.

A new group of hikers arrived that afternoon, and we were asked to put our trail mix and shaving lotion into one tent. This caused some confusion but was taken in good humour and was eventually sorted out. The whole affair was a popular topic for the skits on Friday evening, our final night in camp.

My wife, Carolyn, and I have camped and hiked with this unique nonprofit organization for many years, and during that time we have made many long-lasting friendships through the common bonds that we share with our fellow hikers: an appreciation of camaraderie and of the beauties of mountain wilderness hiking.

Full Circle: The Bruce to Banff

DAVID WALLACE

My daughter Sara was already an experienced hiker on the Bruce Trail at the age of seven. Words such as escarpment, drumlin and limestone were part of her vocabulary. It was time to show her some more of Canada and some different hiking scenery. The mountains of the West were calling us. Skyline Hikers of the Canadian Rockies was the organization that would help the family get into the backcountry.

We drove across the country to Banff and stayed at a friendly B-and-B near the town centre. Saturday evening we attended the pre-hike orientation meeting, where we studied maps and met the camp personnel. There was a volunteer camp musician, a doctor, two hosts and several hike leaders. Meals would be provided by experienced cooks, and our baggage would be taken into the backcountry by pony trains.

We were up early on Sunday morning for breakfast and our last hot shower for a week! We then climbed aboard buses that would take us to the trailhead in Kananaskis Country. We were awed by the snowy peaks around us and made comfortable by all the friendly people in the group.

The hike in was long and included a knee-deep river crossing and significant elevation gain. The camp was a hillside of tents with chimneys to vent wood-burning stoves. There were also some large communal tents and several single-occupancy biffies. We headed to our assigned lot, "Prolific Meadows," to lay out our sleeping bags.

The first night's camp dinner offered plenty of hearty food, and after each course, we changed seats at the long tables. It was an excellent way to get to know our fellow hikers.

Following dinner, everyone assembled in the doughnut, a large circular tent with no roof and a blazing fire in its centre. This was the group meeting place where daily plans and evening entertainment were shared. We learned that there were hikes for sketching, fishing, the study of alpine flowers and even a bridge-building party. Each evening after dinner, groups reported on what they had seen and done that day — and each day the tales grew taller!

The last night in the doughnut was skit night. Each tent entertained us with wild tales of ridges climbed, bears sighted, avalanches narrowly missed, with songs and skits enhanced by amazing props — where did they find them in the wilderness? Everyone was moved by the camp doctor's recitation of a Robert Service poem. Inspired by his description of this great land, we all sang "O Canada" with gusto.

Back in Banff we experienced culture shock — so many people, so much noise and traffic. But that first hot shower was heaven, and how we appreciated soft beds, modern plumbing and a chance to catch up with the news of the world.

Our family enjoyed the Kananaskis Skyline experience so much that we returned the following year to camp at Sunset Pass in Banff National Park, and after a gap of six years, we went to Head Creek in Kananaskis. At one of these camps we met a camper who was knowledgeable about edible wild plants and had us tasting all kinds of unusual fare. A talented camp musician, Gerry, gave juggling lessons, and Sara became skilled in that art. We also met a geologist who talked about his work in mining and was thrilled when he found an abandoned gypsum mine on one of our hikes.

Back home, we regaled anyone who would listen with our tall tales of the Rockies. We told friends the true story of how one evening during dinner someone called us all out of the dining tent to see a grizzly bear and her two cubs on the mountainside. In my version of the story, the bears were just outside the camp, close enough for us to look them in the eyes. In Sara's version: "Dad, they were so far away you had to use binoculars to even see them!" I suspect the truth lies somewhere in between — and beyond the electric fence encircling the camp!

Two decades later, Sara is a geologist. She has spent several years flying into remote sites by floatplane and helicopter in the Yukon, Northwest Territories, British Columbia and Saskatchewan. Sometimes it is a small crew of four who camp under canvas and collect rock and soil samples and make maps. At other times it is a drilling site with a crew of several dozen, including wildlife officers and Native guides.

Sara knows how to plan and purchase the necessities for wilderness camping in the North, and northern landform terms are a large part of her vocabulary. And she now has the answer to bear encounters: she has bear spray, bear bangers and a firearms license. So far she has not had to fire a warning shot — or at least she has not told her concerned parents about it yet.

On a recent trip back to Ontario, Sara was happy to join us on a hike on the Bruce Trail near Milton. As she pointed out features of the escarpment, I felt as if we had come full circle. You never know where hiking the Bruce Trail will lead you.

Hiking in the Rockies

HARRY REGU

Following an enjoyable winter sport outing in the Banff–Lake Louise region, our small group (two couples) took off in September 2009 to revisit the same area for the purpose of hiking. We flew to Calgary, climbed into a rental car and soon thereafter were on our way. It is not absolutely necessary to have a vehicle at hand if one is planning to stay in one of Banff's many accommodation facilities, there is a shuttle-bus system available at the airport that provides door-to-door service to one's accommodations. Also, Banff has three public bus lines to take visitors to the most popular places of interest in this bustling, tourist-oriented town. Other tours offer scheduled trips to various locations throughout the National Park System.

As far as hiking is concerned, there are as many as 30 half-day or full-day routes available close by, with up to 20 additional hikes worthy of consideration. It should be mentioned that our foursome had no intentions to undertake overnight trips; such ventures, even though readily available, require different planning and preparations. Even daytrip routes need to be looked at closely, and it is important to remember that it is not distance that matters, but rather the degree of difficulty, which is based mainly on level of elevation. Whatever the case, the potential hiker should definitely obtain a map before starting out on a trip in any part of the Rockies. Also, it is strongly advised that you take along at least one companion. (Note: In certain parts of the Lake Louise area, park regulations specify a minimum of four hikers per group. Cell phones are recommended but may not have the necessary connection services in certain areas.)

In the hike descriptions that follow, the emphasis is placed on location and trail aspects; no attempt is made to elaborate on details pertaining to scenery:

1a) Bow River/Hoodoos and 1b) Tunnel Mountain: 7.4 kilometres in total. Both hikes offer excellent viewpoints. Route 1a takes you close to several weird-looking rock towers plus a platform overlooking the wide band of the Bow River. Route 1b requires a moderately steep ascent to the top of Tunnel Mountain, which provides vistas of Banff and the valley.

2) Sulphur Mountain: The hike is a challenging 5.5 kilometres long with a steep climb, but the hiker's reward is the spectacular scenery at the summit.

Lake of Little Fishes became Emerald Lake, which in turn became Lake Louise, honouring Princess Louise Caroline Alberta, daughter of Queen Victoria.

— Photograph by Harry Regu

A 1-kilometre boardwalk — erected primarily for the convenience of those who reach the top via the gondola ride — leads to the Sulphur Mountain Cosmic Ray Station, a National Historic Site, and allows for an interesting scenic walk with additional viewing possibilities. If desired, a 1.6-kilometre one-way access trail starting at the Banff Springs Hotel and ending at the Upper Hot Springs may be chosen, but we substituted this with a relaxing dip into the sulphur-laden pool — far better than taking a bubble bath, we all agreed.

3) Sundance Canyon: This 6-kilometre trek starts just past the Bow River Bridge and offers diverse options. Along its route one finds the Cave and Basin National Historic Site. The Basin was once a bathhouse. Debates over ownership of this site led to the creation of Canada's National Parks system. A well-constructed nature park displays such natural attractions as showy orchids (in season) and sulphur springs that spout directly out of Mother Earth. The trail soon merges with a paved bicycle path. This path winds its way along a tributary of the Bow

River before climbing gradually to end at the start of a small loop. The loop leads around the canyon and is used for hiking only. Our attempt to use a mountain-biking trail as an alternate return route turned out to be a poor choice, since the main route is more picturesque; live and learn!

4) Lake Minnewanka: Instead of spending a day trekking along one of the two longer routes in the area (Alylmer Pass or Aylmer Lookout), we opted on an easy walk around Johnson Lake (3 kilometres) followed by a moderate climb up the Stewart Canyon (about 3 kilometres one way from the lakehead). Neither tumbling waterfalls nor swirling rapids were to be seen, but the view was quite appealing.

5) Plain of Six Glaciers (Lake Louise): No visitor leaves this area without walking along the shoreline of picturesque Lake Louise. Since a round-trip is not possible, we chose a 5.3-kilometre one-way trip to the well-known teahouse, located a short distance from one of the glaciers.

A Mountain Experience

FRANK BOUMA

In the days when we belonged to a Farmers' Club, our monthly meetings included educational and social activities. At one of them, we had as speakers Bill and Audrey Snel. They told us about their 1995 trip over the Chilkoot Pass, leading to the Klondike gold fields. This awakened my interest in doing the same thing.

In August 2005 we headed off to the Canadian Rockies with the Skyline Hikers organization, who host five camps of about 50 people for a week each, with about five days of real hiking.

A highlight of that trip came on the second day, when we went to Mount Bolton, a 2706-metre peak in the Kananaskis. Together with 14 other hikers, we gazed down on the green prairies. The week included several more hikes and all kinds of weather.

The next hike was in August 2006. The very first day was up to Snow Peak (2750 metres) in the Palliser Pass. It was a 17-kilometre hike with a change of over 875 metres in elevation. We arrived at the base of Snow Peak with about 30 people. Once there, the message seemed to be "If you want to go to the top, you are on your own." We continued on in three groups of about ten people each.

Up we went, and the crowd thinned out as we went higher. The trail was fairly steep, with some vegetation. The remaining five of us regrouped and looked things over near the top of Snow Peak. Ray, the most experienced mountain hiker, said that he was going to try to go to the top. Gord nodded his head and Erica went on, too. That left Linda and me, a little sheltered from the wind, looking around for a while.

We were within reach of the top — 100 or 150 metres to go — but we were on our own and the path was narrow, rocky and steep on the one side. And we had to go down again, too.

I would have felt safer with a rope connection.

Linda said, "We did pretty well in our attempt. Let's go back, my grandchildren need me a little longer."

I replied, "I promised my wife not to take any chances."

Later, I heard the comment that it takes as much courage to go back than to go on. That day, we did not conquer Snow Peak.

The next day, our group went to Panoramo Peak, 2,590 metres.

Banff National Park

MARY McGEE

When I was asked to write about a memorable hike, I found I did not have an immediate answer. A hike can be memorable for a variety of reasons, both pleasant and unpleasant. I will not forget one of my early hikes with the Toronto Bruce Trail Club on the Niagara section of the Bruce Trail. It was early December, and I was dressed for fall. The unseasonably low temperature, combined with wind and snow, left me so cold, my mouth went numb and I could not speak. Following that experience, I expanded my hiking wardrobe to include several fleece items and warmer boots. Nor will I forget hiking in the Lake District of Argentina and the thrill of coming face to face with horses. And I am sure I will always recall how quickly I descended a narrow trail near the mouth of C level Cirque in Banff National Park after my husband sighted a female grizzly and two cubs. But the hike that I have come to think of as most memorable is one that I enjoyed for its dramatic beauty and variety of scenery, the endurance required by its ruggedness and length, and the pleasant company of family and friends for its seven hours' duration.

In the summer of 2004, my husband and I were fortunate to spend five weeks living in Canmore, Alberta, a beautiful mountain town located near Banff National Park's eastern entrance. Our time was spent hiking in the mountain parks and in Canmore itself. Towards the end of our stay, we joined longtime friends for a 17-kilometre hike in Banff National Park. The hike began at Moraine Lake, climbed into the meadows of Larch Valley, ascended Sentinel Pass, and then descended into Paradise Valley.

The hike required a car shuttle, so one car was left at the parking area for the Paradise Valley Trail on the Moraine Lake Road. It also required other hikers, since we were a group of four hiking in area restricted to groups of six or more. The restriction provides grizzly bears the habitat they need while helping protect hikers, something I appreciated after an encounter with grizzlies just two days earlier. We had only a short wait, at the trail sign for Larch Valley, until we could combine with another group.

The hike began at Moraine Lake, which is noted for its dramatic backdrop of peaks, popularly referred to as the Valley of the Ten Peaks. Shortly after a kilometre, switchbacks began for a steady uphill climb through a forest of Engelmann spruce and alpine fir trees. After another kilometre, the ascent became easier and the trail passed through stands of larch. It then entered a meadow that afforded a panoramic view of the Ten Peaks.

In Larch Valley, we encountered small pools of water and patches of snow. There we enjoyed easier hiking before having to tackle switchbacks up a steep talus slope to Sentinel Pass, the highest point reached by a major trail in the Canadian Rockies.

The summit of Sentinel Pass lies between Pinnacle Mountain and Mount Temple, which is the third-highest mountain in Banff National Park. Erosion of rock formations has created spires that, standing like sentinels, gave the pass its name. So we took time, both during our ascent and at the summit, to appreciate the surrounding grandeur and also to pose for photos.

After the 200-metre ascent to the summit, I thought I was over the worst, but the descent through boulders and talus was steep (500 metres) and long (over 2 kilometres) and proved more challenging than reaching the summit. But with the help of hiking poles and sometimes a proffered hand, I made it to the intersection with the Paradise Valley Trail, about 9 kilometres from our starting point.

There we had a choice of proceeding straight along the valley floor or selecting the higher and more scenic route past Lake Annette. We chose the latter, which required us to cross a major rockslide, which I recalled from a hike ten years earlier, when my husband and I completed the 18-kilometre Paradise Valley Circuit.

At 2100 metres above sea level, the slide provided the best viewpoint of Paradise Valley, whose name suggests the area's great beauty. We then continued on past Lake Annette, which is noted for its extraordinary view of Mount Temple.

As we approached the end of the hike, we were ready to sink into comfortable seats, remove our hiking boots and enjoy the feeling of accomplishment.

So wonderful are the memories of that hike. I recall a perfect summer day of warmth and sunshine. However, the photos suggest otherwise; we were in rain gear and fleece, and the skies were mainly cloudy with a few small patches of blue. But the photos do support my memories of majestic beauty and, judging by the smiles on our faces, of a fun-filled day.

The Plain of the Six Glaciers

MICKEY MacDONALD

The question is often asked, "What was your favourite hike?"

Reviewing past hikes that visited such places as the Peninsula section of the Bruce Trail, Gatineau Park across from Ottawa, Frontenac Park near Kingston, Cape Breton Highlands, and the Rocky Mountains area close to Calgary, brings back pleasant memories.

However, if I had to pick just one, I must go with the Lake Louise area in the Canadian Rockies.

The start of the hike is the parking area of Lake Louise in Banff National Park. The hiking path takes you along the north shore of the lake for 2 kilometres. We saw rock climbers attempting to scale vertical rock faces. They usually succeed, but I cannot explain why. We enjoyed the view of the lake with its blue-green colour and the mountains in the background. This attractive lake colour is caused by silt-sized particles of bedrock called rock flour, generated by glacial erosion.

Beautiful scenery lies ahead, and the mountain wildlife includes marmots (whistlers), chipmunks, goats, pikas (rock rabbits), and fortunately no bears.

The steady climb began toward a viewpoint of the base of the Upper Victoria Glacier (also known as the Abbot Pass View Point), 5 kilometres away. The trail follows the glacier till. Here the silence was interrupted by the loud rumbling of an avalanche across the valley. Numerous creeks feeding Lake Louise can be seen along the route.

We enjoyed the views of Mount Victoria, Aberdeen and others, and we were almost inspired to climb these peaks, until reality set in and we realized that we did not have the skills. To prevent hikers from falling into deep crevasses, chains are located on a section of the trail. Alpine wildflowers greet you as you continue the climb.

A side trail can be seen at the 3.5-kilometre point. It leads to Big Beehive, Mirror Lake, which we had visited on a previous day by taking another route. Using this side trail would make an interesting loop hike back to Lake Louise.

The climb continued through glacial moraine and above the valley slopes, and we reached the famous Teahouse after an hour and a half, at the 5.5-kilometre mark. Here we could see why the trail was given the name Six Glaciers: spectacular views of Aberdeen, Upper and Lower Lefroy, Upper and Lower Victoria, and Popes glaciers.

Everybody paused here, and we took a tour of the famous Teahouse. We had reached an elevation of 2100 metres, 370 metres above Lake Louise. The Teahouse was built in 1927 by the CPR and was one of five that were built for guests of that railway. In 1959, Joyce Kimball purchased the Plain of the Six Glaciers Teahouse from the CPR. Today, one of her two daughters, Suzanne, runs the operation. In the early spring, a helicopter drops supplies for the season (June to end of Thanksgiving), and fresh supplies are brought in by backpackers weekly. Employees stay five days then go down the mountain for a two-day rest. The prices for food items are reasonable, with a pot of tea around $2.75. Seating is provided on two levels, with some outdoor benches.

Some hikers end their hike at the Teahouse, but we continued the climb along the ridge of a mountain to the Abbot Pass View Point, a distance of one and a third kilometre.

The steeper climb leads to a land of rock and ice directly beneath Mount Victoria and the Plain of the Six Glaciers. We were now 7 kilometres from Lake Louise. There were no trees present, only loose rock and ice. We were warned not to continue on the route ahead, which would have taken us to the famous Abbot Pass and the Abbot Shack. This route, known as the "Death Trap," is a deep gorge path between Mount Victoria and Mount Lefroy. The Abbot Shack is at an altitude of 2900 metres and was built in 1922 by the CPR. The pass and the hut were named after Philip Abbot, a climber who fell to his death in 1896. The shack is now operated by the Alpine Club of Canada and is open to visitors, but it must be approached from the other side, in British Columbia. From our vantage point we could just glimpse the Abbot Shack. A few of us scrambled up a short distance and had to slide down on scree. Meanwhile, the roar of another avalanche could be heard in the distance.

It was time for lunch — and what a lunch spot — above the treeline, with avalanche activity, glaciers and mountains all around, and the Continental Shelf before us. "Hello, British Columbia!"

Looking back on our trail, Lake Louise could be seen in its glory, and the return journey began.

While hiking back, the words of poet Robert Bridges (1844–1930) came to mind: "And as I turn me home, my shadow walks before me."

I Survived the Crypt Lake Hike

MONTY JONES

On Sunday morning, September 25, 1983, I was hiking on the Crypt Lake Trail, in Waterton Lakes National Park, Canada. It was snowing lightly, but not enough to obscure my vision. I remember the wind blowing into my face before I was attacked by a grizzly bear. I was singing softly when suddenly I saw the head of a bear below the trail, about 50 feet to my left. I had no way of knowing that 8 feet away there was a partly consumed bighorn sheep carcass on which the bear, a female grizzly, and her two yearling cubs had been feeding.

I first noticed the bear as she was coming toward me. She ran faster as she came closer, but I do not think she made any noise. The bear grabbed me by the front of the leg and I fell to the ground. I was carrying bear spray, but I could not reach it. I did not fight the bear but tried to keep my head down. I think I was mauled for approximately a minute or a minute and a half. I remember the grunting and low growling sounds between the bites.

Just before the bear left, she nosed the ground around me and made low growling sounds for about 15 seconds. I think I lay there for about 10 minutes.

I was not thinking too well and got up and started to climb a tree, getting about 6 feet off the ground. The bear returned and pulled me to the ground. This time however, I had my bear spray out. At the precise moment I hit the ground, I let the bear have it directly in the face with the full force of the spray. The bear released me and ran off into the bush. Luckily I was able to escape, and I received medical attention for my superficial wounds.

The next morning two armed wardens and I approached the attack site. Tracks on the snow indicated that at least three grizzlies were around. Just below the trail, we found a sheep carcass on which the grizzly bear family had recently fed. We left the carcass and returned to where the attack had taken place. As we were walking from the tree I had climbed, the lead warden saw the bear family approaching the carcass. The mother bear charged almost as soon as she saw us. The warden shouted at the bear to warn and deter her, but she did not break stride as she charged through the bushes. I focussed on a tree that looked good to climb if the situation escalated. I also thought of playing dead if I were among the first to be attacked.

In the silence after the shots, I could hear my heart pounding. The bear lay still. Her cubs had run off. Given the personality of this bear and the circumstances, it seemed unlikely that she would have stopped her charge without attacking us.

On Monday, August 16, 2010, I returned to Waterton Lakes National Park to hike the Crypt Lake Trail with my friend Sophie. The trail is advertised as one of the most spectacular day hikes in Canada. Access to the trailhead is by boat. On this particular day, approximately 30 people ventured forth on the hike. The trail switchbacks for 2.5 kilometres (1.6 miles) past a series of waterfalls and continues steeply up to a small green lake before reaching a campground. The final ascent from the campground to Crypt Lake causes the most problems, especially for anyone who suffers from claustrophobia or acrophobia. A steel ladder bolted to a cliff face leads into a natural tunnel that you must crawl through on your hands and knees. The next part of the trail is along a narrow precipice with a cable for support. The lake at the end of the trail, nestled in a hanging valley, is no disappointment. The steep dark-green walls of the cirque rise more than 500 metres (1,640 feet) above the lake on three sides. The international boundary is at the southern end of the lake.

The entire hike is an 8.7-kilometre (5.4 mile) one-way in-and-out hike, so all those people who are truly claustrophobic or acrophobic have the advantage of being mortified twice.

We had reached the lake without any major problems, though Sophie had been a bit nervous on the ladder and along the cable section of the trail. We enjoyed a wonderful lunch break sitting on the international boundary with one leg in the U.S.A. and the other in Canada.

It was not until we were on our return trip that lightning decided to strike twice. I was approximately 10 metres in front of Sophie when I heard her yell, "Bear!" Apparently, this was the third time she had yelled the word out. Meanwhile, I was looking directly down the trail trying to figure out which tree I had climbed in 1983.

After the word "bear" finally registered, I spun around. There, between us, was the biggest grizzly I had ever seen in my life. It must have been 10 feet long from snout to tail and weighed 900 pounds. To my surprise, he only turned slightly to acknowledge our presence before continuing his stroll up the embankment.

Once again I had survived the Crypt Lake Trail hike!

Whistler Flute Bowl

KATIE CAMANI-CONNELL

To some, skiing and snowboarding may simply be viewed as a form of outdoor exercise, a casual pastime or a vacation hobby. To local residents of Whistler, British Columbia, it is a way of life. The weather report is not just used to determine wardrobe selections for the following day, but to plan and organize everything you do.

I recall one morning in particular from my time living in Whistler during the winter of 2010. After experiencing a dry spell of nearly three weeks, rumours of a brewing storm rippled across the village like wildfire. Not just any storm, but an epic dump that would smother our mountains with fresh powder and extend the entire riding season into the summer. By early evening, the village had transformed into a ghost town, as everyone buckled down in anticipation of the day ahead.

My alarm went off before the sun had fully risen, and a nervous, hopeful sense of excitement crept under the covers and reached down to the tips of my toes. A feeling similar to that of Christmas morning moved through my body. After donning all the necessary gear and fueling up with a warm breakfast, I began the

Christmas comes early to Whistler. — Photograph by Katie Camani-Connell

trek with a peaceful walk through the quiet village. With the exception of a few footprints, the snow remained untouched and covered the ground like a fresh, fluffy blanket.

The ride up the gondola was almost silent, making the already slow-moving cabin appear to creep along at an even more sluggish pace. The flakes continued to fall so thick around us that the very mountain we were gliding up remained hidden from view. Time was passed by adjusting goggles, buckles and bindings, in hope of making everything just right for the upcoming ride.

It literally took every ounce of self-control not to strap on our boards at the top of the lift. The vast sea of powder was just begging to be ridden. But knowing what was ahead forced us to hold off. Instead, we continued on to the chairlift, which took us even higher up into the snowy abyss. At this point the wind began to prick at our exposed skin like a million tiny needles, wet and sharp. By the time we got to the next and final chairlift, our faces were numb from the abuse and the only pain was a slow and steady burn.

When we finally unloaded at the top of the chair, we were faced with a blur of white. Although the snow seemed to have stopped falling, the wind was blowing so fiercely that it continued to blur our vision. Many who came up the lift with us considered this to be the top of Whistler Mountain and eagerly began strapping on their bindings, anxious to cruise down the blustery slope. Our group was not swayed. We hoisted our boards and skis and began walking up toward the Flute Bowl's peak. As we set off, the winds started to calm and the whirling snow slowly began to settle. The sun could be seen very slightly behind the clouds, and we could only hope that the heat would burn away the storm clouds before we reached the top.

After several minutes of hiking, the cold wind quickly ceased to feel like a stabbing bite to the face and more like a pleasant relief. I could feel my heart pumping harder and the sweat seeping slowly through each of my trusty thermal layers. We all opened our vents in a modest attempt to stay comfortable. The snow continued to settle, and it seemed as though with each step the sky became clearer. With the top in sight, we tried to quicken the pace, but our bodies felt twice their regular weight. Each step was a battle, an attempt to gain enough momentum to prevent sinking into the fresh snow, while at the same time trying to remain stable and avoid slipping on the icy ground below the surface powder.

A new wave of adrenaline seemed to take over as we neared the top, and when we finally reached it, the scene literally took our breath away. My eyes could not seem to see far enough to take it all in. The mountains spread out in all directions for as far as the eyes could see. Each peak was covered in a frosty layer of fresh snow so perfect in appearance that it could easily have been mistaken for a fluffy white sheet spread across the land. The sun was shining and seemed to make the scene around us glow as if it were a scene from a movie instead of real life.

The moral of many stories, in both hiking and in life, is that, in the end, it is about the journey and not the final destination. This, however, was not one of them.

The Chic Choc Mountains: Quebec's Best Hiking

BILL MUNGALL

The Chic Choc Mountains lie just 16 hours' drive east of the Greater Toronto Area, in the interior of the Gaspe Peninsula. Many accomplished Quebec hikers deem the region to be their best hiking area. The province markets it as "Eastern North America's newest mountain destination," for its wide range of accommodations as well as its unusual and dramatic scenery and wildlife. And it is an area of superlatives. *Chic choc* is Micmac for "insurmountable cliffs," and the views from their peaks were deemed "intense" by my backpacking companion, my 19-year-old daughter, Lisa. Think 800-foot peaks atop three Niagara Escarpments. The region also has the highest density of moose in Quebec. We spent four days without seeing a soul, but the path was rife with moose scat and hoof prints, and we did have the occasional sighting. The only caribou herd south of the St. Lawrence, stranded after the last ice age, loves the open plateau and peaks. The area allegedly has the highest density of black flies, too — so bad that the campgrounds come with communal "bughouses" for meal preparation. Luckily for us, by late summer the bugs had disappeared.

We planned up an 11-day, 155-plus-kilometre route on the International Appalachian Trail (Sentier Internationale Appalache), cherry-picking what we felt to be the best part. The IAT/SIA was the 1994 brainchild of Dick Anderson, then Maine's Commissioner of Conservation. Anderson organized a joint committee from New Brunswick, Quebec and Maine, and by 2000 he and his committee had extended the trail from the Appalachian Trail terminus in Maine, across the length of the Chic Chocs, some 1110 kilometres, to Forillon National Park on the Gulf of

St. Lawrence. This feat inspired a Newfoundland committee to begin work, now nearing completion, on an extended International Appalachian Trail, which runs along the western side of the Long Peninsula.

Our shuttle driver dumped us off at a trailhead at Lac Matane at 4 PM. We looked up, a bit daunted by the fact we had to finish 3,100 feet vertical in 7 kilometres in order to reach the campsite by dark. Just doable, we thought, but we had not reckoned on the straight-up style of the climbs, nor the fact that it would be completely dark by 8 PM (the latitude is level with Ontario's Kapuskasing). Switchbacks and even diagonal grades were nonexistent. The many spruce blowdowns could not be climbed over, and detours around them slowed us considerably. We stumbled into the campsite a half hour after dark. We really enjoyed the quality of the campsites, though, with a choice of shelters, tent platforms and, in a few, spacious eight-bunk refuges that had been built for skiers and offered big woodstoves on which to dry out the gear and cook. And outhouses with room enough for hanging the food packs out of reach of bears (everyone used them for this purpose). These also housed spiders, to Lisa's horror. At our third camp, she opted to do her business well to the rear of the shelter one evening and was interrupted by a magnificent 1,300-pound bull moose, who made his presence known to her when only 12 feet away.

We strolled from peak to saddle to peak for the next four generally sunny days, stunned by views, the isolation and, in many places, clear cuts that extended as far as the eye could see, except for the few kilometres around the trail. The hiking was tough in places, but tolerable.

As we reached the bare crest of Mt. Blanc, wind and rain blasted us violently. We reached an old cabin at the peak just in time. The cabin literally rocked from the blasts, but we cooked lunch and even caught a nap in the two bunks while waiting for the storm to let up. From there, the trail became easier and better maintained, without hazards, and we passed the days without incident.

But atop Mt. Nicole Albert, a sinister-looking peak we reached on day four, we were packing up from a late lunch when Lisa's jacket, wrapped in a ball, rolled and vanished into the only crevasse we saw on the entire trip. I climbed in and started down a muddy 45-degree slope in hopes of retrieving it, but some 50 feet down, I began an uncontrollable slide into the inky oblivion. I barely managed a handhold to stop myself. I looked below with the flashlight. Seeing nothing but blackness, a veritable anteroom to Hades, I quit while I was ahead. Our mood darkened in the rain as we slid down the trail off this peak. This was a harrowing descent due to its steepness, and a very scary plank suspension bridge at a lethal height above a raging torrent reminded me of an Indiana Jones movie.

On the last day, we crossed the big, barren plateau of Mt. Albert, where we saw more caribou and 5 acres of snow that had not yet melted! We descended to reach our shuttled car at the park's interpretive centre, beside the only road that crosses the range.

Our shuttle driver had mentioned that German and American visitors have recently discovered this hike, so you can count on more crowds in the future.

Hiking Grand Manan

SUSAN PREYDE

My husband has been having an affair for over 25 years — with islands. We were married on Prince Edward Island. After visiting Pelee Island, in western Lake Erie, in 1985, we have been visiting two or three times per year since.

Where are the Preydes going for vacation? Chances are an island somewhere. Islands hold some kind of spell over him. And so in 2007 we were drawn to Grand Manan, an island one and a half hours south off New Brunswick's Fundy coast.

Though closer to Maine than New Brunswick, Grand Manan is a Canadian island. A scenic highway winds down its east coast through picturesque villages with names like Seal Cove and Grand Harbour. Few roads push west across the island, as Grand Manan is tilted; the east side lies gently against the sea. Hundred-metre cliffs burst up out of the water for almost the entire length of the west side of the island. Along the top of those cliffs is a spectacular hiking trail some 40 kilometres long. Many hikers are drawn to the impressive wild landscape of the western side of the island, with its rough terrain and views of other Canadian islands and of the American mainland across the Grand Manan Channel.

The west side trail is blazed by tin-can tops and bottoms painted red and nailed to trees. For the most part, the treadway is easily followed, but there were a few places where other trails intersected and we had to hunt for the circle blaze to find the correct direction.

The further we got from access points, the more rugged the trail became. We hiked through rocky ravines and thick forest and along dramatic cliff edges. We found the trail to be quite well looked after, though some trimming was needed, particularly at locations far from access points. Like the Bruce Trail, this trail is maintained by volunteers.

An islander told us a tale of a couple who tumbled off the cliffs "a few years ago," and only one survived the fall. We already had a great deal of respect for the cliff edges, but that story kept us back even further, where possible, from the 100-metre drop.

On one occasion I did not get much hiking done as I instead sat on top of the cliff and watched a fishing boat bring in the catch from a herring weir. For landlubbers like us, the sight of fishing boats, seals, dolphins, whales and seabirds drew us landlubbers to various perches around the island for hours at a time.

The east side of Grand Manan is home to more gentle trails, such as those in Anchorage Provincial Park and at Castalia Marsh. The east trails offer strolls on boardwalks, beaches and tidal flats. In addition, the discovery of treasures such as hermit crabs and various shells, including the unusual shells of sea urchins, added to our walks. We poked along, turning over shells and rocks and sighting flora and fauna not found in Ontario.

An archipelago of islands lies off the east side of Grand Manan. Uninhabited Ross Island is accessible on foot or by vehicle at low tide and is home to white-tailed deer, eagles, an abandoned lighthouse and 7.5 kilometres of trail. White Head Island, named for a prominent white quartz cliff that rises 23 metres above sea level, is accessible by a small car ferry. Some of White Head Island trail follows the roadway, but with a population of about 200 people and the number of visitors limited by the capacity of the ferry crossings, the roads are pretty quiet.

Grand Manan has over 75 kilometres of trail. In our week there, we hiked less than half of the trail system. There is so much to see and do. We were so enchanted that we even took a trip to the library to use the Internet to check out real-estate listings on the island. We plan to return to hike the sections of trail that we missed the first time around. Grand Manan is a naturalist's and hiker's haven.

In this case, I am okay with my husband's affair!

A Fun Day at Fundy

JESSICA SLOMKA

If you ever find yourself travelling down the easternmost stretch of the Trans-Canada Highway 2 and are looking for a day's worth of adventure, I recommend you take a hike or two around the Bay of Fundy in New Brunswick and Nova Scotia. You can go for a day hike if you wish or you can do longer hikes around the bay. I chose to do a series of day hikes, travelling by car to different locations and camping out along the way.

My hike began with a descent along a trail of dirt paths and boardwalks into the cool, mossy Acadian forest, thick with ferns and red spruce trees. The trail broke through the forest onto a very coarse sand and rock beach at Point Wolfe. It was mid-tide, so the Point Wolfe River was completely flooded by ocean water, so much so that I could not see the river at all! At maximum low tide, the Point Wolfe River flows out to the main bay and a large gravel bar is exposed. I walked along the shoreline at low tide, and I could see the different beach benches formed from different water levels, as well as the intertidal communities that lived on the exposed rocks. The rocks on the north shore are green-blue metamorphosed volcanic rocks that are one billion years old! On the south shore, there is a high, steep cliff made of rocks that formed during the erosion of huge ancient mountains. I found several souvenirs of this rock along the drowned gravel bar of the Point Wolfe River. That night I camped out at Point Wolfe campground in Fundy National Park.

I continued my adventure along the Bay of Fundy north to Herring Cove. Along the way, I cooled my feet in the rocky Point Wolfe River where it runs underneath a covered bridge. To get to Herring Cove, I took a short hike through a spruce forest that opened to a sandy beach. On the beach, I saw rock beds tilted almost vertically. These rocks include sandstone that formed in a large ancient river and conglomerate that can also be found at Point Wolfe and Hopewell Rocks. Herring Cove beach was completely vacant, but I could see several kayakers checking out the many caves found in the shoreline rocks.

I also visited the Bay of Fundy in Nova Scotia. As I waited in a one-car line-up (the one car being mine) caused by construction on Glooscap Trail near Memory Road, I rolled down my window to say "Hi" to the friendly-looking construction

Hopewell Rocks, Fundy National Park, New Brunswick. — Photograph by Melissa King

worker holding a stop sign. He was 21 years old and grew up near Parrsboro, my ultimate destination. He told me of his grandmother in Toronto; his brother who was also holding a stop sign at the other end of the construction zone; his boss who drives like a maniac; how he bought a new car in Ontario and raced his brother all the way home to Nova Scotia; and his own business plowing snow. He also told me of a hidden treasure he recently discovered along the Bay of Fundy, with a beautiful view of the ocean and rocks. He insisted that I visit it and instructed me to turn left down a dirt road that is easily overlooked but marked with a wooden sign for Broderick Lane.

Sure enough, my first attempt to find this road was a failure. I drove right by it, just as he had warned. On my second attempt, I turned right onto Broderick Lane and travelled down the dirt path until I reached an open field with a single lighthouse on the edge of a cliff. I got out of my car and looked out over the Bay of Fundy. This sight was indeed a hidden treasure for hikers, as it looked out to rock islands eroded into arches large enough for boats to pass through. From the cliff top, I could see steep red cliffs of glacial till and a beach that stretched along the coastline. I climbed down to the rocky beach, where I found large sand-gravel foresets in the side of the cliff I had been standing on. I put my feet in the icy water and decided I would pass on the idea of swimming.

I continued my drive along the Bay of Fundy shoreline on Glooscap Trail and reached the small town of Parrsboro. Apparently Parrsboro has some Toronto Maple Leafs fans, indicated by a painted wooden Leafs sign in the front window of a house. Aside from Leafs fans, Parrsboro is the home of the most interesting rock and mineral shop. Called the Parrsboro Rock & Mineral Shop and Museum, it contains rocks, minerals and fossils collected from all over the world during the past 70 years or so. It is located at 349 Whitehall Road and cannot be missed because there is a large green dinosaur on the front lawn. When I entered the shop, I was greeted instantly by the owner, Eldon George, the man who discovered the world's smallest dinosaur footprints. A specimen is on view in the shop. He was friendly, humble and happy to get his picture taken with visitors in the shop.

I was very lucky to get a glimpse into the wonders of the Bay of Fundy, but there is still much more to see and discover. For those of you who decide to venture to Fundy, I suggest you bring a camera, a backpack for collecting rocks and fossils, a journal, a good pair of hiking shoes and, most importantly, a sense of adventure.

The Skerwink Trail

KATHY HODDER

N ewfoundlanders say, "There is no better place on earth than Newfoundland on a sunny day." And it was on a sunny September day that a friend and I set out to discover the Skerwink Trail, a hiking highlight of the Discovery Trail. The Discovery Trail is Highway 230, which extends from the Trans-Canada Highway up to the tip of the Bonavista Peninsula, so named because it was this point of land that Giovanni Caboto (John Cabot) first spied land on June 24, 1497, after his difficult journey across the North Atlantic from Bristol, England. Today, numerous hiking trails along this coastline allow walkers the opportunity to experience the pathways that early settlers would have used when travelling from village to village and to access vantage points from which to scan the horizon for ships at sea.

The Skerwink Trail is located at the outport of Trinity East, 2 kilometres off Highway 230 and just north of the better-known historic town of Trinity. The entrance to the trail is well marked and has a designated parking area. The local area was the recipient of funding in 2009 to improve trail maintenance and to put in a necessary boardwalk and steps. Fortunately, the manmade structures are located only on the actual footpath, and no barriers have been placed on the cliff edges. The trail is a 5.3-kilometre loop and can be explored from either direction. We found it fairly easy, but there are some elevations to climb.

The beginning part of the trail runs along an old rail bed before veering across an old farm field towards the ocean. We had to immediately curtail our desire to stop and pick wild blueberries, which were growing profusely. After passing through a copse of aromatic fir trees, we looked ahead to our first view of the ocean and the most amazing sea stack. Sea stacks occur all down this stretch of coastline and have been given names over the years — the "flat fish" because of its resemblance to a flounder, the "music box" because of the sounds created when the wind blows around it. The greatest challenge in walking along the headland was to keep going. One constantly wanted to stop and look at the view or to take photos or to check out the wildflowers and plants. Some of the windier areas were covered with petrified fir trees. The new steps made the ascent easy. As we approached the main headland, there was a wonderful spot to look back and to look ahead. We stopped for lunch at the headland overlooking Dog Cove Beach. Looking back, we could see the town of Port Rexton, as well as a fabulous view of the sea cliffs. This is the only place where an interpretive sign has been placed, as well as a bench for anyone who does not want to sit on the ground. From this vantage point, one can look ahead and see the Skerwink Rocks and a nesting site for kittiwakes. In June and July, this would be a marvelous spot to see whales and numerous seabirds.

Just further ahead was Skerwink Head, which is the turning point in this loop walk. Here, I crawled towards a spot to look down into spectacular crevices in the cliff wall. As we rounded the Head, we saw the most breathtaking view of the town of Trinity, which was settled in the 17th century. Today, it is a major summer tourist destination. It was worth the walk just to get this bird's-eye view of the town.

We then began our descent down the trail, much of which now has manmade steps. Again we crossed various types of terrain and more petrified fir forests where the trees create their own crackling music. Just before the final descent, there is a stunning view of Sam White's Cove, a beautiful protected cove and beach, formerly the site of a thriving fishing merchant's business. Once we crossed the beach, it was an easy walk past two small ponds — at one time, important sources of fresh water for local farmers — back towards the town.

The Skerwink Trail is not for the hiker who is interested in simply racing to the finish line. The mere 5.3 kilometres are meant to be savoured. In its short distance, it probably has more breathtaking vistas than most trails. And it is a delight for the geologist, the botanist, the photographer and the historian.

The Skerwink Trail

PAUL LEWIS

Located on the southern coast of the Bonavista Peninsula, just east of the town of Trinity, lies a hiking trail with lots of surprises!

I hiked this trail on July 1, 2009, while on a trip to northern and eastern Newfoundland with the Halton Outdoor Club. Even though this hiking trail is only 5.3 kilometres long, it took us 2.5 hours to complete.

This was a Canada Day that I will never forget!

The Skerwink Trail. A spectacular 5 km- (3.2 mile-) loop trail, that takes you through dense forest, along cliff-edge paths and over berry bogs via wooden walkways.

— Photograph by Paul Lewis

The trail starts on an old railway bed at the town of Trinity East. The weather was dull and cloudy when we started. The first kilometre is not all that exciting, since you first follow a rail trail and then turn into the woods for a while. Then you climb for a while and then the excitement begins. You come to a lookout overlooking many sea stacks and turquoise water. Then you walk a few yards and you come to another lookout, overlooking a different bay with different sea stacks! Then you hike on, and you come to more lookouts. Then a few lookouts and staircases later, you can look across to where you have been! Since I was near the front of the group, I could see the end of our group at the lookouts across the bay. I walked back to join the rear of the group so that I could take in this gorgeous scenery a little while longer! I had seen pictures of this trail taken by some of our club members who hiked here in 2005. (I was on the same trip, but I did a different, longer hike that day.) This time I took lots of pictures, thinking this was the only part of the trail that was this scenic. By now, the sky was starting to clear, and there was some blue sky in my pictures.

When I walked past where I had turned around before, I was surprised to find even more lookouts! Then the trail came to an exposed point, and I thought once again that the scenery was done, and we were going to have to head inland. Well, the trail came back out of the woods again and up more stairs to even more lookout points! (They have done a great job of building lots of wooden staircases on this trail!)

We came to another exposed point with lookouts on both sides. By now the sun was shining bright and it was getting warm. The sea was now blue instead of grey! We lay sunbathing for a while, taking in the scenery. Then it was up more stairs, and I thought once again that the views would disappear, since we were heading inland. I was proven wrong once again, as we came to another lookout point looking in a different direction, overlooking Trinity Bay. You could now see the town of Trinity in the distance. There was also an iceberg floating in the distance across the bay. Even though the trail leads inland, you can still see across the bay to Trinity.

Then finally the views disappeared and we went into the woods. Then we came to a side trail that went off to the right, with a sign saying it went to a lookout. Two of us decided to go and explore. After a very big climb, you were rewarded with a high 270-degree view! After coming back down, we were treated to more views over another bay and a rocky beach below. The trail comes down onto this rocky beach. There were more sea stacks to be seen from the beach.

This is the point at which my camera ran out of battery power! I thought to myself, we cannot be all that far from the end of the trail, so I will run back to the bus and get my other camera and come back. Well, the trail ended up being another kilometre to get back! The trail went around a small pond and then along a wide track to finish where we had started. I grabbed my camera and ran back. Just before I got back to the beach and the bay, I met the rear of our group! I now needed to run longer to get back to the beach to get some pictures. I took my pictures and ran back to join the rear of our group. Bruce Power, our local Newfie guide, from Branch but now living in St. John's, was hiking with the rear of our group. He has been our guide on all of our Newfoundland adventures (this was my fourth trip to Newfoundland with the Halton Outdoor Club).

I told Bruce that the Skerwink Trail, the trail we had just hiked, had more scenery per kilometre than any other trail I had hiked in my life! This trail had over 50 lookout points over just 3.3 kilometres of trail (since the first and last kilometre were not all that scenic). In addition, there was another kilometre of trail to the high lookout. This trail topped the La Cloche Silhouette Trail in Killarney for scenery per kilometre, even though the La Cloche Silhouette Trail still wins for overall scenery, since it is 80 kilometres long versus Skerwink's 5.3 kilometres!

Bruce was quite moved when I said this, since he is a very proud Newfoundlander!

So there you have it. If you want a short hike with lots of scenery "off the beaten track," head to Trinity, Newfoundland, and hike the Skerwink Trail.

I later learned that this trail had been selected by *Travel and Leisure Magazine* as one of the top 35 walks in North America and Europe in its August 2003 issue.

Newfoundland's East Coast Trail

JUDY LEENEY

The East Coast Trail, on the Avalon Peninsula in Newfoundland, goes south from St. John's along the Atlantic coast for 220 kilometres to Cappahayden.

One of the most scenic hikes is Fort Amherst to Blackhead. It is listed in the map guide as 10.6 kilometres, requiring 4 to 7 hours. Not a long hike, but rugged.

The parking area is in St. John's Southside, on the coastal road across The

Narrows from the Battery and Signal Hill. Park and walk down the road 600 metres to the trail. You start with a steep 500-metre climb up a washed-out track. The map guide kindly points out a resting spot on an old cistern 100 metres up. A 400-metre climb brings you to the top of the cliff, with spectacular views back to Signal Hill and St. John's. For the next 3 kilometres there are ups and downs across rocky ridges, but the trail stays on top of the cliff with great viewpoints. Pitcher plants and other ferns and lichens can be seen in the occasional boggy sections. At the bottom of Freshwater Bay, you can see a rocky causeway-like structure known as barachois. The trail crosses the barachois.

You pass a number of small ponds (not "lakes" in Newfoundland). At 3.8 kilometres, the trail turns left and begins a sharp descent down the Ennis River. Early in the spring, this must be quite a sight, but when we followed it down in July, it was steep and rocky but mostly dry. The trail comes out to the bay and then heads for the barachois that was visible from the cliff top 3 kilometres back. There is a mostly natural structure that was partly washed out in 2001 but rebuilt. Watch for the stepping-stones built into the rocky structure; they make crossing the barachois a much easier task. As you cross, you will see large pieces of rusted, twisted metal. Amaze your friends by telling them this is the wreck of the SS *Thetis* from 1936. In fact, all shipwrecks are clearly marked on the East Coast Trail maps.

After crossing the barachois, the trail climbs again and continues along the cliff edge. You have about a 5-kilometre hike left to reach the community of Blackhead. The map shows a string of interesting features: Sly Rocks, Sly Boots, Peggy's Bag and Peggy's Leg. The trail ends in Blackhead. If you continue 100 metres from the parking area across a footbridge into the village, you will come to a small grocery store that sells ice cream. A pleasant treat at the end of a hike!

The Spout

WANDA FERGUSON

A few years ago, Manuel and I made our second trip to Newfoundland. Our goal was to pick up where we left off from our first hiking trip to "the Rock," when we explored the west coast of Newfoundland, primarily Gros Morne National Park.

This time, we wanted to see what the east coast of Newfoundland had to offer. Upon researching Newfoundland's hiking opportunities, we were immediately attracted to its East Coast Trail, especially since I had already conquered Canada's West Coast Trail. Although much of the trail appeared to be a work in progress, it seemed that there were still a number of good day hikes from which to choose. According to the trail description, it would take us "past towering cliffs and headlands, sea stacks, deep fjords, and a natural wave-driven geyser called the Spout."

The Spout immediately caught my attention, so I checked the trail map and was pleased to discover that it was close to St. John's. The trailhead was said to be easily accessible, with good parking, and the hike was about 15 kilometres round-trip and listed as difficult/strenuous. I read no further. This was the trail for us.

The day of the hike, we got a later-than-normal start from our campsite. The trailhead was relatively easy to find, and we arrived there around lunchtime. The first part of the trail was a long grunt of a climb for a couple of kilometres, from the parking lot up to a high cliff at the edge of the Atlantic Ocean. According to our map and trail guide, the trail was then supposed to follow along the edge of the cliff, which eventually descended back down to the shoreline and the Spout. Once we reached the edge of the cliff, the trail was relatively flat and easy to follow. There were not many blazes or markings by Bruce Trail standards. It was basically a well-worn footpath along the edge of the cliff.

The views were absolutely stunning. We were walking along a cliff several hundred feet above the Atlantic Ocean, which was on our left. On both sides of the trail, there were a few stunted trees and some brush, but in many places, it was an open wind-swept plateau.

From the moment we started the hike, Manuel was totally in awe of everything, all of the views, all of the flora and all of the fauna. In other words, he was stopping constantly to admire something, be it a bird or a tree or even a rock. Initially, I did not mind, but after a couple of hours of this, I grew somewhat impatient and started walking ahead of him. A couple of times, I walked ahead and then waited for a minute or two while he caught up.

After a few stops, however, it seemed that his breaks were growing longer and my patience was growing shorter, so I decided to "stretch my legs a bit" and hike directly to the Spout. I thought it likely that Manuel would catch up to me quickly, as he always does, and if not, we could always meet at the Spout.

After about 15 to 20 minutes of hiking by myself, I still had not seen any sign of Manuel, so I stopped and waited for a while. I looked at my watch. It was more than half an hour since I had last seen him. That was too long. We would never make it to the Spout and back to the car before dark unless I hiked back to give him a bit of a prod. I called his name repeatedly, with no answer. So I walked back in the direction from which I had come, still calling his name. Eventually, I ended up back at the spot where I had last seen him standing on the edge of the cliff and gazing out at the ocean, looking for whales and birds of prey.

It had been over an hour now since I had last seen him. The trail was a single footpath along the edge of a cliff. There were no side trails, and there was really no apparent way for two people to miss each other while hiking towards one another. We had not seen another person all day. It was at least a couple of hours back to the car. There was no chance that he would have returned to the car without me, and he was well aware that our destination was the Spout.

At this point, there appeared to be only two possible explanations: 1) that inconceivably we had somehow missed each other on the trail, or 2) the unthinkable, that he had fallen off the edge of the cliff into the ocean below. It is difficult to describe the range of emotions and overwhelming sense of panic that began to envelop me, but I had to think this through rationally and weigh my options. It was getting late and I had two choices: 1) to turn around and commence hiking towards the Spout again, in the unlikely possibility that I had somehow missed him the first time, or 2) to hike back to the car and drive into town to get help to search for him before it became dark. Against my better judgment, I chose the first option. At every spot where the trail came to the edge of the cliff, I stopped and looked for his footprints and any sign that he may have slipped and fallen over. I even looked down at the rocks below and called his name.

Eventually, I arrived at the Spout. The geyser, although small, was unmistakable, with water spurting up every 90 seconds or so. I tried calling his name, but it was pointless because the crashing of the waves easily drowned out the sound of my voice. I waited there for a few minutes and then, for reasons unknown, walked a little further down the trail towards a primitive campsite that I had read about in the trail guide and had mentioned to him before the hike. Upon reaching the campsite, I suddenly heard some noise across the clearing, and then amazingly, he appeared from the bush on the other side.

Dozens of questions ensued. It turns out that immediately after I had started walking ahead of him, I had managed to find the one and only place where it had been possible to accidentally step off the trail. It would have been no more than a 15-to-20-second detour, but long enough for Manuel to get ahead of me on a mostly flat but constantly winding trail with lots of shoulder-height brush on both sides. I had completely forgotten that I had taken this very short detour.

When Manuel failed to catch up with me in a few minutes, he had started hiking at an increasingly fast pace, so there had been no chance of me catching up to him, especially after having backtracked for so long. After an hour of hiking without seeing me, he too had become worried that I might have fallen off the cliff into the ocean. The inevitable question was why he had not waited for me at the Spout, but instead kept walking down the trail past the primitive campsite. Did he not think that I might be worried? His answer brought me my first laugh all day. He asked what I was talking about. What geyser? He never did find it. Oh… that big rock with the water spurting out of it way back on the trail? Is that what I meant by a geyser? It turned out that the entire time he thought a geyser was some sort of sea stack or other similar rock formation akin to Flowerpot Island on the Bruce Peninsula.

After a huge sigh of relief, we both headed back on the trail and made it to our car shortly before dark. It had been a long day of hiking — more like 25 kilometres than the intended 15 — and a day that we will always remember.

Green Gardens, Newfoundland

MARY ROSE

This turned out to be the hike that had it all — wild, unspoiled natural beauty, variety of terrain, flowers, woods, streams, cliffs, the sea, and encounters with wildlife. Of course an iceberg, a few puffins and a whale or two would have been nice, but let us not be greedy.

We started off under a crystal-clear forget-me-not blue sky (yes, this was Newfoundland), so it was warm and bright as we began our trek up a gently sloping hill. The land was like a moonscape, with sandy yellow rocks and a few shrubs here and there, but this seemingly barren land revealed unexpected treasures at our feet — buttery yellow lady's slipper; bright pink, purple-fringed orchids; and deep, dark red pitcher plants.

At the top of the hill, we came to the inevitable fork in the road. A choice had to be made: should we take the short route and go down to the beach, returning the same way, or should we take the long way round? Of course we chose the latter and followed the trail as it took us up and around until we found ourselves amongst green conifers. We then started a deep descent down, down, down, right to the bottom of the valley, where we encountered our first challenge. We had to cross a stream. So off came our boots and socks, and we waded carefully across, clinging to rocks to keep our balance as the water cascaded around our bare legs.

Once across, we followed the trail up and down through the woods. Finally it began a descent that brought us to the same creek but much further downstream. After we had waded across once again, I felt myself drawn to the noise of the sea and walked down the beach nearby to watch the breakers crashing onto the shore. I realized to my horror that the waves were also crashing against the headland further down the beach and that there appeared to be no way to could get around them. Would we have to retrace our steps? A call from behind alerted me to the fact that the trail went inland and up the headland.

It was a very, very long climb up. Just as I was beginning to feel we would never reach the top, I heard a noise. We had disturbed a moose that had been sleeping on the trail! Luckily it was not a crotchety old moose but an inquisitive young one. It was so inquisitive that it decided to come down the path and investigate us. I did not want to be investigated, so I took off into the bush at the side of the trail (thankfully, it was not boggy), followed by my companion. Did we think it could not see us peering around a tree? It looked at us, and we looked at it, and then we carefully worked our way around the shrubs and emerged further up the trail. It was amazing how fast we covered the last section to the top of the headland.

And the view was magnificent! The turquoise sea stretched out before us, the cliffs on either side sloped down to the foamy water sparkling in the sunshine. The land stretched out on both sides as far as the eye could see, forming bays and inlets. This was the perfect place to stop and eat lunch and ponder the meaning of life.

Now that we had achieved the summit and enjoyed the beauty of the land, it was time to set off on the homeward journey. We followed the path, which led us into woods, through fields where sheep safely grazed, and into meadowlands, and always the sea was there at our side, glinting in the sun, creating a backdrop to the swathes of blue iris and yellow flowers that grew right to the edge of the cliff. Eventually the path led down to the shore, and we could feel the power of the waves as they battered the strange, dark formations that spiked upwards toward the sky while the frothy white water swirled around their bases. This was truly awe-inspiring. It was wild and beautiful and we had it all to ourselves.

But as all hikers know, if you go down, you have to go up again, and so we turned inland and began the long trek up through woods, past a campground. Soon the landscape began to change. The soil turned from rich fertile brown to dry-looking yellow ochre. The vegetation was becoming more like that of a desert, with cactus-type plants and sandy-looking boulders. This was familiar. It was similar to the moonscape-like landscape that we had encountered at the outset of our hike. We realized that we were nearing the end of the trail. We rounded a headland and found ourselves on top of a hill, and there, down at the bottom, looking like a tiny beetle, was our car. It is always the greatest relief at the end of long day's hike to know that the car is where you left it. All that remained was the gentle plod down the hill. We stepped around the beautiful gems of flowers growing in amongst the rocks, and our Greatest Hike Ever was completed.

*Green Gardens is located on the west coast of Newfoundland, south of Gros Morne National Park.

Our Gros Morne Adventure

JANE KENYON

I had dreamed of hiking and backpacking in Gros Morne National Park, Newfoundland, for as long as I could remember. My dream became reality when Phil — a retired accountant and trained wilderness hike leader who led backpacking expeditions — offered the trip. So the trip, the guide, the date and the group were all set, and I was ecstatic. Each person and couple were responsible for their own camping equipment, food and clothing. Phil would act as guide, leader, motivator and instructor as needed. We had a perfect combination: independence, the camaraderie of a group, and the support of a guide.

On July 25, 2009, the group met at the Park Visitor Centre in Gros Morne. There would be no single designated trail on this expedition, no markers, no defined route. We would be entirely in the wilderness and dependent on our navigational devices and Phil's experience to guide us. For safety, the park provided us with a transponder, which they could use to locate us if we became lost. Phil also had a GPS spotter that would allow us to call for medical aid if necessary. Fortunately, none of this was needed.

Along the channel through Western Brook Pond, Gros Morne National Park, Newfoundland.
— Photograph by Gillian Stead

Our last evening before setting out was spent arranging gear and clothing, preparing lunches, and discussing the weather possibilities, which at that moment were miserable — wet, grey and heavy. The long-range forecast, however, was good. When we woke to the same grey weather the next morning, we were a little disheartened. It is no fun to backpack in rain and wind, but the adventure had to begin. After an excited group photo at the start of the hike, we had an easy walk across a boardwalk east towards Western Brook Pond. On the coastal plain, the land spreads out flat along the shoreline. The fiords and mountains rose dramatically in front of us to form the massive, flat-topped Tablelands. The scene is breathtaking. Hundreds of millions of years ago, an ancient seabed was thrust upward by tectonic activity to reveal the Earth's mantle. These rare geological formations made it feel as though we were heading into a prehistoric landscape.

Our first challenge was to cross a river. We had to discard boots and socks, roll up pants, don water shoes and wade carefully with backpacks into the rushing white water. A cable attached on either side of the river enables hikers to negotiate the torrent. It was a struggle and a balancing act, but we all made it safely across and relatively dry.

We hiked through the bush for an hour before reaching our first campsite, at Snug Harbour, at the mouth of the fiord. The low cloud and mist hanging over the water made the scene mysteriously silent and subdued. The two young moose that walked directly through our campsite further enriched the atmosphere. We were finally in "the Wilderness."

Incredibly, for the next six days we had fantastic weather: not too hot, not too cold, no rain except slight drizzle on the last day as we got off the trail. One morning we awoke enveloped in mist and low-hanging cloud, a magical start to the day. The warmer days with no wind were the most challenging, as the insect life was voracious. The black flies and deer flies plagued us relentlessly. Most of us had never experienced such an onslaught. Thank goodness for bug jackets! With movement and good use of headscarves, long sleeves, pants and bug spray we made ourselves somewhat comfortable.

Each night we camped on a lake, on platforms if available. Each site was unique, and we enjoyed spending our evenings in a variety of settings. We experienced star-studded skies, including one with northern lights, others with unknown sounds in the night. Each site was equipped with an outdoor toilet, positioned discreetly in the bush, and a bear box for the safekeeping of our food supplies. The sites are minimal, for low impact on the landscape, and added to the feeling of really experiencing wilderness camping.

Our encounters with animals were magical — the goofy moose on our first evening and on three other occasions, and on our last day a proud caribou standing sentinel high atop a rocky outcrop, outlined against the sky and seeming to proclaim, "This is my land. I am king here." We had a brief view of an arctic hare and an even briefer view of a bear swimming in a lake — spotted as we left one of our campsites! The huge bear paw print that we saw in the mud on the trail one day gave us pause (paws). A lone baby duck kept us company and entertained with its diving and fluttering one evening. A ptarmigan mother and her chicks hurried past us one day on the trail. And of course the abundance of insects kept us busy!

This hike is challenging, we all concurred, but also so very wonderful, and we all felt we had achieved a great goal in many ways. You need to be physically fit and emotionally strong. Our group was incredible, with everyone looking after themselves whilst also working together as a team.

The Best Beer I Ever Had

PAUL TOFFOLETTI

In 2003, I visited Gros Morne National Park with 45 other people from the Halton Outdoor Club. The park is a UNESCO World Heritage Site. The first few days were spent hiking area trails that varied from green waterside pastures to the Mars-like red terrain of the Tablelands. It was not until the sixth day that we had a clear, sunny sky to hike up the "Holy Grail," Gros Morne Mountain.

We left the town of Rocky Harbour at 8:30 in the morning. This is a rather remote area of Newfoundland, and considering that it was a summer weekday, I did not think there would be too many people at the park. When we got to the parking lot, I was surprised to see it filled with over 50 cars and I thought, "So much for remote." We had been told ahead of time that the top of Gros Morne is windy and much cooler than down in the parking lot. The elevation of Gros Morne is 2,644 feet above sea level, and we all looked like we were dressed for December, even though it was 26 degrees Celsius in the parking lot.

We had a guide with us who knew all the trailheads. She told us that the hike would be about an hour and a half of uphill climbing just to get to the base of Gros Morne. She also explained that once at the base, there were two routes up to the top. One is a steeper climb over rocks, and the other follows a long trail that gradually rises. She recommended the steep, rocky route up and the long route down.

We started the hike along a well-worn path, and after an hour and a half of continuous climbing we came upon a flat clearing where we all turned to our left and had a great view of lakes and hills below us. After a few minutes, our guide told us to turn around, and there stood a massive barren granite outcrop similar in shape to Ayrs Rock in Australia. This was Gros Morne.

There were a number of tents set up like an Everest base camp but without the garbage. We could see the long, rising trail that our guide spoke of but could not see the other route. She pointed it out: a steep, eroded gully in the rock that ran from the base to as far up as we could see. As I looked, my eyes played tricks on me and I could swear that the rocks were moving. As we got closer, I realized that the rocks were not moving, it was hordes of people making their way up. A few people in our group decided that they would take this route. They never made it, as their legs gave out and they had to turn back. The trick is to take the hardest but quickest way up. This section would take at least another hour to climb.

Finally at the top, I buttoned my windbreaker all the way up and pulled my hood over. The wind is so strong that over the years people have made walls from available stones, lying behind them to get a break from the wind. It was a great view — the Gulf of St. Lawrence to the north, the Long Range Mountains to the south, hills and pastures to the west, and an amazing fjord, known as Ten Mile Pond, under my feet to the east.

After regrouping with a few others from the club, we started to make our descent, on the other side of the rock, where the long trail leads back to the base. It would have been too hard on our knees to go back down the way we came up. It was at this point that I thought I might run out of water. I had brought 2.5 litres and had less than half remaining. I asked the others, and they too were low. It would be two and half hours before we got back to the bus. So we pushed on. With half an hour to go, I was starting to get tired and had a dry mouth. I could not wait to get back to the bus, as I had another litre of water on it.

It was 4 PM when we finally stumbled into the parking lot and began to head for the water on the bus. On the way to the door, I passed by one of our members. She was standing beside some bushes and going through her backpack. I noticed an empty beer bottle near her feet. I pointed at the bottle and said, "This is such a beautiful place, and some idiots have to leave their garbage behind." She looked at me and replied, "Yes, I agree. You should go see the mess of beer bottles that has been left on the other side of the bus." As I turned the corner of the bus expecting to be disgusted, I was stopped in my tracks. My jaw dropped, my eyes opened up, and I must have had a huge smile on my face as the others standing nearby laughed. There was a cooler full of cold beer. It seems that after we got off the bus that morning, our driver went to town and picked up some beer, pop and ice. He already had the cooler in the bus. I was like a kid at Halloween time…no, make that Christmas because it was a surprise.

I would also have a few laughs while watching the expressions of others arrive and see the cooler. Of all the "after hike" pub stops I have gone to, this was the best beer I ever had.

"Tankdelardfereltanstringt"

BONNIE ZINN

My trip to Newfoundland in 2008 surpassed all my expectations. From the day we landed at Deer Lake and settled in at Dave and Vera's Anchor Down Inn at Rocky Harbour, until we departed A Bonne Esperance House on Gower Street to head for St. John's airport and home, each day was an adventure and a new hiking experience.

From the west coast's exhilarating Gros Morne climb to the East Coast Trail's magnificent ocean vistas, the trails that I had heard so much about and long anticipated all lived up to their reputations.

And then there were the unexpected, the trails that neither of us had heard of, that we came upon by chance as we drove across the province. Nothing could beat the Alexander Murray hiking trail at King's Point for a cardio workout, and the rewards were a beautiful waterfall en route and a great view once you reached the top. We encountered a black fox while walking trails at Long Point lighthouse. I managed to trap a bee in my pants while on the Badger's Park Trail, but we both came through the ordeal unscathed.

One hike I remember with particular fondness is the Bay Roberts Heritage Trail. We discovered this trail at French's Cove after making a detour to visit the town of Dildo. (Though we originally intended to simply take photos by the town sign, this turned out to be a lovely coastal stop.)

Upon reaching the trailhead, I ambled along ahead of my hiking partner, who was booting up. Not far in, I met a man returning from his daily walk. It was a very pleasant exchange, though at times I had trouble understanding him, as his accent was very strong. His parting words were "Tankdelardfereltanstringt." I detained him long enough to get him to repeat it, and when I deciphered his words, I heartily agreed.

The well-worn trail meanders through meadows and blueberry patches, past root cellars and beside an old gravesite overlooking the ocean. It takes you out on the edge of high cliffs and then leads to rugged rocks where you can carefully clamber close to the crashing waves.

It was an afternoon that combined so many good aspects of life — fellowship with a friend, perfect weather, Mother Nature in all her power and splendour — and a chance encounter. "Thank the Lord for health and strength!"

EASTERN CANADA 139

Middle Falls at Letchworth State Park, New York. — Photograph by Caitlin Mirra

UNITED STATES

Beautiful Letchworth State Park

MARIE-JOSEE BLOUIN

I truly enjoy hiking and discovering new places to visit. Packing your lunch in the morning and going for a three-to-four-hour hike is pure delight. Walking in nature brings such a sense of peace and quiet. It is also excellent exercise with many benefits.

The most memorable hike I have done in the past few years would definitely be at Letchworth State Park in New York State. I was there two years ago with a group of hikers. It was a three-day bus trip. The walk around this park was absolutely breathtaking. We spent three days enjoying the picturesque view while hiking along the canyon. We stayed at the Quality Inn about 45 minutes outside the park and commuted every day by bus.

We walked on a trail along the gorge. There are three falls — called upper, middle and lower — at the end of the park. These three falls are absolutely beautiful, and I took many pictures all along these hiking paths. To view the lower falls you must go down a staircase. The middle falls and upper falls are right beside the Glen Iris Inn, a small hotel located in the park. We even saw some people rafting down the river.

I also went on a hot-air balloon ride. What an experience! Getting in the basket and taking off into the sky — wow! To my surprise, the takeoff was very smooth. The basket is stable as you move into the air, and there is no sense of motion at all. The landing is a different story. The last 10 metres before touching the ground are pretty rocky. The basket goes side to side, and you have to hold on to the edge so you do not lose your balance. I had the chance to take many pictures from up in the air. It was an incredible 45 minutes that I will never forget in my lifetime. Flying over the gorge and letting the wind carry you to an unknown destination is a pretty amazing feeling. Something everybody should try once!

I definitely recommend hiking and visiting Letchworth State Park. You are guaranteed memorable hours of pleasure. Please do not forget your camera. You will want to capture your memories. Enjoy and have fun!

Hiking Down a Mountain

MARTI OBREZA

Hiking down a mountain in thunder and pouring rain is an adventure. For those of you who have never hiked up and down a mountain, I recommend accepting the next invitation. It is a great experience. However, a word of caution: going down is a lot tougher on your legs than going up. Of course, the definition of a "mountain" is relative to where you live, and I would not advise an attempt on the Himalayas as your first mountain climb. If you are from Toronto, the Adirondacks are a good place to begin.

This particular hike started off a cloudy day, I think — it is all foggy to me now — but I know it was early because our leader, who I will not name, to protect the innocent, likes to get up at 4:30 and be at the trail by 7 AM. Well, probably even earlier, but he had some more relaxed hikers with him. There were eight of us in total: six diehard hikers, me, and one other fit hiker who enjoys a good challenge. I probably had done the least hiking of the group, but I trail run and am pretty fit.

At the start of the trail, you are on soil with lots of rocks jutting out, so you do need some ankle support. Slowly the rocks get larger and larger, and eventually you are on large rock faces, sometimes at almost 90-degree angles, and you have the chance to play billy goat. Yes, I play in my mind as I hike. I think of myself as different animals from time to time.

I really enjoyed gradually climbing and climbing. Time flies as you look up ahead and wonder what is around that next corner, especially when you can see how far you have climbed as you look at the view to your side. It is spectacular, and I can hardly wait to get to the top. Working hard is fun. It is great to feel your heart pump — Pump it! Pump it! goes a song I like from Black Eyed Peas (again I digress) — and you know that you are alive and well.

Reaching the top was great. We sat on the rocks, enjoyed the view and had lunch. Everyone climbs at their own pace, so the group rejoined here. The last two, a couple, arrived just before we heard thunder. Oh-oh, that is not good when you are on top of a mountain. It began to rain. I saw a flock of people gathered around someone. They all had rain ponchos on. The man in the middle was the park ranger. The ranger said firmly, "You need to get down below tree line as fast as you can. Leave now." We fled down the mountain like a bunch of lemmings in rain capes.

The rain was coming down hard, and we were on rock. Those of us who worry about slipping (that would be me) must be careful with each step. But it was pouring buckets now.

We reached some fir trees and squeezed ourselves along a narrow path between rocks and trees. Meanwhile, water poured down the narrow path like a small tidal wave and soaked our hiking boots. As the water swished around us, we sometimes grabbed onto tree branches to maintain balance.

My, oh my, I really enjoyed the trip up, but I did not realize it was going to be like this on the way down.

As we continued down, we discovered there were some huge ladders that we

The Adirondacks in the sunshine.
— Photograph by Peter von Bucher

would have to go down, some of them leaning in such a way that we had to climb down forward, being careful not to trip on our capes and go over the cliff.

Then came huge boulders that we could not possibly jump down from, so instead we slid down on our butts. All the way, I was careful, though getting dirty and bruised. In front of me was an experienced mountain hiker. He would gain ten steps on me and then wait for me to catch up. He was whistling and extremely calm. No big deal for this guy.

Our group had separated. At one point, when the rain slowed down a bit, I suggested we drink some water and grab some energy, and two other fellow hikers passed us by. They looked quite happy walking through the mud, and they were going pretty fast.

When we arrived at the lake with a bridge over it, we saw so many others who had made it down the mountain of adventure. They were standing around, talking, laughing and feeling good that it was all over.

When you are in the midst of it all, it does not matter if it is easy or not; once you climb a mountain, you have to get back down the mountain. As they say, what goes up must come down.

The Final 4,000 Footer

JOHN EGSGARD

Have you ever given yourself a task and wondered after some time if you would accomplish it?

The White Mountains of New Hampshire are a rugged collection of peaks and valleys with trails more challenging than many in the Alps and the Rockies. Forty-eight of these peaks have elevations of over 4,000 feet. In 1973, I challenged myself to climb all 48 peaks. It took me 20 years to do so. Fortunately, my wife had a place on shores of Newfound Lake, within one to three hours' drive of every 4,000-footer trailhead. Thus, every summer, I had the opportunity to add more peaks to my list.

The highest peak is that of Mount Washington, at an elevation of 6,288 feet. Mount Washington is infamous for sometimes having the "worst weather in the world." In 1934, the observatory on the summit recorded the world's highest surface wind speed, 231 miles per hour. The temperature there has never risen above 72 degrees Fahrenheit. More than 100 people have died on Mount Washington, almost all due to weather-related complications.

Because of the open spaces on many of the peaks, one has to be careful to avoid climbing during thunderstorms. A few years ago, the leader of a group of hikers climbed a rock to warn her hikers of an impending storm seemingly miles away. She was struck by lightning and died. This took place on one of the most beautiful trails, the Franconia Ridge Trail, which runs 4.9 miles from Mount Lafayette (5,089 feet) to the top of Mount Flume (4,328 feet). Mount Lafayette and its adjoining peaks on the Franconia Trail were my first 4,000 footers.

The most challenging hike was up to the two peaks of Tripyramid (4,180 and 4,140 feet). The Tripyramids are best known for their slides, exposed slabs of rock that are visible from long distances. They offer great views while hiking and make for a unique trail. The rocky slides below the North Tripyramid and the South Tripyramid on the Mount Tripyramid Trail become dangerous when wet — as I discovered in 1979.

The longest climbs were to Owl's Head (4,025 feet) and Mount Isolation (4,004 feet).

Owl's Head Mountain occupies a narrow valley created by Pemigewasset Range to the east and the Franconia Range to the west. More than ten 4,000s surround Owl's Head. Needless to say, it is one of the more remote major summits in the White Mountains. It took my son, Erik, and I eleven hours to make the 18-mile trek from trailhead to summit and back.

As its name implies, Mt. Isolation's remote location makes this trip either a full-day in-and-out hike or part of a multi-day traverse of the surrounding ridges. Erik and I made the 16-mile return trip in just under 10.5 hours. On this hike, I accused Erik of tripping me on the return, as I stumbled and fell face-first in a puddle of muddy rainwater.

Although Erik accompanied me on several hikes, I have actually had 15 different companions. I made only three climbs solo: Moosilauke (4,910 feet), Passeconaway (4,060 feet) and Whiteface (4,000 feet).

On several climbs we stayed overnight at one of the Appalachian Club's huts. There are eight huts, with the distance between huts equivalent to a day's hiking. Information about these huts and about hiking the White Mountains can be found at the Appalachian Club's website, www.outdoors.org.

After 20 years of hiking, I was ready on August 6, 1993, to climb my 48th 4,000-footer. All of my family — my wife, Lyn, and my three children, Jennifer, Erik and Neil — accompanied me. At 4,170 feet, Mt. Cabot is the highest peak in New Hampshire's North Country, offering spectacular views from the site of a former fire tower just southeast of the summit. On our ascent, we stopped on a ledge and were approached by a Canadian army helicopter, which we decided, was there to salute my final climb. As we approached the summit, my family suggested that I go alone. At the summit, under the Cabot signpost, there was a bottle of champagne. How did it get there? Our children revealed that they had hurried up before me to deposit the bottle — a pleasant surprise. What a happy way to finish a task that I wondered if I would ever complete.

Climbing "The Rockpile"

GRAHAM STEAD

This is a tale of an ascent of Mount Washington. At an elevation of 6,288 feet, it is the highest summit of the Presidential Range in the White Mountains of New Hampshire. For Jane and me, the climb almost did not happen. Our four-day trip by car to the White Mountains had been a wet one. After the 12-hour drive, we arrived in Franconia Notch in a torrential downpour. Our windshield wipers could not keep up, our camping plans seemed to be crumbling, and we bailed to the nearest motel.

We did camp and hike in Franconia State Park for the next couple of days in drizzle and cloud, with partial views of dizzying heights whenever the weather broke. The final morning saw us at the Cog Railway base station, where we had hot tea while watching the steam trains start their long climb to the summit of Mount Washington. Suddenly, we saw an unfamiliar sight — the sun! We decided to set off upward and see how far we could get.

There are several trails to the summit, and we chose to ascend on the Ammonoosuc Ravine Trail. The trail starts off gently by following the south bank of the Ammonoosuc River. After 2 miles, we reached the aptly-named Gem Pool, a stunningly pretty spot where sunlight occasionally sifted down through the brilliant green all around. The huge volume of rain over the previous days was now evident in the mountain stream torrents and up — way up — in the splendid waterfalls cascading over the ravine.

Immediately after the Gem Pool, the trail rises steeply through the forest on the ravine wall. A fairly long section followed, with good footing and an enormous number of stone steps, ideal to get the heart pumping. About halfway up, we came across a side trail posted to a waterfall. Could this be the one we had viewed from far below? We decided to explore, and after a short walk we soon arrived at our viewpoint. We found ourselves on a rock ledge with a fork-tongued flume dropping towards us before disappearing into an abyss beyond the ledge and pool where we stood. We were now out of the trees and could see for miles in every direction and, far below, our starting point. An absolutely stunning spot for sure — we had a Kodak moment!

Alas, we had to leave, as time was slipping away. As the climb progressed through the forest, the trees thinned and became smaller, opening up spectacular views into the distance. Eventually, we surpassed the tree line and entered an alpine zone of bare rock and boulders. Through wisps of mist we saw the shape of a building ahead. This was the Appalachian Mountain Club's "Lake of the Clouds" hut, which sits in the saddle between the Mount Washington summit cone and Mount Munroe. How could we turn back now, with the summit in view and only 2 miles away? We continued upward, now on the Crawford Trail, traversing the part known as "the Rockpile." This is an agonizingly steep switchback over a jumble of granite boulders.

Clouds whipped across the antenna of the Observation Complex at the summit. Exhausted, we finally reached the top. It was a strange feeling! We had just hiked up a wild mountain, and suddenly we came face to face with tourists in shorts who had reached the summit via Cog Railway or the second route on the other side. Our late start left only time for a quick snack and pictures before beginning our descent via the Trinity Heights Connector Trail, off the summit to the Westside Trail. This then crossed over the Cog Railway Line and joined the Gulfside Trail. To our right, the clouds suddenly opened up to reveal the Great Gulf, an enormous gully in the side of the Presidential Range. The view was outstanding, down the valley and beyond, thousands of feet below.

Then, as quickly as it had been revealed, the Great Gulf was once again covered in a shroud of mist as the clouds moved back in. We passed beneath the summit cone of Mount Clay to the right and picked up the Jewell Trail, which, above the tree line, is more suited to mountain goats than hikers. Jane found it especially difficult as condensation formed on her glasses, obscuring and distorting her vision on a section where you needed all of your senses. Eventually, the Jewell Trail snaked into shrub trees and then mixed northern forest surrounded us. The descent from here was fairly gentle, as the trail followed the north shoulder of Burt Ravine. About halfway down, there was an open view of the ravine with the Cog Railway Base Station far below. Before reaching our destination, there were a couple of stream crossings, but none as spectacular as those of the Ammonoosuc.

With our loop complete, we had hiked about 9 miles and gone to the clouds and back. Ever since driving the Auto Route several years earlier, it had been my desire to do the summit the hard way. A "Mount Washington — Hike It" sweatshirt gift from my daughter a while back had also prompted me to make the climb. So, it gave us great satisfaction to finally "get the badge!"

Ontario hikers, be informed that within a 12-hour drive you have mountains — and bloody big ones at that!

The Panorama Trail

MAC McDANIEL

Yosemite is one of the "crown jewels" of the American National Park system. It is located on the western slopes of the Sierra Nevada Mountains, which naturalist and parks advocate John Muir referred to as "the Range of Light." It is best known for its polished granite cliffs, its huge monoliths, its hanging valleys and towering waterfalls, its giant sequoia groves, its pastoral meadows, and its biological diversity. A hiker's mecca, it boasts 1300 kilometres (800 miles) of hiking trails, but its heart is Yosemite Valley, only 11 kilometres in length and just over a kilometre in width.

Yosemite Valley was discovered by a militia group while chasing Indians shortly after the mid-19th-century California gold rush began. Soon there was a growing concern about the impact of commercial interests and, in 1864, President Abraham Lincoln signed the Yosemite Grant, the first instance of park land being set aside by the U.S. federal government for preservation and public use. It was the first preserve in the world to be protected for its scenic grandeur and was the precedent for the 1872 creation of Yellowstone as the first national park.

The park is most closely identified with Scottish-American naturalist and preservationist John Muir, who first arrived in 1868 and who wrote of this place: "We are now in the mountains and they are in us, kindling enthusiasm, making every nerve quiver." Muir quickly became an advocate for further protection, especially against overgrazing of the meadows and logging of the giant sequoias. Muir went on to found the Sierra Club, which in the 20th century became the most important conservation organization in the America.

There is an often-told story of a newcomer to the park approaching a veteran ranger and asking him, "What would you do if you had only one day in Yosemite National Park?" The grizzled old-timer replies, "Madam, if I had only one day in Yosemite, I would go sit by the Merced River and cry."

Of the park's many hiking trails, my favourite for an introduction is the Panorama Trail. It lives up to its name, with every turn bringing another dramatic vista. This is what Yosemite is all about: massive granite cliffs, classic glacial features, and waterfall views.

The Panorama Trail is 8.5 miles in length (13.5 km) and ranges in elevation from 4,000 feet (1220 m) on the valley floor to 7,200 feet (2200 m) at Glacier Point.

Because of the elevation change, most hikers choose to begin at Glacier Point and hike down to the Happy Isles trailhead. Thus, they park in the valley and take the day's first tour bus to Glacier Point, a ride of slightly more than one hour. (Confirm the bus schedule the night before; it is subject to change. Also, this is a "fair weather" hike; review conditions at the Visitor Centre before leaving for Glacier Point.)

The trail is not difficult, but people with knee problems should be aware that the descent is 3,200 feet, and they may wish to use hiking poles. As well, the Mist Trail section features over 600 steps carved into granite!

An alternate approach for those in excellent shape (and who wish to avoid the bus from Yosemite Valley) is to take the 4 Mile Trail from the valley up to Glacier Point and then the Panorama Trail to return. The total distance is 14 miles (22 km) and it is strenuous, but it is the ultimate Yosemite day-hike, with an unmatched range of scenery.

Although the temptation when getting off the bus is to begin the Panorama Trail immediately, make sure to walk the short trail to Glacier Point. John Muir made instant conservationists out of politicians by bringing them to this overlook. With its sheer drop into the valley, the view includes landmarks such as Half Dome, El Capitan and the full length of Yosemite Falls.

Then begin the well-signed Panorama Trail. As the name suggests, the panoramic views of Yosemite Valley are incredible. The trail crosses Illilouette Falls after 2 miles (3.2 km) and then continues partially uphill along the Panorama Cliff. A must-see detour on the hike is a 100-metre walk to Panorama Point. It is 0.8 kilometres after crossing the bridge over Illilouette Creek, and the views are truly spectacular.

At the top of Nevada Falls, the trail joins the Mist and John Muir Trails to descend to Happy Isles. (The John Muir Trail is longer and has fewer views, but it is less steep. Take it instead of the Mist Trail if your knees are hurting too much!) Here, the Merced River flows over the steps of the Giant Staircase, from the top of Nevada Falls to the trailhead, a drop of 1,900 feet (580 m). Nevada is 594 feet high; Vernal is 317 feet. As you descend the rock steps beside the falls, the spray will cool you down, but it can also make the route slippery, especially in the spring and early summer. However, in the spring, the falls are at their eye-popping best.

With 1200 kilometres of trails, Yosemite can become addictive for any hiker. The only downside of a park of such beauty is the crowds who also want this experience. As a general rule, the farther from the valley floor you get, the fewer people you will run into.

On Higher Ground

"Twinkle, twinkle little star; how I wonder what you are; up above the world so high; like a diamond in the sky…."

One gangly arm somehow disengaged from the sleeping bag and floated upward, plucking hundreds of sparkles from the surrounding blackness.

Minutes before, a pale-blue sky had somehow morphed into a sea of lava, menacingly encroaching, threatening to engulf the tents and sleeping bags below. The girl turned awkwardly onto her left side, only to be impaled by some vaguely unfamiliar firmness.

"Oh shit," she thought. "The professor." Earlier, she had begun shivering uncontrollably, and he had so generously volunteered to zip their two sleeping bags together for warmth.

In San Francisco, one hour prior to hopping in a van headed for Yosemite National Park, she had hastily purchased a thin nylon sleeping bag appropriate for use on any warm summer night. She had never imagined how much the temperature would plummet after sunset so high above the tree line.

"Dear God, please keep him asleep and, if you please, please let me live until tomorrow. I promise never to smoke that shit again!"

Two weeks earlier, after being designated the family emissary, I had boarded a flight to Los Angeles in order to rekindle our familial relationship with Uncle Joe. Years before, he had relocated to California after his first nasty divorce. (Rumours have it that he subsequently perished in the arms of some nubile 16 year old.)

These were the '70s — sex, drugs, rock and roll, and a most peculiar yet popular American west coast pastime, jogging. How odd it appeared to a teenaged middle-class intellectual wannabe from Montreal to see people regularly running for no particular reason to no particular destination, only to return home to immerse themselves in huge outdoor tubs of hot water. For hours, they would simmer at 90 degrees Fahrenheit, drinks in hand, inviting known or unknown passersby to join them. Alas, this would be the fate of the next generation, boiled and pickled to death before inception.

I had befriended Uncle Joe's second ex-wife's nanny, Claire, a rather muscular and intimidating girl sporting some really unusual tattoos. At any opportunity, rain or shine, she eagerly volunteered to apply and reapply my suntan lotion with unusual fervour. To her credit, I never once developed sunburn. As well, she was exceptionally talented at baking amazing brownies, whose main ingredient was some type of secret herb that left me feeling sort of jet-lagged yet giddy, delighting in the humour of any asinine conversation.

After a couple of weeks, I was desperate to escape the madness of this large and "plastic" city. The Los Angeles smog was stifling. My chest ached, my eyes were filled with grit, and in absolute desperation, I threw myself through the doors of the first tourist bureau I could find. My saviour turned out to be a very sympathetic university student who recommended I visit Yosemite National Park, which he promised would reveal spectacularly diverse scenery and clean mountain air. This park was located approximately 200 miles or a 4-5 hour drive east from San Francisco. The route followed I-580 east to I-250, east to Highway 120, then east into the park. Apparently, vans seating up to 20 people departed twice daily for the park.

The next day, I boarded a bus to San Francisco and plunked myself beside an amazingly clean-cut, well-groomed, bright, interesting and engaging young chemist. After several hours of great conversation, I totally anticipated a wonderfully romantic evening with "Mr. Right for the moment." Alas, two hours after arriving in trolley land, my bubble was burst, my ego deflated, etc., etc. "I'll be leaving you when we get to Polk Avenue," he announced. "I'm looking to get picked up tonight." Picked up? I understood only that in some way I was terribly inadequate.

After being so readily dumped, I felt embarrassed and humiliated. It was one of those rare hot and humid summer nights, and I was parched. Hoping to find something cold and wet — quickly, somewhere, anywhere — I entered the closest bar, which at first glance appeared to cater predominately to women. Within minutes, a very friendly statuesque redhead slid onto the barstool beside me. She smiled warmly, muttered something about my gorgeous dark tresses, placed one hand on my thigh, ordered two scotches, and asked me where I was spending the night. The feelings of unreality were overwhelming. I just didn't get it. Men were dumping me, women caressing me, and I really needed to get out of this place fast. I escaped my predator's grip, dashed out, hailed a cab, and 15 minutes later, with great relief, entered my sanctuary, a lovely B&B with a magnificent view of the Golden Gate Bridge. Slumber was most welcome.

At 8:00 the next morning, I boarded a bus, destination — paradise. Only one unoccupied seat remained, next to Marty, a Harvard professor who had done a considerable amount of hiking and backpacking in the Appalachians and White Mountains. He explained that Yosemite National Park encompassed both the low and high Sierras. Hikers often hire guides, along with beasts of burden, to spend a week or two exploring the more remote higher altitudes. (Apparently, there are now lottery draws for the chance to visit this supposedly pristine and unadulterated alpine topography.)

Marty had chosen to hike to the summit of the Half Dome, a 16-mile or 10-to-12-hour round-trip hike up to an elevation of 8,800 feet above sea level, approximately 5,000 feet above the starting point at Yosemite Valley. He anticipated spectacular views of Vernal and Nevada Falls, Liberty Cap, the Half Dome, and from the summit, a panoramic view of Yosemite Valley. I struck up a conversation with two girls from France and two guys from Switzerland, all of whom were experienced alpine hikers. By the end of our bus ride, we six had made a pact: all for one and one for all. We were determined to tackle the Yosemite icon, the Half Dome, together.

That night, we six new best friends broke bread and camped out under the stars. The night sky was clear, the air balmy, and the next day's forecast promised a high of 85 F. The ranger had suggested that each person carry one gallon of water for the day, as well as a purification filter. The only treated water available was at a drinking fountain located about 2 kilometres from the trailhead. Since there was no trash removal service on the trail, it was expected that nothing be left behind. Apparently, black bears were quite prevalent, and it was suggested that food and backpacks not be left unattended and that visitors not feed the animals, such as squirrels, Steller's jays or chipmunks, that might be sharing the trail.

I lay in delicious anticipation of my first mountain hike. The plan was to set out at 9 AM and spend the next night at the summit, above the clouds.

The hike was interesting, in that the terrain varied considerably, beginning in shaded forest and eventually climbing up to a number of flat, open viewpoints. Soon came "the Stairs," exposed rocky surfaces winding up toward the heavens, with several thousand-foot drops on either side. How I wished that instead of sporting tennis shoes, I had purchased a pair of sturdy hiking boots and hiking poles. By noon, the temperature was 90 F, and the sun's rays were relentless.

My two French female companions generously offered to carry my knapsack. They were smirking and muttering derogatory comments about how stupid I was to embark, so ill prepared, on such an arduous hike. But then again, for me, ignorance was truly bliss, as there had been no time for me to contemplate, ruminate and eventually talk myself out of the hike.

After five hours of steady climbing, enjoying magnificent viewpoints, our group arrived at the base of Half Dome. I was totally unprepared for the last 400 feet to the summit, the ascent up the cables. Thankfully, some hikers had, on their way down, discarded their hiking gloves, which proved invaluable to me. Otherwise, my hands would certainly have become blistered and bloodied.

After a one-hour climb, hands and arms aching, I finally reached the summit, an unexpected large, flat surface. I promptly made my way to the main attraction, a protrusion at 8,838 feet. The air was clear and thinner than I had ever experienced. I was giddy, intoxicated by the panorama: river canyons, valleys, waterfalls, lakes, bald peaks — in other words, breathtaking!

We six hikers set up camp and spent the next couple of hours sharing the sandwiches, dried fruits and nuts, and, nectar of the gods, several bottles of cheap no-name California wine.

The temperature was dropping dramatically, and I layered on every article of clothing I had brought with me. Martin was preoccupied with something he had just rolled. He offered me a drag. Sure, why not. I began shivering uncontrollably, never imagining that it could be this cold in California in the middle of summer.

Martin adeptly zipped my rather inadequate sleeping bag to his subzero scientific marvel. For the first time in my rather sheltered life, I surrendered to the ways of Tennessee Williams' rather pathetic character, Blanche, in *A Streetcar Named Desire*. Out of necessity, I relied on the kindness of strangers. This was just the beginning.

Sunrise proved much less eventful than the rather dramatic and terrifying sunset, but thankfully my pleas for mercy had been granted and I did indeed live to see another day.

After a communal breakfast of something resembling wet sawdust, our group packed up our gear and prepared for the descent. Approaching the edge of the summit, I was suddenly winded by gut-wrenching dread. I froze, panic-stricken, paralyzed and acutely aware of my terror of heights. After several embarrassing moments of uncontrollable sobbing, I could finally verbalize the reason for my histrionics. The Swiss hikers had a marvelous belly chuckle at my expense, and Friedrich, the true mountaineer, mentioned something about a similar incident having occurred on a recent alpine outing with his girlfriend.

With his back facing the edge of the cliff he asked me to face him, place each of my feet on top of each of his, place my arms around his neck, close my eyes, and most importantly, keep my mouth shut.

As Friedrich expertly descended the cables with a somewhat hysterical me on toe, so to speak, I prayed as I had never done before. In fact, this was a far more dramatic encore of the previous night.

After finally reaching the base of the Half Dome, the group expressed a communal sigh of relief. Apart from my mildly bruised ego, considerably strained knees and two swollen ankles, the remainder of my descent was a breeze!

That evening, we splurged on dinner at the lodge and reminisced over the wonders of the previous 48 hours. The Europeans had decided to extend their stay to include three more days of hiking; Martin was to resume teaching at Harvard; and I was to commence my pre-med year at McGill University.

Exhausted, I crawled into my sleeping bag for one last slumber under the stars. I was convinced that the past two days were but a prelude to many awe-inspiring, humbling and glorious encounters with God and nature.

During the ensuing years, the great outdoors would repeatedly prove to be a comforting and reliable antidote to life's common and not-so-common stresses and to my episodic periods of existential angst. On this particular summer's night in July 1972, I felt particularly blessed and certain that all was right with the universe.

The Gila Wilderness

CHARLES HILDEBRANDT

The whip-poor-will called all night: *Whip poor wheel, whip poor wheel.* The last note of his monotonous cry a higher pitch than the first. Now coming from nearby, now from far away, it is the sound of the wild, the mark of the Gila Wilderness and the mountains of the Continental Divide.

The land is the ancient home of the Pueblo people, but the name "gila" is of Spanish origin and should be pronounced the Spanish way, "*he*-la." The first Europeans to come to this region were Spanish-speaking people, adventurers, lured by the silver hidden in small pockets within the mountain flanks. They lived, pioneer fashion, in rip-roaring communities with names such as Mogollon and Pinos Altos, and their money flowed freely. Stagecoaches ran to and from Silver City, the closest community where supplies could be obtained. But when the easy silver gave out and mining became unprofitable, the adventurers left and their communities declined. Today, they are ghost towns.

With the miners gone, cattle rangers took over, expert riders, completely at home in the saddle, the cowboys of the Old West. But more profitable surroundings opened up for them, and they too left the Gila Mountains. The territory reverted to its original wilderness state. Now, more than ever, the Gila is an alpine landscape, superb in its natural beauty, challenging in its isolation.

We took the trip in the early '80s, twelve experienced backpackers who had come to explore the wilderness, to escape the crowds and to rely on their own resources. The Gila Wilderness is a fitting locality for such an expedition. More than

Gila Cliff Dwellings National Monument is found within the Gila Wilderness of New Mexico.
— Photograph by Caitlin Mirra

half a century ago, the renowned naturalist Aldo Leopold convinced the federal government to pledge: "This part of the Continental Divide being traversed by the Gila River is forever to be kept in an unimproved condition."

As a result, we have the Gila Wilderness area, known by few yet easily accessible by a paved road that winds its way through splendid alpine scenery from the town of Silver City, New Mexico.

We came to see the untamed hinterland where the Gila River tumbles down from the mountains and then flows swiftly through the valley that gives the area its name. The ravine is narrow and the embankment steep, and the trail meanders back and forth through the river. At the height of land, we took the appropriately designated No Name Canyon to cross over from the West Fork of the river to the Middle Fork, where water is more plentiful and where a couple of hot springs let us clean the grime off our feet.

Whip poor wheel, whip poor wheel. Few have seen this drab bird of the night. Inactive at daylight, his leaf-patterned body resting on the limb of a tree, his camouflage is perfect. If flushed, he will flutter away on seemingly unsteady wings and all that is left is his call, the three piercing notes that penetrate the stillness of the night and give yet another dimension to the mountains, the river and the land of the original residents.

Testimony to the Pueblo's past prevalence is found in the natural rock caves that abound in the area. It is here that the Pueblo people made their homes. The largest of the caves, now designated a National Monument, was discovered some hundred years ago and has become a much-visited tourist attraction.

The Pueblo were farmers who lived in harmony with their surroundings. They knew how to use the land and cultivated traditional crops of corn, beans and squash. They erected partitions in the caves and set up wooden supports for ceilings, which in the arid climate of the American southwest remain intact even now. With more than 40 separate and self-contained rooms, the cliff dwellings appear like a prehistoric version of today's apartment buildings.

Deep inside the Gila, hidden in the walls of the cliff, are more caves. No maps mark their location, and the wall of sandstone that forms their base has become brittle and unstable, but the timber to shore up the ceilings is still there, proof that these caves too were made habitable.

The secluded area is a haven for animals. We were lucky to catch a glimpse of the beautifully coloured coral snake, reputedly deadly poisonous yet, like most snakes, shy enough to slither away into the dense vegetation. We saw many uncommon birds, such as the dipper, who walks below the water. We observed skunks and porcupines and heard the cry of a mountain lion, said to live in the highest region. We were pleased by the display of large bats that came close to our campfire. And, when we sought a change from the wilderness, we drove to Pinos Altos, where we partied and danced the evening away in the only saloon that still exists after the departure of the miners.

A Day Hike in the Grand Canyon

HENRY GRAUPNER

My most awe-inspiring and physically challenging hike was in the Grand Canyon. It was a few years ago, when my knees were stronger than they are today.

On the way home from a business conference in Phoenix, in late October, I drove to the Canyon through an early snowfall, booked a motel room for two nights and arranged for an early wake-up call the next morning.

By seven in the morning, I had started my descent from the South Rim via the South Kaibab Trail, about 4 kilometres east of the Grand Canyon Village. I had planned to take the Bright Angel Trail back up, but a recent washout had closed it. So it was the Kaibab Trail in both directions.

I was on my own, so I had only myself to commune with about the size of the Canyon, the scenery, the overpowering silence (most of time; there were a few sightseeing flights during the day), and the amazing colours, which change from rim to rim, from one level to another, and from hour to hour.

Leaving the snow behind me at the rim, I spent just over three hours walking steadily downhill, except for two short stretches of about 100 yards each. Some of the things or persons you meet on the way down include:

- A notice saying that unless you are exceptionally fit and experienced, you should go no further if you plan to return the same day. Needless to say, but with some trepidation, I pushed on.

- Two park wardens, at different points, checking to see how much water you are carrying. I had enough to pass. There is no water source on the trail between the rim and the river. I did not use any of mine until I was on the way up.

- Notices asking you to step to the outside, unprotected edge of the trail to allow mule trains to pass. I plead guilty to ignoring these notices. I felt sure that the mules were more surefooted than me, so I stood on the inside when they came.

View from the north rim of the Grand Canyon. Billions of years forever etched in stone.

— Photograph by Alaskaphoto

Signs on the trail and all the guidebooks warn that it takes twice as long to walk up as it does to walk down. I therefore set 11 AM as the time I would turn around, wherever I was. However, at 10:15 AM, I was standing on the centre of the suspension bridge, one of the two built across the Colorado River, each wide enough for hikers or mules. By the time I reached the river, the temperature was well above 30 degrees Celsius, and I was carrying various layers of upper-body clothing that I had been wearing when I started.

Other writers have fully described the flora and fauna in the canyon. I can confirm that there is life in that desert. I saw many lizard-type creatures in the shade of the sparse shrubs that grow in the dry soil, as well as a small snake now and again. From time to time, I met or was overtaken by mule trains carrying either sightseers or supplies for the campground near the river. I saw few other signs of life for most of the day. There were occasional hikers with backpacks, indicating they were planning to stay in the canyon overnight or slowly struggling up to the rim. But on the whole, I was alone, seeing and hearing no one, free to contemplate the isolation I felt and to marvel at the natural wonder and size of the Grand Canyon.

At the time, I was professionally involved with the construction of a million-plus-square-foot building in Toronto. I imaged throwing a few thousand such buildings into the canyon, where they would completely disappear into its immensity.

The climb back up took six hours, including many rest stops. In fact, towards the end I think I was standing motionless more often than Grand Canyon Village.

I was happy to make it back to the top. When I got there, all I wanted to do was to get into my car, drive back to my motel room in the Village and to soak in a hot bath. However, a young woman from a party of seven who had made the return ascent that day asked me if I would take a photograph of her group. Although I felt like saying no, naturally I said, "Sure, be happy to." I forced my jelly-like knees to stand firm while the group posed. But no sooner had I finished than each of the other six members of the group came to me with their cameras. I never again wanted to take a photograph of another group on a trail.

In my many years of hiking in Ontario and other countries, I have never found any trail so grueling as on that day, especially the last two or three hours, but the whole experience was so very worthwhile, I am happy I did the hike.

My Great Grand Canyon Adventure

RON SIMPKIN

The Grand Canyon Rim-to-Rim hike had been on my bucket list for about 20 years, and finally, at the age of 68, I decided I had to do it now or never. So, in 2008, I signed with a Grand Canyon outfitter to do it.

I contacted the outfitter on arrival and made sure everything was organized for our departure on Thursday morning before setting out to see the country.

On Thursday, they came to my hotel and picked me up at 4 AM, along with two other participants whom I had not met before. It is about a five-hour ride from Flagstaff to the North Rim, and we arrived about 10:30 AM. The outfitter supplied everything: knapsack, sleeping bag, mattress and tent. All I had to bring were my own personal things and my camera.

We left the North Rim about 11 AM and headed down the trail. And down we went. And down. By the end of the day and a little over 6 miles, we would drop about 5,000 feet.

It was hot and getting hotter the further down we went. We took full advantage of the watering faucets along the trail. We doused our hats and bandanas well at each one to cool us down. The first significant sight we came across was the Supai Tunnel on the North Kaibab Trail. It is a manmade tunnel that allows the trail to pass through.

From here, the vistas become more and more magnificent as they spread out below us. Our first night's stay would be at Cottonwood Campground, still four hours away and definitely the focus of our attention.

We stopped for lunch about 1:30 PM, and our guide Kevin whipped up the largest wrap I have ever had, with chicken, lettuce, red pepper, cucumber and mayonnaise. It tasted better than one made at any restaurant — or maybe we were just plain hungry. With orange juice, boy, it hit the spot.

After a bit of a rest we set off again. This was the hardest part of the hike, all the downward walking. The next spectacle was Roaring Springs, a creek coming out of the wall of the canyon a couple of hundreds yards above the trail. We followed it down for the rest of the day.

We finally arrived at Cottonwood about 5 PM. I found myself very much dehydrated and out of sorts. When I took off my T-shirt, it was white with salts that I had lost through perspiration, even though I had drank about a gallon of water, a bottle of Gatorade and the orange juice. My electrolytes were severely out of whack. I sat and had two large bottles of Gatorade and felt fine half an hour later.

We set up our tents for the night, then headed over to Roaring Springs Creek to have a swim. It was more like a wade in a bath full of ice cubes. The creek is ice cold when it comes out of the wall, and it had not been able to pick up much warmth. It certainly did refresh us after the heat of the day, though. Back at the campsite, Kevin made a supper of spaghetti and meat sauce, rolls and butter, with cheese and crackers — a wonderful meal with good food and new friends in an exquisite place. (I must say, at this time, Kevin carried all the food, cooking equipment, snacks, etc. His pack must have weighed 75 to 80 pounds.)

After supper Kevin took out a star map. We tried to figure them out. In addition, Kevin told us tales of his adventures in the canyon. We were scheduled to rise at 5:30 AM, but we all toddled off to bed in the splendour of that first night.

With every sunrise, the topography of the canyon changes by the minute, startling views of crags and walls a kaleidoscope of changing colours, shadows and blue, blue sky above. Over the next four days, we experienced many exciting moments, such as meeting a black widow spider and a ringtail cat, never mind rattlesnakes. We saw a couple of California condors soaring over the South Rim and took heart at their flight. We were now experts, having enjoyed our lecture at Phantom Ranch on day two, and we discussed them thoroughly.

On our last day, we met a lot of hikers on the trail, most of them day-walkers from the South Rim. Some were neither dressed appropriately nor carrying enough water. They were putting themselves in danger, as the hike down is faster and easier than the climb back out in the afternoon sun.

It was tough going, and we inched our way along. The rim seemed no closer, and then all of a sudden, Kolb Studio loomed in the distance, and we picked up our pace. The end was near; our goal would be reached.

Another hour and we were there — people, cars, buses and flat land. We congratulated each other. It was 10:45 AM. We are done. What a feeling.

We did a tour of the South Rim, the Kolb Bros. Studio, and picked up some souvenirs. Then our van picked us up for the ride back to Flagstaff. After a shower and shave, we rested with a meal at a table with chairs.

This was a very exciting and happy day for me, a day of fulfillment, with memories to last a lifetime.

A typical cottage on the island of Saba. — Photograph by Euro Color Creative

CARIBBEAN & SOUTH AMERICA

Winter Escape

ROSS McLEAN

S aba is known as "the Unspoiled Queen" of Caribbean islands. Located a short distance southwest of St. Maarten, this 5-square-mile island is dominated by Mount Scenery, a potentially active volcano that rises to 2,877 feet at its summit and offers views of seven surrounding islands. Part of the Windward Islands, Saba has a stable population of only about 1,500 and is a special municipality of the Kingdom of the Netherlands. It boasts some of the best scuba-diving in the Caribbean, as well as an extensive network of hiking trails.

Although first settled by Europeans — some of them pirates — in the mid-1600s, the island's first road wasn't completed until after World War II. Prior to that, Dutch engineers thought the topography too rugged for road construction. It was only after a local resident took a correspondence course in road engineering that a vehicle route across the island was established. Formerly, homes on the island were connected only by hiking trails.

About 15 years ago, a call came to Bruce Trail volunteers in Ontario. The island's Saba Conservation Foundation recognized that its future lay in ecotourism, and it hoped to develop a land-based park to compliment the Marine Park that surrounds the island. The old footpaths would form a magnificent hiking network, and the varied terrain and vegetation, combined with a sense of history, would stimulate the curiosity of any hiker. An intrepid group of four travelled to the island and began assisting in the restoration of the trail network that foundation hoped would attract tourists. That program continues today.

To me, the most spectacular track is the North Coast Trail, which has been called "one of the world's great hiking trails." Veteran Bruce Trail hiker and volunteer Sandra Purchase captures the essence of the magic of hiking Saba:

"Our small group of winter weary hikers are admiring the glossy greens of the giant elephant ears and enjoying the intricate silhouettes of the tree fern against the blue of the ocean, when James, our guide, steps off the trail, ties his knife to his long walking stick, reaches into the trees and cuts down a prickly green fruit

— sour sop, a perfect cold drink at the end of our hike. But that is hours away yet. We are on Saba's most challenging and rewarding North Coast Trail. Most of the trails of Saba, like this one, were created by early settlers. Now, they are being restored and maintained by the Saba Conservation Foundation with assistance from Bruce Trail volunteers.

"As we walk, we pass under the lush moistness of the high rainforest canopy. Then we skirt around steep guts looking into the tops of leather leaved balsam and fragrant leaved bay trees. Our path climbs upward. A cluster of white lilies hiding under the dripping foliage of an elephant ear is thrilling. Many things delight us – the yellow bracts of the wild plantain, the delicate pink fronds of the wild begonia, the giant bunch of bananas that James cuts for us. As we head onto the most challenging part of the trail, a sudden downpour drenches both the hikers and the trail. With James' guidance and the help of strategically placed handholds, we move precariously along ridges with sharp drop-offs. Goats watch as we pick our way along the trail. Tall trees stretch above us, the rocky coast far below.

"As quickly as it came the rain stops. We are breeze dried as we come up through a section of sparse coastal forest and finally out onto a windswept grassy slope, high above the bluffs overlooking Diamond Rock. The bleating goats and the wild cries of the soaring frigates and tropical birds exhilarate me. The wind sweeps through the tough grasses, past the red crowns of the barrel cactus, drawing the eye to the spectacular azure blue of Cave of Rum Bay.

"Leaving the bluffs behind, the trail leads us through the remains of the pirate village of St. Mary's. The rainforest has long since overgrown the village, but we catch glimpses of it in stone walled terraces, stone cisterns, and fragments of blue Delft pottery and old glass. James remembers his childhood when the terraces were still farmed. Often he would descend the steep bluffs to Cave of Rum Bay, spear fish and climb for hours back to his family's stone cottage in time for his mother to cook the fish for supper.

"After another hour of hiking in the deep shade of mango, papaya and redwoods, then swinging over a slope on a massive vine and a lucky spotting of a sleek and harmless black racer snake, we finally descend to Wells bay and Saba's only road. A short ride and we are in the picturesque town of The Bottom. On the green and white verandah of the Family Deli, the friendly staff brings us our frothy sour sop drink. We enjoy crispy fresh fishcakes and delicious tamales with cold beer…a lovely ending to a delightful day experiencing just a few of the many jewels in the crown of Saba, the Unspoiled Queen."

Almost a Miracle

HEINZ NITSCHKE

I want to share a story about something that happened on one of my group trips. It was the second-last day of an 18-day journey that had taken us to the Galapagos Islands, the City of Quito and to Yachana Lodge, one of the finest upper Amazon jungle lodges on the Napo River in Ecuador. The visit and hikes in the upper Amazon jungle had been our last outing.

My group consisted of 16 Canadian hikers, mostly from the Bruce Trail clubs, as well as some friends that I normally hike with on the Oak Ridges Trail. The bus trip from the lodge on the Napo River (near the town of Tena, capital of the huge jungle province of Napo) back to Quito takes in the better part of a day. It is all uphill and covers just about every terrain one can think of, including a pass at over 4000 metres just before entering the City of Quito at about the 2500-metre level. Many kilometres of this roadway run through the jungle. The road is very narrow, often unpaved, and in some places partly washed-out. This part of our journey made it a real adventure.

After many hours in the bus, with no air-conditioning, we all decided that we needed a break and something to eat. Our driver was familiar with the area and drove us to a small village called Beaza, which had a small restaurant, the only one for miles around. And it had a fairly respectable restroom. A Canadian would call the village of Baeza a one-horse town, with a few houses here and there, nothing else. If you blinked driving through it, you would surely miss it.

While we were in the restaurant, we heard some commotion and loud talk outside. Some of us went out to see what was happening. As we came outside, we saw people running up the street towards a small row of wooden houses about 100 metres away. Thick black smoke was billowing from one of the small structures.

By now the crowd had grown, and one could hear desperate cries for *agua*, water. People seemed to appear from nowhere carrying cooking pots or plastic pails of water.

The sun shone brightly in an almost cloudless sky as flames shot high in the air from the back of one of the houses and black smoke came out of the cracks, windows and roofs of two others.

All the houses were attached to the one in flames. If the fire could not be brought under control, all houses on that side of the street would surely perish. In minutes, some people in the crowd wrapped bandanas around their mouths to protect them from the smoke and rushed into action. Doors were kicked in and window frames were broken in order to remove larger pieces of furniture and save family possessions from total destruction. Men ran feverishly, carrying as many things as possible from the houses to the other side of the street, away from danger. All furniture and other goods ended up in one big pile.

Roughly 15 minutes had passed since the fire started, when all of a sudden the sky darkened and rain started to fall. Seemingly from out of nowhere, one single, very dark cloud had formed right over the small village. All around this cloud, one could still see the blue sky and the sun shining on the mountains across the valley.

The rain was so heavy that we had a hard time seeing the restaurant, only a hundred metres away. The townspeople kept on working, trying to save what could be saved, while we ran back to the restaurant for cover.

It rained — no, it poured — for roughly ten minutes. Water rushed from roofs and down the fairly steep street. Then, as fast as the rain had started, it all of a sudden stopped. When we left the restaurant again to check on the damage caused by the fire, the sun had reappeared, and the cloud that had caused the heavy downpour had moved on and had almost disappeared. In its place, a big, beautiful rainbow had formed just behind the small houses.

Looking closer now, we saw that a shed behind the house had totally burned down, and there was lots of damage to the house.

We learned that the people who lived in the house were at work somewhere and would find a very rude surprise when they came home. Still, all houses were standing and saved.

Knowing how little people in these parts of the country earn, our group took up a collection of money and left it with the restaurant owner to be handed to the victims of the blaze. It would go a long way in helping fix the damage.

Later, in the bus, on our way back to Quito, we still could not stop wondering where that small black rain cloud had appeared from.

Years later, I am still wondering. Was this a miracle?

Hiking the Inca Trail

Lonely Planet rates Machu Picchu as "South America's best known and most spectacular archaeological site." To me, using the Inca Trail to get there, as did the Incas themselves, is an important element in properly appreciating it.

The trail is certainly not for the faint-hearted. There are many steep ups that will challenge the heart and lungs of pretty well anyone, particularly at high altitude, and there are many long, steep downs that will challenge anyone with knee problems. Well-constructed Inca steps do help. The scenery — mountain peaks, river valleys and changing vegetation — is awesome, and there are many interesting ruins en route.

Sixteen of us started off before dawn, with two guides, in a bus from the Plaza de Armas in Cuzco. The bus deposited us at the village of Chilca, where our porters were assembled. It was from here that we commenced the hike, initially along the side of the Urubamba River.

The daily routine started with breakfast in the dining tent, during which the porters dismantled our sleeping tents. After breakfast we hit the trail, to be overtaken by the porters trotting along in their flip-flops with camp equipment. By the time we got to the lunch spot, the dining tent was up and lunch preparation was under way. In the evenings, our tents were erected before we arrived at the campsite

On the first night, there were no facilities for washing, and the toilet was a pit dug in the ground within a tent. We camped near the village of Wayllabamba, which had a small soccer field nearby. Ten of us from our hiking group played soccer here — an altitude of 2750 metres (9,000 ft) — with our guides, Jose A and Jose B, the cook, and some of the porters. I pulled a muscle in my leg slightly during this and was apprehensive about the hike the next day.

On our second day, we were told to set our own pace up to "Dead Woman's Pass," 1440 metres (about 5,000 ft) above us, at an elevation of 4200 metres (almost 14,000 ft). Our crop of youngsters took off like gangbusters to tackle the slope. I had a feeling that they might burn themselves out, and I set off at a more sedate pace. Sure enough, I steadily passed members of our group who had overexerted themselves early in the climb.

I was relieved to find that my muscle-pulled leg was not functioning too

CARIBBEAN & SOUTH AMERICA 167

View through the ruins, Machu Picchu, Peru. — Photograph by S J Francis

badly, and after about half an hour, I caught up with Sebastian. We hiked together for a while and speculated that Dead Woman's Pass might be visible when we rounded a hillock ahead. When we got there, however, all we could see was the trail going up and ever up as far as we could see. Sebastian let out the most heartfelt "Bloody Hell!" I had ever heard and collapsed on a rock. Johnny and Ed, from our group, were there too, similarly discouraged by the view ahead. I left the three hares resting as I tortoised doggedly on.

I was the third of our group to reach the pass. Jose P, who was already there, gave me the thumbs-up salute. Cyrill, a Dutch fellow, was there too.

On our second night at high altitude, icy-cold mountain-stream showers were available. I and one or two others braved these — wetting, stopping the water, soaping, and then turning the water on again briefly to rinse the soap off, emerging gasping from the chill.

During the night, the temperature dropped below freezing, and I slept wearing a toque. We all wore day clothing in our sleeping bags to keep warm. One fellow said that he used every garment that he had with him.

Towards the end of the third day, after numerous steep ascents and descents, our guides described the route and let some of us go ahead as they stayed with the rest, some of whom were suffering from diarrhea and altitude sickness. We reached the camping area near the Winay Wayna ruins at about 4 PM. Here, at lower altitude, it was warmer, and the shower, which was supposed to be hot, was at least lukewarm.

On the fourth and final day on the trail, we were awoken well before daylight for a hasty breakfast before heading off on the last lap of our journey. In the darkness, the caterpillars of light from the flashlights of different groups could be seen bobbling along the path. The target was to reach Intipunku in time to watch the sun rise over the site that we had come so far to see. I would like to be able to report the glory of that sunrise over Machu Picchu, but regretfully it was obscured by cloud — a small setback in an overall hugely worthwhile excursion.

Shortly after leaving Intipunku, we arrived to find Machu Picchu almost deserted. It would not be until late morning that the buses would bring the multitude of day visitors who had taken the train to the nearby village of Aguas Calientes. Meanwhile, we hikers had the opportunity to explore the ruins and marvel at the surrounding mountain scenery in relative calm. Nobody really knows the original purpose of Machu Picchu. The most popular theory is that it was a retreat for Incan head honcho, emperor Pachacuti.

The Inca Trail Highway: El Choro

DARCI LOMBARD

When I trekked off to South America over ten years ago, the popular four-day hike from Cuzco to Machu Picchu was definitely on my list of things to do. Not having planned my entire journey before I left Canada, I knew little else of hiking along the Incan trail system. As is par for the course while backpacking, I was fortunate to meet up with a small group of travellers with similar interests and who were heading in the same general direction. This is how I discovered El Choro.

Though not as famous as the trek to Machu Picchu, this three-day journey covers one of the better-maintained portions of the historically significant Incan highway system. The trail begins north of La Paz, Bolivia, in the breathtaking Cordillera Real mountain range, and follows approximately 50 kilometres of the ancient Inca highway from high Andes down to the lush, tropical Bolivian cloud forest known as the Yungas, which bridges the Bolivian *altiplano* (high plain) with the Amazon Basin.

I joined a motley crew of Israeli, Dutch and Chilean backpackers who had befriended one another in San Pedro de Atacama, Chile, and had just spent eight days traversing the breathtaking salt flats in Uyuni, exploring the unforgiving silver mines in Potosi, and meandering through the mystical witch markets and vibrant streets of La Paz. Now we found ourselves standing at La Cumbre, the start of El Choro, deposited there by a good-natured, toothless taxi driver from La Paz. With our scantly packed gear and our spirits brimming with enthusiasm, we began our trek.

At an altitude of 4650 metres, La Cumbre is in thin air. We began our journey gasping for breath, pushing forward, cloaked in a cloudy mist. After some time, the clouds cleared, exposing a windswept landscape of brown and grey, a dull backdrop for the bright blue alpine lakes and snow-capped peaks of the majestic altiplano. This is where the condor flies, and we were constantly on the watch. Vegetation is sparse in these high altitudes, imparting a moon-like appearance on the surrounding land.

The initial portion of this trail is an upward climb to the Saddle, the highest point along the trail at 4900 metres above sea level. For the unconditioned hiker, a 40-pound pack feels behemoth on one's back at these high altitudes. Beyond the Saddle, we passed by an ancient *tambo*, an old stone outpost where Inca messengers rested during their travels.

The terrain and rapid decline into the Yungas is challenging, and to put things into perspective, note that the entire Choro Trail runs parallel to one of the world's most dangerous highways, the "Highway of Death." On average, more than 25 vehicles disappear each year over the precipice of this road. It has become a popular highway for extreme mountain bikers because of its hairpin turns and rapid descent. I was thankful we were walking calmly on foot into the Yungas rather than descending madly by bus to Coroico on the deadly road.

Our first night's camp was a frigid stay in the small village of Chucura, elevation 3600 metres. We woke to find two young children gazing suspiciously at us through our tent door. With a giggle and a mad dash, they ran off, bringing back an old man in need of "Aspirina for his aching tooth. After sharing some medication and tea with this local farmer, we continued our descent.

The transition from the desolate landscape of the altiplano to the lush vegetation of a tropical cloud forest on the second day of our trek was impressive. Barren rock turned to green grass-covered patches, and in turn the landscape transformed yet again to a lush, tropical paradise bursting with bromeliads, orchids, ferns and a variety of birds and butterflies. A warm yet leisurely descent led us to our second night's camp near Choro, alongside the Rio Chucura, where we enjoyed the welcoming warmth of a tropical evening, a delicious camp meal and good company.

The following day, we continued to marvel at the awesome views as we travelled along the trail skirting this expansive valley. We enjoyed frequent rest stops alongside refreshing waterfalls, reveling in the most fantastic views over the valley as we continued our descent. We passed near Cotapata National Park, where I hoped to get a glimpse of the spectacled bear, the only surviving species of native bear in South America. No luck.

Our next stop was Casa Santillano, home to Tamiji Hanamura, a kindhearted, gentle Japanese man who has lived on these premises since 1940 and who maintains the beautifully sculptured gardens around the Casa.

From here, we neared our journey's end with a short hike to Chairo (1300 m), where we soaked our tired feet in the nearby river before catching a bus to the peaceful town of Coroico. Sitting on the terrace of our hotel, enjoying a bottle of wine, we recapped our great descent, some 3600 metres from the expansive, majestic snow-capped Andes Mountains to the lush Bolivian Yungas.

Pulpit Rock, above the Lysefjord, Norway. Look down, look way down.

— Photograph by Harald Høiland Tjøstheim

EUROPE & NEAR EAST

Preikestolen

JENNA LEVI

With a height of over 604 metres above sea level, Preikestolen, or Pulpit Rock, is the massive shoulder of rock that juts out over the edge of the Lysefjord in Norway, providing hikers with a breathtaking view of the Kjerag plateau. Located in Forsand, a municipality of Rogaland county in Norway, Preikestolen receives nearly 100,000 visitors during the summer months, making It one of Norway's most visited natural attractions.

Travellers to this incredible piece of nature have various options for beginning their trek. Ferry service is available from Stavanger to Tau, and from there a bus will bring you directly to the start of the trail. For those with their own means of travel, parking lots are available at the same location. Due to the incredible growth in popularity of Preikestolen, it's best to visit early in the morning, before the rock becomes too infested with tourists.

The actual path to Preikestolen is about 3.8 kilometres in length. Although a mostly uphill rocky path, the trail leads hikers through beautiful green forest, along rocky landslides, across flat plains of rock, and finally skirts the mountain itself, the wide path sometimes shrinking to a mere foot or two in width.

It will take the average hiker around 1.5 to 2 hours to complete the clearly marked trail, and there are incredible photo opportunities of the Kjerag plateau. If you have time, be sure to bring your swimsuit, as on top of the mountain are a couple small freshwater pools, perfect for washing off the dirt and sweat from the first part of the trek.

Although Preikestolen has its fair share of beautiful views, the landscape is not the only thing that lures visitors to this site every year. Visitors daring enough to walk to the very edge of the cliff and swing their legs over the side leave with more than just a nice view. There's something about sitting on the edge of a deadly cliff with no safety rope or harness, with nothing holding you there but gravity, that is extremely humbling and yet liberating. With a base of only 25 by 25 metres and standing 604 metres above sea level, you not only feel like you are sitting on the edge of the world, but on the edge of life as well.

The Swansea Valley

ELSIE JONES

The Swansea Valley encompasses the upper reaches of the River Tawe area in South Wales. Notable towns and villages in the area include Clydach, Pontardawe, Ystradgynlais, Ystalyfera and Abercraf.

The upper Swansea Valley is also the site of Dan yr Ogof Caves, said to be the largest show cave complex in Western Europe. South of Abercrave, the valley was formerly a region of heavy industry, including coal mining and iron making.

The Swansea Canal was built along the valley in the late 18th century to serve the local industries. There were originally 36 locks on the canal to raise it from sea level at Swansea to Abercraft. The Swansea Canal Trail follows the line of the Swansea Valley from Clydach to Abercraf.

There must be something about the sea air around this part of the Welsh coast that produces talent, as Dylan Thomas, Richard Burton, Anthony Hopkins and Catherine Zeta-Jones are all from the region.

I was born in Ystalyfera on December 31, 1920. I attended infant school in Ystradgynlais and primary school in Pontardawe. I remember going on hikes with my younger sister Gwenni. We would head out with a sandwich lunch. There were no marked trails. We just followed the sheep tracks up the valley. Our mother had told us not to go down towards the canal. On the other side of the canal was the common area. The gypsies had their caravans there, and it was understood that if you were naughty, the gypsies would take you.

The gypsies sold laundry pegs and lace. In addition, they could tell fortunes. My mother also told fortunes. Eventually, she would run away with the gypsies.

I remember that the valley and mountains were covered with woodland routes that rose higher and higher until it was possible to gaze back down to the distant coastline. In season, we would pick winberries. They grew wild and resembled black currants.

When I was young, there were ample opportunities for walking, from leisurely local strolls to adventurous long-distance hikes. With the new "Right to Roam" law, the whole of southern Wales can now be your playground.

The Ups and Downs of Life

JACQUELINE HOLMES

The red double-decker bus shuddered and rattled along the steep, winding road leading to the Seven Sisters Country Park, part of the famous South Downs Way National Trail. In celebration of my 60th birthday, my friend Sheila and I were going to climb the Seven Sisters, a challenging up-and-down cliff-top trek of approximately 9 miles. Although Sheila and I were both born in Manchester, England, we were both Toronto residents when we met several years ago while hiking along the Toronto section of the Bruce Trail. Here we were, years later, staying at a small family-owned hotel in the seaside town Eastbourne, an hour from London's Gatwick Airport, and on my 60th birthday found ourselves sitting on a spluttering bus on our way to the start of this cliff-top hike.

Unfortunately, after further huffing and puffing, our bus finally wheezed to a halt. We passengers were asked to leave until a replacement bus could be arranged. The morning mist ebbed and flowed around the high, lonely countryside. We could hear the distant bleating of sheep and the sound of waves hitting the beach hundreds of feet below. The bus conductor took this opportunity to have a ciggie break. He walked around his bus, giving each wheel a swift kick, then looked under the hood — to no avail. Eventually the replacement bus arrived and we were once again on our way, perched on the front seat of the top deck, eager to continue our adventure.

Once off the bus, we spotted a tearoom, so decided to enjoy morning coffee and a plate of scones and cream before setting off. We had our full "British Breakfast" two hours previously — eggs, bacon, sausages, tomatoes, mushrooms, baked beans and anything else one could fancy. The sea air gives me a feeling of tremendous wellbeing, together with the belief that I am entitled to whatever food I wish to eat. Sitting in this café's little courtyard, gulls overhead, lashings of thick, fresh cream on our scones — what more could I want on my 60th birthday?

The Cuckiloere Estuary, the entrance to the Seven Sisters Coastal Walk, is supported by several agencies, including the National Trust and Natural England, to ensure the future of this beautiful area where wildlife can thrive and all can enjoy the fabulous landscape. An easy access trail, about 2 kilometres long and suitable for impaired mobility, wheelchairs, etc., leads directly to the water's edge. It was along these gentle, meandering paths that we walked together with a group of local sheep until we reached the windblown shingle beach. We dipped our bare feet into the sea, shrieking in shock at the cutting coldness. This is where it all begins.

Looking back towards the first cliff, the First Sister, I suggested we could save a little time and energy by easing our way up what appeared to be, from a distance, an old goat path. So up we went, gingerly holding onto tuffs of dry windswept grasses. Two teenagers whizzed by. We climbed slowly inch by inch. The path became steeper. I felt horribly afraid for my own and also for Sheila's safety. She is older than me, and her husband would surely kill me if anything happened to her. Suddenly the teenagers came back into view, only this time sliding on their stomachs almost knocking us off the cliff in their haste.

We had to make our move to safety, arms spread-eagle, bums in the air, one crablike move at a time until we finally reached a place where we were able to turn around and dig our heels in to secure ourselves. Sheila and I looked at one another, our faces and hair caked with chalky dust, our clothing a disaster. It appeared as if we had been dragged through a hedge backwards. What a mess. We laughed and we laughed till our tears streamed through the chalk dust. A small group of people, including the teenagers, had watched our slow but steady return to solid ground. A man sporting a trilby hat said in a posh BBC voice, "For a while there, we didn't think you'd make it down. But we are jolly glad you did."

We brushed ourselves down as best as we could, then walked back to the pathway clearly marked Coastal Walk and started to climb to the crest of the First Sister. The going was tough. I later learned from a member of the Eastbourne Rambling Club that we should have started our trek from the other end, from Eastbourne, because that way the ups are less and the downs steeper.

When we had finally huffed and puffed our way to the top of the First Sister, the winds were so strong we could not stand upright. The seagulls swirled and swooped above us, their cries lonely and sad. The wafting scents of gorse and heather surrounded us as we trudged further along. There are railings along the sides of the cliffs, with warnings not to tread beyond marked areas. We could see several birds' nests perched precariously along the edge of the cliffs. The Seven Sisters National Park is a dream for birdwatchers. A lone fellow walker pointed out a group of raptors, including sparrow hawks and hovering kestrels. The information centre at the Cuckiloere Estuary supplies maps and information upon request.

We stopped only to drink water and watch ships passing along the English Channel. Birdwatching would have to wait for another time!

Birling Gap is a popular attraction for locals and tourists. With four out of the Seven Sisters completed, we were compelled onward by the sight of the weather-beaten refreshment building in the distance. We quickened our pace because not only did want a rest, we deserved another treat. With a big pot of hot tea in front of us, accompanied by four fat custard tarts, we sat by the window to watch children climb down a steep iron ladder to the pebbly beach below. Dozens of children scampered in and out of the waves, their bodies shiny and smooth as baby seals, their thin arms and legs blue from the cruel temperature of the English Channel, but their cheeks rosy red. One would shout and wave to his mum and dad, "Hey, look at me," as he'd swim further out from the beach than was allowed, causing his dad to splutter through his beer that if his little beggar knows what's good for him, he'll get right back!

With our pot of tea finished and every last crumb of our custard tarts demolished, we said goodbye to this lovely scene and attacked the final three Sisters.

We were almost on the crest of the sixth Sister when my legs began to feel wobbly. Sheila's knees were bothering her, as well. The wind was still strong, and every uphill step became a battle, but despite our aches and pains we trudged along faithfully to our happy destiny — a fish-and-chips supper. We looked back to see those mighty, magnificent cliffs, splendid in their white chalkiness, like a giant rolling cake, the grass on top as icing, and ahead the little red cliff-top lighthouse.

Finally, we reached the crest of the seventh Sister. We could see Eastbourne nestled in the distance. Walking briskly, we'd be there within the hour. Discussing fish-and-chips shops makes the time pass quickly. Where shall we go? Shall we sit down in the restaurant or walk along the prom with our meal wrapped in newspaper, listening to the sea, having a laugh about old times and reflecting on this wonderful day.

Fish and chips wrapped in newspaper were the choice of the day. So here we were, strolling along Eastbourne Promenade, eating our generous portions of fish and chips sprinkled liberally with vinegar, salt and pepper, the gentle wind rolling in from the sea. The gulls circled overhead hoping we'd throw them a chip.

What a hike! What a friendship! What beautiful countryside!

A Walk in the Wallops

DOROTHY SCOTT

"**A**ll leaves cancelled, even SOP's. Six PM curfew. Carry gas mask at all times. No private phone calls. Mail censored. And nobody, civilians included, to travel more than 15 miles from home base without a special permit."

It hadn't rained for two days and it was the off day — came off last shift at 2300 hours and not on again until the night shift.

Beds properly made with the "biscuits" (mattress) neatly piled and the "sandwich" of sheets and blankets set on top. Buttons and shoes polished, smalls washed and hung out, fresh collar and neat tie.

The others were hitchhiking to Salisbury (just within the 15-mile limit) to go to the pictures. I decided to go on a walk.

Signed out and took the road to Middle Wallop village, having first stashed gas mask in a convenient thick hedge. MPs generally stuck to towns and main roads. They had been a real pest lately, all this top-secret stuff going to their heads. Some even had the effrontery to demand that the gas mask satchels be opened, displaying contents really suitable to such a container: spare stockings, lipsticks, handkerchiefs, letters, darning, Penguin paperbacks, knitting, but, curiously, no gas masks.

It really was a beautiful day: early June, all shining with the last hawthorn still in bloom in the hedges, buttercups glistening in the lane edges and somewhere a cuckoo commenting on the follies of mankind.

As I neared Grately Station, a cheery voice called, "Good afternoon." the district nurse was on her way to a confinement. She puttered by on her mechanized bicycle with the medical bag in its basket.

About halfway down the return road, I heard voices and realized that this lane was no longer unfrequented. Ahead the trees were looped together with camouflage nets. Parked closely, tight against the left verge, was a convoy of amphibian gun carriages, all facing south. The sentry was smoking and yakking with a pal, so my swift vault over a farm gate went unobserved. Running the gauntlet of inevitable wolf whistles was not part of the plan.

Before me was a wheat field. Path around the perimeter looked fairly well trodden, possibly a right of way rerouted to avoid the standing grain. Yes, that was it — a stile in the hedge just about opposite the gate. And, super, from the top of it I could see a marked path straight across the next field, a very uncared-for field. Surely the farmer wasn't so rich that he could afford not to put in a token crop so as to collect the subsidy? Rather curious clump of trees, that in the middle, possibly one of the tumuli that marked the graves or maybe habitations of pre-Roman dwellers? Anyway the path went right to it and so did I. Once out that gate at the other end, I knew that I should strike the Allington Road, which came out just a few yards from the "Joint."

I managed to avoid the worst of a very large bramble as I descended from the stile and set forth towards the grove. Speculated idly on its existence — site of ancient religious rites or perhaps a coven? Oh, no! These trees had camouflage netting too.

"What are you doing here?" The speaker was from a good school and not long left it judging from the very clean second-lieutenant's pips, a marked contrast to the corporal's tapes on his companion, who was wearing a sardonic expression and leaning against a tree.

"Just going for a walk."

"Don't you realize that this is a firing range?"

"Top secret," added the corporal.

"Aren't you supposed to have flags or sentries or barbed wire or something to warn people?"

"Well, we do."

"Not at the stile."

"The stile? What stile?"

By this time, several other soldiers had drifted up to observe the fun. Obviously, an embarrassing situation for the lieutenant.

"Higgins, you and Tonks take barbed wire and seal up that stile. Use the older stuff, not the new roll. Then Tonks, do sentry duty all along the perimeter. Corporal, please escort this lady to the gate and set her on her way by the sunken path — and this all comes under top secret. Understand, everyone?"

We walked very fast indeed to the gate, where, in fact, there was a sentry.

Together, they rolled aside a mass of foliage near the gate to disclose a path hidden between two hedges. The path would lead me to Salisbury Road. I retrieved my gas mask and checked in before curfew, just in time for supper.

Hadrian's Wall is the most visited historic site in Northern England. It was built by the Roman Emperor Hadrian to establish territorial boundaries and secure Roman Britain.

— Photograph by Ian McDonald

Hadrian's Wall

VALERIE DOBSON

"**W**alk in the footsteps of the Roman Legions." Many hike descriptions of walks throughout Europe begin with this appealing introduction. My husband and I chose a route that is probably the most distant from Rome: Hadrian's Wall. The Wall, built as a barrier between the conquered lands of Albion (England) and the lawless land to the north, was started by the Emperor Trajan as a turf barrier. When the Emperor Hadrian visited the area in AD 122, he ordered a stone wall to be built along the same line between the Solway Firth and the North Sea, marking the northern extent of Roman territory.

Next we had to decide how much of the route to cover, allowing time to visit the museums and forts. We decided on the 135-kilometre coast-to-coast walk, travelling from east to west in nine days. That would give us time to walk at a gentle pace and spend some hours immersing ourselves in its history.

So what made this a favourite walk? It has something of everything: lovely rolling countryside, small northern country villages with good pubs (my husband's "must have"), it's steeped in interesting history and there's lots of site/ sightseeing.

The trail starts just east of Newcastle, at Wallsend, at the Segedunum fort. The Romans built their forts to a standard plan. The site has been exposed in such a way that the "playing card shape" plan is evident. There is a small museum with a tower that provides an aerial view of the layout. What's more, there is a reconstructed Roman bathhouse.

We visited Segedunum and admired the small piece of Wall remaining there before starting on our first day's walk to Heddon-on-the-Wall, some 24 kilometres distant. Walking beside the tidal part of the River Tyne, we left Newcastle, an important city once famous for its coal mines. Its industrial base has changed, but it is an interesting city architecturally, both new and old, especially its nine bridges. Leaving the city, we walked beside the Tyne for most of the day until our path led away from the river, through fields, past the house where George Stephenson, inventor of the Rocket steam engine, was born, and up to Heddon-on-the-Wall.

The next day, on a glorious September morning, we rounded the corner out of the village to discover a fine piece of Wall. It is 3 metres wide and was originally 6 metres high. The Wall was more than just a "wall"; it formed a part of the fortification. The entire project included a wall ditch 9 metres wide on the north side and a vallum, an earthwork consisting of two earth walls with a ditch between them, on the south side. The vallum seems to have been intended to keep the civilians away from the military establishment. Archaeologists estimate that the three Roman legions that constructed it would have used one ton of stone to build a single yard of the Wall.

Men were stationed along the Wall at the 80 mile castles, up to 32 men at each mile castle. Evenly spaced between each of the mile castles were two turrets. There were 16 forts irregularly spaced in the vicinity of the Wall, each housing from 500 to 1,000 men. If that sounds like a lot of "Italians," bear in mind that to be a Roman citizen a man did not have to have been born in Rome. As Roman armies conquered Europe, some of the people from the newly acquired territories became Roman citizens.

We walked alongside amazing stretches of Wall with views of beautiful rolling countryside dotted with magnificent oak and sycamore trees. We counted the stiles and kissing gates as we passed from field to field, reaching as many as 46 in one day. On the bright side, it meant there was less need to worry about closing gates to keep the stock in.

We visited Chesters Fort and Housesteads Fort, the latter being high on a hill. The Vindolanda Fort, with its civilian surroundings, is particularly interesting because archaeologists have found the delicate remains of writing tablets, which have been treated so that the writing can be read and interpreted. As well as providing military information, some mentioned earlier, notes of a personal nature have been discovered, including one that thanks a friend for a gift of oysters and some asking for socks and underwear.

As we neared Carlisle, the major town of Luguvallium to the Romans, the land became flatter. After visiting the excellent museums, we left Carlisle, following the river for a while to the marshes beside the Solway Firth, with views across the estuary — Scotland to the north and the Lake District to the south.

Had we had more time, we could have continued along the coast beside the Irish Sea, visiting Stenhouse Museum at Maryport and Ravenglass Roman Bath House. What we actually did was take the appropriately named AD122 bus back to Newcastle. The little bus takes the Military Road for most of the journey, and we were able to look to the north and see hikers walking beside the Wall, enjoying the same fine hike we had just completed.

Walking Stevenson's Way

DAVID BEEVIS

In late September 1878, Robert Louis Stevenson set out to walk from Le Monastier, in Velay, France, south to Saint-Jean-du-Gard, Cevennes, a journey of just over 190 kilometres, which he accomplished in 12 days. Stevenson used a small, slow donkey, Modestine, to carry his gear and published his account as *Travels with a Donkey in the Cevennes*. In May 2007, Micheline and I set out to follow him.

Although donkeys are available for trekking throughout France, we travelled without one, our heavy luggage instead carried from inn to inn prebooked through a French hiking company. The route passes through the Velay, Gevaudan, and Mont Lozere regions of southern France before arriving in Cevennes.

It has been suggested that Stevenson thought his whole route lay in Cevennes because that name was marked in big letters over a large area on some maps available in the mid-1800s. Certainly Stevenson did not have the benefit of detailed maps, and he even discussed his route with villagers one evening using the inn's cups and glasses as markers. Fortunately, in 1978 the Cevennes tourist board decided to publicize Stevenson's Way. The tourist board produced a passport for the route that lists accommodations, and the route is now well marked as GR No. 70 of the French hiking federation, which has also produced an informative French guidebook.

We started our hike from Le Puy-en-Velay, which is easily reached from Lyon via the rural rail system. Stevenson could be said to have started from Le Puy because it was there that he commissioned his "sleeping sack" of green waterproof cart-cloth lined with blue sheep's wool. The Velay is a plateau dotted with the eroded remains of long-extinct volcanoes and cut by the valley of the Loire, which we crossed at lunchtime on our first day. Climbing slowly from the start at 630 metres, a 19-kilometre hike through pleasant countryside led us to Monastier, at 930 metres, where a cairn marks the start of Stevenson's Way proper, or "Le Stevenson" as the French call it.

The second day was similar, climbing gently on quiet country roads or unpaved roads and tracks. At Goudet we lunched at the inn where Stevenson had stayed, now very much expanded. Here we crossed the upper Loire again, currently the subject of a hydro dam proposal. We continued climbing steadily to the hill town of Pradelles, at 1150 metres. Unlike Stevenson's day, when few people seemed to have travelled anywhere, we were served coffee by a Scots woman with a Greek surname, who had moved to France so that her son could learn the language.

As Stevenson had crossed the bridge over the Allier River into the town of Langogne, it had started to rain; 109 years later, we found that some things have not changed! Villages in this area had communal ovens and laundries. We met a group of villagers maintaining the tradition by firing the oven and cooking bread. It had taken three days to get the huge stone oven warm enough to cook, but the street was filled with the smell of fresh bread, which they offered us free.

The next stage took us through Gevaudan, a heavily forested area that for three years in late 1700s was terrorized by the "Beast of Gevaudan."

Stevenson next travelled to the monastery of Notre Dame des Neiges, which in those days was quite remote, in forest at 1084 metres. We stayed just long enough to appreciate the peace of the visitors' chapel and to buy a bottle of the monks' wine.

After descending through small valley towns, our route now climbed 513 metres over Mont Lozere, still marked by standing stones to guide travellers in bad weather.

The route then led us down to Le Pont-de-Montvert, at the head of the dramatic Gorge of the Tarn, now very popular with kayakers and river rafters. At the lower end of the gorge stands Florac, one of the two capitals of the Cevennes, with spring-fed fountains in its squares. After the quiet tracks we had been following, the traffic in Florac was a shock. Here time went back, not to Stevenson's day, but to the late 1960s, as the town has become very popular with hippies.

From Florac, the trail climbs up a long valley reminiscent of some sections of the Bruce Trail. The trail next followed typical Cevennes ridges through the Forest of Fontmort, much like a managed southern Ontario forest, to St-Germain de Calbert, which we found as quiet as Stevenson reported it to be.

We tried to enjoy the last stretch of trail, a rugged descent to the valley of the Gard, but we did finish well before Stevenson's original arrival time of 10 PM.

In Saint-Jean-du-Gard, Modestine had been found unfit to travel further, and Stevenson had sold her with some regrets. We enjoyed a meal in the courtyard of our hotel and looked back over a very enjoyable and memorable trip: 11 days of hiking 168 kilometres of quiet trails and back roads, with good food, good accommodations and beautiful countryside. It took a while to realize that we had maintained the same daily pace as Modestine!

Hiking in Austria

JOËLLE MARTIN

In early June 2003, six members of the Beaver Valley Bruce Trail Club left for a two-week trip to Austria, combining sightseeing and hiking. After four days of taking in the architecture, art and music of Vienna, we left for an area southwest of Salzburg in the Austrian Alps called the Salzburger Saalachtal. There, through a program called Hiking Without Luggage, we hiked the Route of the Gorges for the next six days.

Every day saw us climb through a variety of sights and terrain — forests, meadows covered with wildflowers, roadside chapels, farmhouses tucked in here and there, cows grazing — always surrounded by the awesome mountains. And of course the gorges! What a build up. Every day brought a gorge more spectacular than the previous one: deeper, longer, with more water gushing through it. Because of the time of the year and the altitude, we had expected to hike in moderate temperatures. But, lo and behold, we hit a heat wave with temperatures of around 30 degrees Celsius every day. The toughest day of hiking saw us climb for six straight hours, followed by two hours of joint-numbing descent. I can still see us at the top, plunging our faces into a wooden animal trough filled with cold, clear mountain water.

A daily reward was coming to the next village and the comfortable, quaint inn where our luggage was waiting for us, and then sharing a wonderful meal. We were also impressed in two villages to find large stainless-steel community swimming pools, which were most welcome after the hot, tough hiking.

This week of hiking was followed by three days in Salzburg, enjoying the birthplace of Mozart and all the famous city has to offer.

The above description is but one example of what hiking is to me. It can be the peace of a short, solitary walk, the companionship of a group hike, the friendships formed over the years, the satisfaction of a goal attained, the development of new skills, a different way of travelling, and more. I hope I will be able to keep on doing this for many more years.

Camino

BILL McMURRAY

It was an auspicious beginning to an almost 800-kilometre walk: my Air France flight was circling Charles de Gaulle airport waiting for the fog to clear when we were hit by lightning. The bright flash and a loud bang certainly caught my attention, but we landed safely. Shortly after that, I connected to Biarritz/Bayonne, where I caught a train to St Jean Pied de Port for the start of my walk along the Camino de Santiago de Compostela.

Starting in St Jean, in the foothills of the Pyrenees, the Camino is approximately 765 kilometres long. It is a pilgrimage for some, a serious walk for others. It proceeds into Spain, then follows a westerly course across the north of Spain, ending in Santiago de Compostela. This route takes you through the Pyrenees, then follows a westerly route through the Basque part of Spain, then Navarra and La Rioja (think full-bodied Spanish wine), the Meseta (the rain in Spain), the Cordillera Cantabria (another region of high hills and picturesque valleys), finishing in Galicia region, with its rolling hills and pretty valleys. The Camino is marked by yellow arrows and yellow scallop shell markings on the road, on sign posts, on the sides of buildings, and just about everywhere you look, so it is, for the most part, fairly easy to follow along the narrow paved roads, such as the climb out of St Jean, along country lanes and beside busy highways.

I had been encouraged to do this walk by several articles I had read in the Globe and Mail and the Sunday Star, and with the encouragement of my wife, Elaine, I departed Canada on August 29, 2003, and started walking on August 30. That first day was quite memorable. Following the recommendation in my guide book, I had taken the easy route into Spain. However, after 30 minutes I had to backtrack to St Jean because the markings ran out and I had no idea where to go. An hour later I was back in St Jean, and I followed the line of pilgrims walking up the Pyrenees. Nine hours after my original start, I arrived in Roncesvalles, tired but with a feeling of having set out on this long journey knowing that I was capable of finishing it.

Walking the Camino, you must be prepared to carry everything on your back, stay at simple hostels and be willing to share facilities with one and all. One's North American sense of privacy has to be compromised. You soon learn to avert your gaze. The hostel in Roncesvalles is a large stone building with bunk beds to accommodate 100 pilgrims. It has no communal kitchen. However, two restaurants serve pilgrims meals for a very modest price. The first communal meal suggested the variety of people and nationalities I would meet along the way. Brazilian, French, Dutch, German, Spanish and Finnish pilgrims all participated in this happy, festive meal. Not every evening was as communal as this first night, but on several evenings during my trip I met up with fellow pilgrims, and we broke bread together and shared a bottle of wine, with a lovely feeling of fellowship

As Spain is a Catholic country, and this is a Christian pilgrimage, many lovely churches are encountered along the way. Every city, town, village and hamlet has its churches. They were all different, starting with the large abbey in Roncesvalles, where I attended a pilgrims' mass before dinner and gloried in the magnificent organ music, to the simple little church in San Juan de Ortega, where after the pilgrims' mass we all gathered in the parish hall and enjoyed a cup of garlic soup prepared by the parish priest. In my diary I wrote: "Have just attended a pilgrims' mass, now eating garlic soup with all the pilgrims — good!! What a wonderfully spiritual event this is. Simple fare, happy people and a wonderful warm feeling. So many tongues." Another memorable meal was shared in a small hostel in the village of Ledigos, which had a communal kitchen where I enjoyed dinner with some English speakers, and to our great joy a group of French pilgrims started to sing, and again I had that wonderful feeling of sharing something special with my fellow pilgrims.

In order to cover the 765 kilometres in a reasonable length of time, one must be prepared to walk between 20 and 35 kilometres a day, which means walk-

The scallop shell, has long been the symbol for the Camino de Santiago de Compostela.
— Photograph by Liane M

ing between five and eight hours at a stretch, including the time taken for a lunch break and a Kit Kat break. Most towns have a small bar/restaurant where you can enjoy a simple pilgrims' meal, with wine included, or there will be a shop where you can purchase groceries for dinner, breakfast and lunch. I ate a lot of crusty bread and chorizo with all my meals, and the bananas I purchased seemed to satisfy my fruit needs. Walking such long distances meant hydrating where necessary, so I always had my water bottle handy, and there seemed to always be a well where I could top it up. If the water were not potable, there would be a sign warning you.

My walking pace is not fast, but it is also not slow, and as a result I sometimes found myself walking alone for several hours at a stretch; other times I shared the road with fellow pilgrims from many countries and walks of life. Even if one is not religious (and I'm not), this journey gives you a lot of time to be alone and think about many things, some of them spiritual. I also had time to share experiences with other people and know that there were as many reasons for undertaking this walk as there were people doing the pilgrimage. One of the people I met and made friends with was a young German girl from Cologne who works for the Catholic Church at Cologne Cathedral. Her strong Catholic faith impelled her to undertake this pilgrimage. We have kept in touch, and she has visited with my wife, Elaine, and I twice in Canada, and we have visited her in Germany.

My final day (October 1) took only about five hours, but it seemed to take forever. I arrived at noon, in time to attend the daily pilgrims' mass in the massive Cathedral of Santiago de Compostela. When I started out on this journey, I insisted that I was not a pilgrim. However, upon entering that massive structure, I had an overwhelming feeling of being one. The church was full of fellow pilgrims, with most of us walking around before and after the mass meeting people we had encountered along the way and renewing recent friendships. It was a very emotional experience, one I wish all walkers could experience.

Before you go, there are some preparations that you should undertake. One is to find a good guidebook. I highly recommend *Walking the Camino de Santiago* by Pili Pala Press. You should also get a Camino passport, which can be obtained from Little Company of Pilgrims Canada. You need this passport to be admitted to the hostels along the way. You must have it stamped at each location so that you can receive your "compostela" (certificate of having completed the pilgrimage) at the pilgrims' office near the Cathedral of Santiago de Compostela.

Hiking with Fred in Malta

MADELAINE PIHACH

When I heard Fred Azzopardi was inviting friends and family to hike with him in Malta, I decided to make this my winter holiday. For three weeks, we enjoyed this marvelous island in the Mediterranean, hiking most days with Fred. We would hop on a bus right in front of our hotel, meet up with him at the bus terminal, and let him pick the bus of the day that would drop us off to explore a section of Malta.

Fred is very passionate about his beautiful country of birth, and he proudly showed us every inch of Malta. Having him as our personal guide allowed our trip in a strange country to be stress-free. Everything was planned for us. The hikes around the Mediterranean Sea were my favourite outings. We explored many coves, caves, harbours, cliffs and beaches. The scenery was stunning, and Fred always waited patiently while we took many, many pictures. Just when I thought I had the best view, a few more steps along the way proved to be even more breathtaking. We visited the village where Fred was born, the school he went to, and where he swam and played as a young child. When signs of aching feet and sore shins became too much for the not-so-seasoned hikers, Fred engaged his friends and family in the rescue. They drove us around, had us over for lunches and drinks, and, just as proudly as Fred, showed us their beautiful country.

The architecture of the cities and villages, especially the churches, was awe-inspiring. Malta has 400,000 people and 365 churches. They range from a small, isolated chapel perched on a cliff to beautiful steeple-topped churches crowning the villages and cities. Every journey inside a church is an event unlike the last one. The eyes look around in wonder at the grandeur and beauty of the domes, frescos, statues and carvings in gold or marble.

Malta's countryside is lovely and very different from that of Canada. There are so many places up high to get a panoramic view of the villages, cities, gardens, rocks and sea at a distance. As Fred says, Malta is a hiker's paradise. It was also very interesting to visit the many grottos, caves, catacombs and temples that date back as far as 5,000 years.

My holiday in Malta was an experience that will always be close to my heart. It is with deep gratitude that I thank Fred for letting me see Malta through his eyes.

Cinque Terre

STELLA PARR

The Cinque Terre (Five Lands) is the name given to five villages — Monterosso del Mare, Vernazza, Corniglia, Manarola and Riomaggiore — on a rugged stretch of Italian coast on the Ligurian Sea. The original fishing villages were reachable only by sea, but a railway and roads now link the villages. The coastline, five villages and surrounding hills have been designated Cinque Terre National Park and are a UNESCO World Heritage Site. Naturally, Cinque Terre is now a popular tourist area.

The park's easier walks feature distances of around 9 kilometres with 335-metre ascents. The harder walks are around 14.5 kilometres with 570-metre ascents, depending on the walk. I chose the easier walks, my friend chose to vary hers.

The first full day was spent exploring the hills above the nearby town of Bonassola, where we had sweeping views of the bay, the town and the chapel at Punta Della Madonna. We then climbed further through wooded areas via the village of Costella to the church of San Giorgio, with its beautiful views of the sea and surrounding villages. We stopped in the village, rested and ate lunch while our guide regaled us with some of the history of the surrounding areas. We then continued to the village of Montaretto, one of the first to be founded in the area.

On day three we took the train to Riomaggiore. The railway was a terrific feat of engineering, with several tunnels cut through the rocky cliffs along the coast. After exploring the village, we headed along the coastal trail called Via dell'Amore (Lover's Path). The path is carved into the cliff, narrow and busy; sometimes you have to wait while people going in the opposite direction pass through. We encountered visitors of many nationalities on the path. We continued on through the lovely harbour village of Manarola to arrive at Corniglia station. We were then invited to either walk up the 377 steps to Corniglia or take the local shuttle bus. You can guess which option most of us selected. After exploring Corniglia, we continued along the coastline to the pretty village of Vernazza, where we took the train back to Bonassola.

The next day, we explored the area to the northwest of Bonassola. We took a short train ride to Framura, then hiked up to the various villages that make up

Framura. After reaching a broad ridge of farmland, we entered some of the best-preserved woodland in the area. We circled around Monte Serra on a beautiful woodland path where we came across many sea pines and chestnut trees. Wild boars are reputed to occupy the woods, but we did not see any. On our way back, we stopped at a small botanical garden, where we saw many of the local plants. The sea views were again spectacular. Some of the small villages have relocated to the hills. Earlier in their history, these fishing villages were routinely raided by pirates in search of supplies. We then descended to Framura and took the train back to Bonassola. That evening after dinner, we walked up the steps to the chapel Punta Della Madonna. The starlit night was beautiful, as were the lights from the town.

Day five was a free day. We could take the train to some of the larger towns in the area, such as Levanto, Portofino or Genora, or simply relax. My friend and I decided to revisit the area above Bonassola so that she could photograph some of the local wildflowers. We came across an orchid and a curry plant (when you bruise the leaves, it smells just like curry). Many of the little villages had a communal water tap, which in some cases was very ornate. We ended up back in one of the stores in Bonassola for a very welcome dish of ice cream, as the weather was sunny and very warm.

Our last day started with a train ride to Vernazza, where we would complete the final section of Cinque Terre by walking to Monterosso. Vernazza is a pretty village with brightly painted houses that flow down to a natural harbour guarded by a rocky headland. The path ascended through woodland with wonderful views of the coast, then descended steeply through lemon groves to Monterosso, where we had the opportunity to find refreshments and explore the old town. Finally, we travelled up through a tunnel and along the beach road to the station to return to Bonassola.

This was a very enjoyable holiday with challenging hikes up and down steps and hills, always rewarded with fantastic views. The food was good and the hotel comfortable, our companions were nice, the guides excellent, the weather very co-operative. Each night we were informed about the hikes for the next day and selected the one we wished to walk. Most nights there were quizzes or games to play or else you could relax at the local bar with a drink and a chat.

Way of the Cross

In the year 2000, I made a pilgrimage to Jerusalem for Holy Week. I decided to walk the route from Pilate's house to Calvary. This is the same route Jesus walked (from trial and condemnation to crucifixion and burial). There are fourteen stations commemorating various events that took along the way.

The word *station* comes from the Latin word meaning "to stand." Every place a train comes to a stop and stands for a while is a station; except we have built buildings at each of those places and for us the building is the station. In this case, we are using the word station in its original meaning. We are going for a walk, and every point along the way where we stop and pray is a station.

In 1342, the Franciscan monks of the Roman Catholic Church were put in authority over the Holy Land. They became familiar with the Stations of the Cross and decided to promote them as a devotional discipline. Of the fourteen stations, eight are preserved in Christian scripture and six are preserved in Christian memory.

The walk begins about 400 metres up the road from St. Anne's Church. There is a ramp on your left leading to the blue metal door of a school. On Friday afternoons at four o'clock (April to September; three o'clock from October to March), the brown-robed Franciscans begin their procession of the Via Dolorosa in the school courtyard. This is Station I. It marks the spot where Jesus was tried and condemned by Pontius Pilate. Station II is across the street. It is here that Jesus was scourged and given the cross. Just beyond it, on the right, is the entrance to the Ecce Homo Convent of the Sisters of Zion, with a basement of ancient pavements, a huge cistern, and a Roman arch in the chapel. The continuation of the arch crosses the street outside.

The Via Dolorosa runs down into El-Wad Road, one of the Old City's most important thoroughfares. To the right, the street climbs toward the Damascus Gate; to the left, it passes through the heart of the Muslim Quarter and reaches the Western Wall. Arab matrons in bright embroidered dresses sail by; black-hatted Hasidic Jews in beards and side curls hurry on divine missions; nimble local Muslim kids in the universal uniform of T-shirt, jeans and sneakers play in the street; and earnest groups of Christian pilgrims, almost oblivious to the tumult, pace out ancient footsteps.

As you turn left onto El-Wad Road, Station III is on your left. This is the spot where Jesus fell for the first time. A few steps beyond, also on the left, is Station IV. The spot marks the place where Mary embraced Jesus. And, on the corner, Station V is where Simon of Cyrene picked up the cross. There, the Via Dolorosa turns right and begins its ascent toward Calvary. Halfway up the street, a brown wooden door on your left marks Station VI. It is here that a woman wiped the face of Jesus. His image remains on the cloth. She is remembered as Veronica, apparently derived from the words *vera* and *icon*, meaning "true image." Facing you at the top of the stepped street, on the busy Suq Khan e-Zeit, is Station VII. This is the spot where Jesus fell for the second time. The little chapel preserves one of the columns of the Byzantine Cardo, the main street of 6th-century Jerusalem, which lines up with the impressive remains excavated to the south, in today's Jewish Quarter. Step to the left and walk 30 metres up the street facing you to Station VIII. This station is marked by nothing more than an inscribed stone in the wall. It is here that Jesus addressed the women in the crowd. Return to the main street and turn right. One hundred metres along Suq Khan e-Zeit from Station VII, turn onto the ramp on your right that ascends parallel to the street. At the end of the lane is a column that represents Station IX. It is here that Jesus fell for the third time.

Step through the open door to the left of the column into courtyard of the Ethiopian monastery known as Deir al-Sultan, an esoteric enclave of this poor but colourful sect. From the monastery's upper chapel, descend through a lower one and out a small wooden door to the court of the Church of the Holy Sepulcher. Most Christians venerate this site as that of the death, burial and resurrection of Jesus. You will find Station X, where Jesus was stripped of his garments. Station XI is where Jesus was nailed to the cross. Station XII is where Jesus died on the cross. Station XIII is where Jesus was taken down from the cross. Lastly, Station XIV is where Jesus was buried within the church. But many Protestants are drawn to Skull Hill and the Garden Tomb, north of the Damascus Gate. A good time to be here is in the late afternoon, after four o'clock, when the various denominations in turn chant their way between Calvary and the tomb amid billowing incense.

Mount Kilimanjaro, in Tanzania, is the highest peak on the African continent and the tallest freestanding mountain in the world. — Photograph by Robert Hardholt

AFRICA & ASIA

Mount Kilimanjaro

VINCE ZVONAR

Our hike-of-a-lifetime started from Toronto on February 14, 2009 — Valentine's Day, which my wife reminds me of every chance she gets.

Once in Tanzania, we drove from Arusha to Lake Manyara National Park. Most of the area looked like desert, with very little vegetation, mostly dry grasses and some low bushes. Seeing children tending their cows beside the road, barefoot with stick in hand reminded me of my own childhood, when I would take our cows to the public pastures. We later spotted our first giraffes grazing on thorny bushes beside a road and were excited to take our first pictures of African wildlife. Game-viewing drives through the park that afternoon and next morning gave us a safari experience as well as a chance to adjust to the time zone change and somewhat acclimatize to the warm temperatures. I would strongly recommend this, rather than starting to hike the day after arriving in Tanzania. After lunch, we drove to Springland Hotel in Moshi, the launching location for our climb. In the evening, we were given a briefing and suggestions by our guide on what to take and how to pack a maximum 35 pounds, which is what porters would carry for the next seven days during the climb.

The Kilimanjaro climb started with an early morning bus ride from Moshi, through Machame Village, to the Machame gate. The Machame route is thought by some to be the most beautiful route for climbing Kilimanjaro, it not only offers scenic splendour but the added benefit of acclimatization. Accommodation on this route is strictly tents.

Our supplies and gear were unloaded and distributed among ten porters. We registered at the gate office and started our climb through the rainforest in warm but comfortable conditions. The trail through the rainforest was a good, wide, mostly gravel-packed path, but it did narrow before we reached the first camp. I realized very quickly that this would be a 5-kilometre-per-hour hike, as I normally hike on the Bruce Trail. One of the first expressions you hear on the trail is "poli poli," meaning "slowly, slowly." After about six hours of hiking, we reached our first campsite, Machame Camp, which is 2980 metres above mean sea level. The tents were being set up and, before we knew it, we were offered warm water to wash our hands and face before a snack was served. Popcorn was our snack after every hike and before supper for the rest of the climb. Our hot dinner was served in a dining tent on a cloth-covered table surrounded by lawn chairs, all very comfortable and unexpected on a hiking trail.

The second day started at daylight with a hot breakfast. The first hour of hiking was through the remaining forest before reaching the moorland zone. After lunch and a short break, we continued up a rocky ridge onto Shira Plateau. In between the clouds, in an easterly direction, we could see the western breaches of Kibo (Mount Kilimanjaro) Glacier. We reached the Shira Camp, at 3840 metres, after about six hours of hiking. After a hot dinner and some fresh fruit, it was early to bed. The temperature in the morning dropped to about -2 degrees Celsius on this exposed campsite, but a down-filled sleeping bag kept me warm.

The next day we started hiking east into a rocky semi-desert landscape. After lunch, we ascended the rocky scree path to the Lava Tower, reaching an altitude of 4600 metres. This was the first time we all felt the effects of reduced oxygen: headaches and tingling sensations in our fingertips and toes. The benefit of acclimatization was beginning to make sense, even with reduced oxygen (or because of it). Descent to Barranco Camp, at 3950 metres, took another two hours. The camp is situated in the valley below the breach and the Great Barranco Wall. By now we were getting used to the routine: snack, warm water before dinner, hot meal, some rest, fill up the water bottles for the next day's hike, then early to bed. This had been the hardest day of hiking so far.

The fourth day was the shortest day of hiking, but the steepest and hardest climb thus far. The Great Barranco Wall is an imposing site, and I don't remember being told the night before that we would climb the wall. This climb was the most "pole, pole," or slowest, topping out just below the Heim Glacier. The view from the top was impressive, and it was hard to believe that I just climbed it. We reached the Karanga Camp, at 3963 metres, after about three hours of hiking. We had lots of free time in the afternoon to take pictures of the Kibo, to the north of us, during breaks in the clouds — and we were virtually in the clouds. We also had time to try out Iain's Blackberry, and it worked, but for some reason my wife did not appreciate a phone call at 4 AM. We forgot the time difference, or at least I did. It could have been the reason why Iain had *me* try calling home.

Our last day of hiking before summiting was through the Karanga Valley, over intervening ridges and valleys, before joining the Mweka route. We turned north onto the Mweka route, heading towards the Barafu Camp. This section is comprised mostly of barren rocks and dust, a desert-like landscape, and about the only animals you see are black birds that looked like ravens. We reached Barafu Camp, at 4600 metres, after about five hours of hiking. The Barafu Camp is totally exposed, and tents are pitched on narrow stony ridges. We were advised to familiarize ourselves with the terrain before dark. On this day, our washroom was set very close to our tents. You did not want to be very loud unless you wanted half the camp to know what you were doing. Before dinner, we prepared our equipment, water, hiking poles and thermal clothing. This time we took great care to prepare our day backpacks and headlamps, and to put new batteries in our cameras for the summit attempt. This was to be our last dinner before our final ascent, but for some reason we were not that hungry. It could have been a case of upset stomachs or perhaps nervousness about our final destination, the peak of Africa.

We went to bed earlier than normal, about 7 PM, as wake-up call would be a mere four hours later, at 11:30 PM. After some tea and biscuits, we started our ascent at midnight. We headed in a northwesterly direction through heavy scree, or what at times seemed to be loose gravel, towards Stella Point on the crater's rim. Hiking through the night did not seem to be as much of a problem as I had expected, but we did stay very close to our hike leaders. For a short period, we were accompanied by distant lightning. Watching the lightning at night from above the clouds was an awesome experience and something I will remember for a long time. Our climb was slow with frequent stops to rest and drink lots of water. You would not think that simply breathing and walking slowly up the hill would be such hard work. My glasses were fogging up, and I had to take them off. No need to worry about pee breaks, though. All the water, about 1.5 litres, seemed to have evaporated through my mouth.

We reached Stella Point, at 5685 metres, had a short rest and continued on to the Uhuru Peak, at 5896 metres, and reached it at about 6 AM, just as the sun was beginning to light up the distant horizon. Taking pictures in front of the congratulatory sign was the first priority. Luckily, I carried my camera inside the pocket of my coat and it worked. After spending about 15 minutes at the top of Africa, we were cold, too cold to linger, so we started the descent to our camp. On our way down, as the sun was coming up, we saw spectacular views of glaciers, and I took some nice pictures. For some reason, going down was easier than going up, and we reached our camp in about two hours. We didn't need any encouragement to take a much-needed snooze before hiking another three hours to our last camp of the hike. I must have been asleep before I hit the ground, and I mean literally. This time the thin mattress did not bother me. Wake-up call came too soon, just three hours later.

We descended to our last camp, the Mweka Camp, at 3100 metres, via the Mweka route. This is where we first noticed the two-wheel stretchers used to bring the injured or sick down the mountain. The trail was not difficult — down the rocks and the scree path into the moorland and eventually into the forest. The rain came during the last hour of our hike into the camp, and we realized how lucky we had been the previous five days, having hiked and slept in dry conditions. To our surprise, the Mweka Camp office had beer available. After drinking what seemed like tons of warm water for six days, that Kilimanjaro beer was the best one I had drank in a long time.

Our last day started early, after a well-deserved breakfast. That morning was the first time that we saw the Mount Kilimanjaro white, completely covered in snow. The day before, when we had rain at a lower altitude, it had snowed at the top. I couldn't help but wonder how the climb would have been with snow on the trail. After a three-hour hike through scenic rainforest, we reached the park gate where successful climbers received summit certificates. After that, it was an hour bus ride back to our hotel in Moshi, where the first order of business was a long-overdue hot shower.

The most pleasant surprise for me on this hike had to be the hot meals that were provided every day on the trail. Sure, the bread got a bit stale after a few days, but hot soups and fruit more than made up for it. After a few days, our cook compromised and switched to crepes, which were almost as good as my mother made when I was growing up in Croatia.

This, for me, was the hike of a lifetime, with great scenery along the way. I could have done without sleeping in a tent and the lack of sleep in general, but it was worth it. The whole experience was awesome!

Mt. Meru and Mt. Kilimanjaro Climbs

JAMES GRIFFIN

It was early in 2005 that we signed on to Isabelle Sheardown's 70th birthday expedition to Tanzania, to climb Mt. Kilimanjaro, at 5846 metres (19,180 ft), Africa's highest mountain.

We arrived in Tanzania mid-September, the dry season and considered one of the best months for climbing. The day after we arrived, we set out on a three-day climb up Mt. Meru to get acclimatized for the longer climb up Kilimanjaro. After a very bumpy ride to Arusha National Park, we assembled at the main gate with our guides and porters. We were surprised to see that our head guide, a park ranger, was armed, but we were assured that the rifle was only for scaring off water buffalo, which can sometimes be mean, especially when alone. Shortly after noon, we were on our way through open grassland and sub-tropical forest. We saw the first of many water buffalo, warthogs and giraffes. After a brief stop for lunch, we climbed for three hours through a continued mixture of forest and grassland, arriving at our first encampment, Miriakamba Huts (2500 m/8,202 ft). The huts were comfortable bunkhouse-type accommodation with solar-powered lighting, but the washroom facilities were primitive. The six-hour climb was steep and relentless, starting with a series of stairs equal to a climb of the CN Tower. This was followed by a narrow rocky trail and a series of switchbacks that were still under construction. The views were becoming ever more spectacular as we arrived at Saddle Hut (3570 m/11,713 ft) in the early afternoon. This was to be our jumping-off point for the final climb to the summit. After a brief rest, five of us did the short climb up Little Meru, another 250 metres. The final climb started at midnight, but unfortunately could not be completed due to a combination of rugged conditions, altitude sickness and lack of time. Meru is in fact harder to climb than Kilimanjaro, something we did not realize beforehand. With only so many days for a trip of this nature, time is against you, and the difference between success and failure very often depends on it.

The next morning we were off for the assault on Kilimanjaro. We were taken on the Machame route, one of the most scenic (there are several routes of various lengths and difficulty), starting at 1850 metres and taking seven days up and down. After signing in at the park gate, a requirement at each camp, we were off, loaded with a big lunch, extra clothes and mandatory 3 litres of water to help prevent acute mountain sickness. Meanwhile the porters loaded up the camping equipment, food and our main luggage.

Two days of climbing through forest brought us to Shira Caves, a camp at the edge of the tree line. The caves are a volcanic version of the caves one sees on the Bruce Trail. It was now below freezing at night, with quite heavy frost on the ground in the morning; however, the sun rises so rapidly at this latitude, and air is so clear, one soon warms up. The third day was very long, involving a steep, steady climb through rock-strewn alpine desert up to 4530 metres (14,860 ft) and then down to Barranco Camp 580 metres below. It was on this day that we saw vegetation and birds unique to Kilimanjaro.

The following morning, having struggled with altitude sickness for some time, Elizabeth wisely decided to go back down. The mountain has claimed many lives from this affliction, including fit porters, who have succumbed without warning. Immediately upon leaving Barranco, we were faced with what is known as "Breakfast Wall." Technically, this was probably the toughest part of the climb and required some caution, but was not too long. The rest of the day was spent going up and down various valleys. It was considered an acclimatization day, as we would not be much higher at the next camp, Karanga, 3963 metres (13,000 ft). The next day involved a steady and, in parts, very steep climb through a barren landscape with vultures, including the magnificent lammergeier soaring overhead. The temperature changed quite often as clouds drifted in and out. We reached the final camp, Barafu, 4600 metres (15,090 ft), in the early afternoon. After an early supper and bedtime in preparation for another midnight start, we got away at 11:30 PM for the final climb. Along with several other groups, we made our way up the steep, rocky switchback trail, a long line of pinprick lights ahead and behind, us and brilliant stars above us. Our guide, Justaz, was marvelous as he guided the sight-challenged James around and up the rock hazards. He maintained the all-important slow-but-steady pace hour after hour, with regular short breaks to drink, eat and gasp the rarified air. "Poli poli" (slowly, slowly), they kept repeating from the very first day. Six hours after we had started, dawn came at last, and by 6:00 the sun was up. Another hour of very steep climbing over scree brought us to Stella Point, on the edge of the main crater; the worst was over. We were all pretty whacked, to put it mildly. We had another hour of gentle climbing to Uhuru, but a challenge as the air became ever more rarified. The summit reached, we stood for the mandatory photos, hugs and congratulations. There was a mixture of elation and sadness with only four of us standing there when there should have been six. The mountain is not forgiving.

Roof of Africa

DEIRDRE DONNELLY

In 2008, I climbed Mount Kilimanjaro in Tanzania. The Maasai people call it the "House of God" or the "Roof of Africa," with a height of 19,340 feet (5895 m). Not even childbirth was as difficult as summiting. You are put to the test physically and mentally. Unless you have severe altitude sickness (HAPE or HACE), getting to the top is achieved through proper acclimatization and, perhaps even more importantly, sheer willpower.

I decided to take the Umbwe route, which is shorter and thus more direct than other routes. It is the least travelled because it is the steepest, but also the most spectacular way to reach Barranco Camp, where the major ascent routes join on their way to Uhuru Peak. It also serves as an escape route for those climbers suffering from altitude sickness, and I encountered a few on their way down (looking very poorly) that gave me pause at the time!

You trek through six incredible and very different eco zones on the way up: farmland, rainforest, heather, moorland, alpine desert and, finally, arctic summit conditions. I was sick the night before I started the climb and continued to be ill throughout the full ascent. On the first day, a torrential five-hour rainforest downpour gave me a clue as to what I was in for and the need to be totally prepared for all circumstances.

On the second day of the climb, about 1 kilometre uphill from Lower Umbwe Caves, I reached "the first rock step." It is a steep rock wall (25 ft/8 m) where you need to use both hands to climb. One of the porters fell off and thankfully was not seriously harmed, but he was sent back down the mountain due to his injuries. What I found shocking was that my guide did not even have a first-aid kit. As usual, I had my own in my pack and was able to provide the necessary bandages, etc., to treat him before he hiked down to the local hospital for proper treatment.

As sick as I felt, it could not overshadow the spectacular scenery. I had booked the climb to coincide with the full moon over East Africa. Clouds had mostly obscured the climbing route, but when I left at 10 PM for the summit attempt, the sky was clear, with the moon illuminating both the mountain above and the town of Moshi below, with its twinkling lights. Meanwhile, the blazing stars of the Southern Cross constellation shone far above me. It is a vision I will truly never forget. Even now, whenever I look up at the full moon back here in Canada, my mind returns to that full moon over Kilimanjaro.

That last night, after days of excruciating discomfort, I wanted to get a head start, since I had not been eating and was vomiting and still had diarrhea, not to mention the effects of low oxygen (hypoxia) on the brain. One climbs at night because in the night cold, the scree trail is firm, and slipping backwards on its surface is minimized. It was certainly the most mentally and physically challenging portion of the trek.

The winds were fierce and the water in my CamelBak bladder froze within the first hour due to the extremely cold nighttime temperatures. I would walk ten paces and then collapse over my trekking poles and count to ten. My guide attempted to get me moving more quickly, but I just did not have the stamina to go any faster. This routine continued for nine hours until I reached the top. After climbing all night, I had indeed made it to the top but was devoid of all emotion other than exhaustion. I could not summon the energy to care that I made it to the "Roof of Africa."

Hiking Mount Kilimanjaro

MICHAEL CURTIS

With the iconic peak in the background and several zebras in the foreground, the T-shirt proclaims, "I have climbed Mt. Kilimanjaro — Have you?"

OK, I bought the T-shirt, thereby stimulating the local economy, because I did the climb — in reality, a walk. Sure, it is not easy, but it is also not that tough. Yes, people have died while attempting the ascent, and no doubt more will, but it is not that hard of a slog. It is a strenuous walk, not a climb! There is no climbing apparatus involved!

I read an article in the *Bruce Trail News* written by a member who hiked Kili in the late 1980s, and it was interesting. The wife was interested in the trip and a photo safari of Kenya, and so, a brief talk with a travel agent friend and the trip arranged. We would fly from Toronto to Paris, then Nairobi, with a transfer to Arusha, in Tanzania, where we would join a tour company called Guerba for the climb up Kili, spread over a week, then have a two-week photo safari in Tanzania and Kenya.

The group of a dozen that we joined had already been together for two weeks, travelling through Tanzania in a well-equipped open lorry with a guide, driver and cook. We were the only Canadians in the group, which was made up of Brits, Aussies, Kiwis and a Yank. We got along quite well! We drove through the town of Moshi to the Marangu Hotel at the base of Mt. Kilimanjaro, where we camped for the evening.

The following morning we met our guides and porters (we carried only a day pack, while we each had a porter who carried our sleeping bags, food, etc.) and travelled by lorry to Marangu Gate (1860 m/6,000 ft), the entrance to Mt. Kilimanjaro National Park. The requisite papers obtained, group and individual photos taken (no digitals), we commenced a four-hour walk along a roadway through a rainforest inhabited by monkeys. After three hours, the roadway became a very good pathway leading to Mandara Hut (2725 m/9,000 ft), where we spent the evening.

The next day we continued along the well-travelled path for 12 kilometres over a period of seven hours. The rainforest gradually gave way to open and rolling alpine meadows with giant heather trees as we gained elevation. We arrived at Horombo Hut (3780 m/12,000 ft) in the late afternoon. Due to the cloud cover, I could see only what lay around me. I could have been in northern Ontario for all I knew, except for the unusual vegetation. I felt no different and had no difficulties breathing. None of our party had any problems. The clue is to acclimatize gradually. If you cannot walk and talk at the same time, you are travelling too quickly.

Now the landscape became more rugged and rocky as we left the alpine meadow zone for the stark desert of rock and dust, which rarely sees precipitation, hence no water available save that carried by oneself and the porters. As we travelled six hours (12 kilometres) to Kibo Hut, at 4740 metres (15,450 ft), we saw a few hardy plants that had managed to eke out an existence somehow. It was during this portion that some of our party had to stop and rest on several occasions. It was best to travel *poli-poli* (slowly) and acclimatize. I felt just fine, not rushing, just taking my time and enjoying the scenery and trip!

We reached Kibo Hut in the late afternoon, with the peak a mere half-kilometre distant horizontally, but some 3,000 feet vertically. We lounged and wandered around, ate supper and retired to the huts, with shared accommodations, since they were double-booked. (I shared with the wife — separate sleeping bags.) We were awoken at 3 AM for the four-hour ascent, in order to witness sunrise over

Africa. A brief cup of tea and a biscuit and we were off, zigzagging up the scree slope. It is loose volcanic scree, and progress was slow. "Poli-poli" was the mantra! I rested on several occasions to catch my breath. The lights of villages were visible on the plains thousands of metres below, clearly visible in the pristine air. Having missed the *pasi-pasi* (faster) group (I am married and remained with the wife's group), I witnessed the slowly growing illumination of the eastern sky as the sun rose and beheld the beginning of a new day over Africa, even as I struggled to the summit of Gilman's Point.

With only a few moments of rest, I was refreshed and ready to walk around. Photos were taken, and I wandered around the area. I felt quite fine, even though I was at 3780 m/18,640 ft. The walk up had been a very tough slog, with a few individuals descending straight down, in the darkness, due to altitude sickness. I drank water copiously, took no medication, and felt just fine. The next time, however, may be different. Altitude affects people differently, and each person's experience can vary. Perhaps I was just lucky. People do die doing the Kili climb.

The descent to Kibo Hut took a mere 30 minutes, compared to the five-hour ascent. We then returned to Horombo Hut for an overnight before returning to Marangu Gate for our certificate and an overnight camp at the Tanzanite Hotel.

On Safari

DARYL W. COWELL

It seemed that Yankari National Park, Nigeria, was officially closed, as it was the rainy season and the animals were disbursed — not a good time for foreign visitors to see the wildlife. However, my Nigerian colleagues from the National Forestry Department apparently arranged a visit for the distinguished Canadian visitor for the next day.

The nine of us — my driver, five colleagues, Samuel, and the park driver — were off to observe the surrounding Guinea Savannah and a riparian forest along the Gagi River, a tributary to the Niger River. All was going well until we descended a steep slope into the riparian zone, where the truck promptly stalled. As it turned out, this was the furthest point along our route from the camp, about 7 kilometres distant. I got out of the truck to take some pictures as the driver assumed a position under the hood. I did not suspect anything at the time, but after what seemed an inordinately long period I looked over toward the truck. Samuel was standing beside the driver, hands on hips and head slowly moving back and forth.

The truck had stalled, normally not a problem, but it seems it did not have a battery. The driver then proceeded to dig dirt out from behind the wheels to assist a roll that would get the truck clutch-started. We then pushed the truck backwards whereupon the wheels became lodged in the holes dug by the driver. It was now approaching 40 degrees Celsius.

I suggested to the ranger that he radio back to the camp so they could come and collect us. He responded, "What radio?" With a smile he suggested that they would eventually realize we were not returning and would send the other truck. My lack of confidence in the second truck being mechanically superior led me to suggest he get his gun and we would walk. He responded, "What gun?"

Nevertheless, the thought of being sitting prey did not interest me, so we headed off on our unplanned hike. We had a total of three small water bottles amongst the nine of us, but there was some shade offered by the overhead riparian forest. The hike started off quite good, and I began to think that this was actually preferred, as I could inspect the terrain much better, get some good photos and hopefully live to see my wife and child again. We walked in loose groups of two or three, with forestry colleagues a few metres ahead of me.

I was getting some great photos of the riparian forest zone and enclosed habitats — meadow marshes, even an animal watering hole with lots of tracks. Hmmm, tracks. Sani Usman, a remote sensing specialist, and I began a great conversation on these matters and soon all were discussing wonderful things. Nigerians, when speaking amongst themselves, generally talk about only two things, food and the price of food, often quite demonstratively.

This had been going on for a short time when the park ranger abruptly stopped in front of us and commanded us to be quiet. It seems that the animals, including some rather large cats, were sleeping in the heat of day, and it was advisable for us to not wake them up. Well, talk of a pin dropping. The tension was clearly rising, and we began to notice the heat for the first time. After a half hour or so, four of my friends were quickly, but quietly, walking toward me in the opposite direction as the camp. I watched them pass me then turned to see a cow elephant standing directly on the path in front of the remaining group. The elephant had come from the direction of the river and made not a sound. That such a large beast could walk through the jungle and not make a sound astonished me. However, that was not my first thought. The possibility of a calf nearby passed quickly through my mind. She stopped on the path and turned to look at us. As I was wondering how fast an elephant could run, she just as promptly turned and continued on into the jungle to our right; again, so silently that for a second we were left wondering what just happened.

An adrenalin rush, tempered by the knowledge that something big could step out onto the path or drop down from above without a sound, created an interesting condition that I had never experienced before. Combined with the oppressive heat, the "hike" became an ordeal for the first time. No more pictures, no more talking, just a focus on getting back to camp. We eventually reached the base of a steep hill and got a second wind when Samuel told us the camp was just over the top. The climb was about all I had left, and when I reached the camp I found myself extremely lightheaded, nearly passing out.

The most difficult experience I have ever had while hiking ended in bliss. It turns out that the camp is located beside a natural spring and swimming hole, the Wiki Warm Spring. I guess the term "hot spring" is relative to the ambient temperature. The whole episode thus ended with the most wonderful swimming experience I have ever had, in probably the most beautiful place that I came across in two months of fieldwork in Nigeria. Oh, and by the way, it turned out that this spring also supplies water for one of Nigeria's best beers — Rock Beer.

Gorillas In Our Midst

ELIZABETH BOJARRA

My hike in Rwanda included gorillas. Yes, you heard me correctly, gorillas! In 1990, I decided to take a trip to Africa. I had read Isak Dinesen's book *Africa: Images of the Wild Continent*, and I wanted to smell the red earth of Africa for myself, dance with the Maasai people and see elephants in the wild. I did all of this and much more. This hike took place a long way from Canada and was very different from my Canadian experience.

I was hiking the savanna, which is open, undulating land with no fences or roads, when I came across a Maasai boy about 12 years old. He was herding goats and cows when our paths crossed. We walked towards one another, eyes drawn by the fascination of the "other," and silently he put out his hand, reached up and touched my fair hair. I reached out and touched his hair. It felt coarse. He then touched my skin, and I did the same to him, and we smiled at one another. It was a magical moment. We both carried on our walk, and I felt joy in my heart.

Yes, the red earth of Africa does have a distinct pungent smell. It is like sun-kissed earth and is very comforting until it rains. It looks hard-packed, but with a little rain it turns into a quagmire. The elephants do not seem to have any trouble with it, and they crossed our path several times. For the elephants, time is running out. They have been reduced from millions to thousands in less than 40 years. Some African nations reported a decrease of as much as two thirds in 2008.

In Rwanda, most of the land is farmed — by women, I might add! Early morning, around 6:00, you see women tending the many gardens. When you look up the mountainsides, only the tops seem to still be forested, everything else is neat little patchwork-quilt squares, some on very steep slopes. One gets the feeling that habitat is running out for all living creatures except humans in this small country.

We started our hike in the Virunga Mountains, from base camp in Parc National, where I could feel the tension in the group of men hoping to be picked to accompany us. They looked very poor and hungry, and their stares made me uncomfortable. Maybe they were thinking, those strange *wazungu* (white people). My thoughts were of Dian Fossey and her violent death. Fossey devoted her life to protecting the mountain gorillas and spent 18 years living in primitive conditions. I feel they would not be alive today if she had not brought world attention to their plight. The cost of my hike contributed to the survival of these magnificent creatures, and I did not begrudge one penny of it.

The forest was lush and green as we started out. There were about 12 of us plus our local guides. We started at the base of the mountain, so walking was fairly easy for the first half hour, and then we gradually started to climb. We walked through thick bush and open meadows, climbing higher up the mountainside. Our guides came across a flat black-and-white worm about 6 inches long and 4 inches in circumference. It had rolled up in defense and felt like leather. I know, because I thought they were afraid to pick it up, so I picked it up and put it at the side of the path so others would not trod on it. The guides looked at me in amazement: Who was this Canadian, anyway?

When we were getting close to the group of gorillas — by the way, they do not always find the group and the two-hour hike up the mountain can be for naught — the guides asked me to come to the front of the group. As I was trudging along and wondering why, all of a sudden a guide with a fearsome-looking machete stepped in front of me and indicated that I should follow him. He then swung his machete and cut down a dense patch of forest to reveal, not 4 feet away, a full-grown gorilla eating vegetation. Its huge hands looked swollen, like rubber gloves filled with water. She looked at me with disinterest — I felt it was a she for some reason. She did not seem upset or alarmed that this white face with eyes as big as saucers was staring at her with a stupid grin. That was my first contact with the family, and it will always stay with me thanks to the sudden introduction.

The whole thing felt like a dream. We quietly stayed with the group for over an hour. There were two youngsters at play all the time we were there, tumbling over one another and rolling in spoor. We dodged them when they rolled too close. The big silverback, at around 400 pounds, was the head honcho and let us know who was boss by charging through our group, bumping us gently with his massive body. He then sat in the middle of his kingdom, surveying us and his group, looking like a fat king on his throne of leaves. Once he had established that he was the boss, he had no trouble with us having lunch with him and his family. We respected his wishes, as we wanted to live to see another day. Sadly we had to leave, but I will never forget the wonderful visit in this strange land with these magnificent animals — so different from Canada. Thank goodness I can hike: it was my own two feet that allowed me to experience this adventure and I hope many more in the years to come.

The Maasai Mountain of God

TONI QUINN

The single-day climb of Tanzania's Ol Doinyo Lengai, the Maasai Mountain of God, the only active natrocarbonatite volcano in the world, is the strangest thing I have ever done.

My trip to Tanzania in 2005 began with a desire to see, and perhaps climb, Kilimanjaro. I was not seeking a sense of achievement by climbing the highest mountain in Africa. It was more important to me to see Kilimanjaro's 5896-metre (19,344 ft) massif rising out of the hot equatorial plains of Africa, yet crowned by glaciers. Global warming is melting these unique glaciers, and they will soon disappear. I wanted to see them before they are gone forever.

As I read about Tanzania, I became intrigued and no longer wanted to limit my trekking to one mountain. I assembled an itinerary, which I called in my journal "Trekking the Volcanoes of Tanzania," all of which formed along the fracture line of the Great Rift Valley. I searched, without success, for a trekking company with this route on offer. So over the Internet, and with some trepidation, I drew up a contract with a Tanzanian outfitter to guide and outfit the trip I had in mind: the Crater Highlands, Ol Doinyo Lengai, Mt. Meru and Kilimanjaro.

A one-day safari in the Ngorongoro Crater, itself an extinct volcano, introduced the Great Rift Valley and the journey to come among its attendant volcanoes. For the Crater Highlands and Ol Doinyo Lengai, I set off from Arusha with a Tanzanian crew: Ole, my Maasi guide; Steve, driver and safari guide; and Obadi, our Maasai cook. Once into an area without vehicle access, an armed ranger and donkey handler joined us. Just before sunset, not far from the rim of Ngorongoro, I began the four-day Crater Highlands trek with a climb of the first of two extinct volcanoes ascended on this trek, Olmoti and Empakaai. We then trekked across a remote part of Maasailand and ended by descending the steep 1,500-foot wall of the Great Rift Valley — an amazing four days.

The second hike was the night ascent of Ol Doinyo Lengai. Next, another four-day trek put me on the summit of Mt. Meru at dawn. At 4566 metres (14,981 ft), Mt. Meru is Kilimanjaro's sister mountain, another extinct and very dramatic volcano. Finally, the seven-day trek up Kilimanjaro ended with the third night ascent of this trip. Contrary to my own expectations, I did experience the wonder of standing on Kilimanjaro's summit, listening to its glacier creak and groan. It is astounding to think that in a week-long trek one can traverse climatic zones equivalent to walking from the equator to the arctic. Ironically, I never realized my dream of seeing Kilimanjaro in its entirety because unheard-of cloud, haze and rain settled over East Africa for the entire month I was there, in spite of it being the dry season. An elder Masaai said that "not in living memory" had they seen such haze. The people of Zanzibar kept saying, "It's a funny rain," completely out of season.

Every day that September was a gift that amazed. Yet in all that dramatic hiking, the bizarre mountain of Ol Doinyo Lengai most fascinated me with its extreme otherworldliness. Even for a volcano, it is an oddity. The cooled lava is white, not black. It is a soda composition, so runoff and airborne ash make Lake Natron below, as well as the lake in Empakaai's crater, exceedingly caustic. As for the climb, imagine walking steeply uphill all night, in pitch darkness except for the circle of your headlamp, working your way up through dust that sinks and drags you backwards on every step, while every so often the volcano trembles beneath you and sends a wave of sulphurous gas wafting around you. That was life, hour after hour. Nothing broke the inexorable uphill struggle and the dark monotony of treading upward except the occasional person passing in the opposite direction, giving up and going down, and once, a warning from the guide not to fall over an edge. Lengai is cone-shaped and steeply buttressed by alternating ridges and gullies that run vertically from base to crater rim. The route climbs one of these narrow corrugations, on its crest, never dropping into the deep, precipitous canyons on either side. The climb is relentlessly steep. Lengai's summit is at 2878 metres (9,426 ft). Estimates of the climb vary from 5,000 to 6,000 feet.

It was not until the descent in daylight that I got a true picture of Lengai's forbidding terrain. Now I could see the exposure on either side of the ridge and the rugged nature of the deep, steep gullies eroded between the buttresses. The long dust sections were hard on the legs, though in places one could ride the dust down. Rocks that should have provided relief were too slippery with dust and grit to relax concentration. It was an endless descent.

We made it down, moving with caution, in three and a half hours, but it seemed much longer. I felt a sudden sense of incredulity over all that had happened. I realized that these had been the strangest hours of my life and that they had encompassed one of the most intriguing and spectacular experiences I would ever know.

Band-Aid Boxes in the Nepal Himalaya

MARLENE ROTHENBURY

If you love mountains, after Nepal, there are no others. The words formidable, majestic and resolute do no justice to how the Himalaya lay on your soul. The mountains reach out to your body and spirit and forge a kinship that will be with you forever. The absolute stillness of a spring morning, with smoke rising through the roofs of thatch-covered dwellings, sweeps you back to an ancient time; you know the mornings have not changed for millennia. You scramble from your tent, knowing the sunny rays will be teasing at the tips of the peaks that you knew surrounded you last evening in the dusky, misty mountain air of the night. Your lungs take in the first icy breaths, and you look around and see the valley bowl you are camped in, each peak — north, east, south, west — tantalizing you with seductive glimpses of themselves as the sun moves upward over the far valleys. Second by second, the peaks show off a majestic new snapshot. On the mightiest, on Everest, snow swirls and races with the winds in endless streams, like a veil in the sun.

Most visitors to the Khumba region will stop at Namche Bazaar in Nepal. A stay of at least one night is recommended in order to acclimatize to the altitude before climbing to higher elevations.
— Photograph by Jason Maehl

The carrot is impossible to resist: the chance to trek with New Zealanders on the 3rd Annual Band-Aid Box expedition to the Gokyo Lakes, in the Khumba region of Nepal's Himalaya range, over 23 days. The primary goal of this trek is to help fund and transport medical supplies and personnel to a clinic in Kharikhola, Nepal. The trek group is comprised of two teams, the volunteer medical team and the trekking team, all of us with one goal: the trekkers offer financial support through part of their trek cost; the medical team volunteers their time, skills and compassion to bring medical support to a community in need.

Some of us are first-timers to Nepal, and the bus drive from Kathmandu Airport to our hotel fills every one of our senses to overflowing — sounds of the traffic, barefoot children in the streets, horns, sights of litter and refuse against the curbs, aromas of flowers, trees, dust, hot white sunlight, brilliant saris, tunics, blouses, lolling sacred cows, smoldering funeral pyres, tangles of electrical wiring, flowerpots, rickshaws, chickens, goats, roast meat and corn, sewage. The haze of the 30 million people (and almost as many cars) forms a cloudy curtain over objects 100 feet away.

We are relieved two days later to fly out of the Kathmandu Valley to the clean, low mountains of Paphlu (2470 m). A whole plane full of trekkers and medics descend on the lone teahouse for lunch. Our excitement is palpable. There is a quick briefing while the camping and medical supplies are loaded into baskets and on the backs of our porters. We are a formidable bunch: 17 porters, 7 kitchen staff, 8 Sherpas, 14 trekkers and 8 medical personnel.

The walking is easy and uphill to our first camp at Ringmo (2720 m). For a first-time trekker in Nepal, my learning curve is steep and swift as I peel away my First World sensitivities. This is Camp 1. By Camp 22, I will be seasoned and relatively comfortable living at the same basic level as the majority of people in this world. All forms of Asian toilets are taken in stride. We join the villagers at the communal hose to wash clothes. The kitchen staff work wonders and produce a varied array of dishes, presented to appeal to western appetites. Some of us, sometimes, choose rice and dal, the staple diet of the Nepalese. Simplicity is the key in learning and adapting to the Nepalese culture.

Our trek schedule has been designed by our leader, New Zealand mountaineer John Jordan, OMNZ, and Allan Jellyman, Trustee of Band-Aid Box, to take us through varied altitudes, up and down, though always gaining, the better to acclimatize us to our ultimate challenge, Gokyo Ri at 5360 metres. The daily rhythm of our trek days takes hold.

We arrive at Camp 3, Kharikhola, and have a bodily sense that acclimatization has begun as we ascend and descend the hills and valleys from Paphlu. This wonderful, bustling village is the very reason we are here. So much to do in 24 hours before the clinic officially opens. Villagers mill expectantly around the small medical facility as supplies are distributed to their respective shelves. The dental chair assembled. John demonstrates the state-of-the-art stretcher to the local people who will use it. The medical team includes Nepalese MDs and nurses, a New Zealand gynecologist, New Zealand eye specialist, and New Zealand nurses. Villagers from across the valley have waited for months for this medical miracle to arrive. In one full day, the clinic is set up and ready for its first patients. We have our first party as the two teams prepare to say goodbye in the morning. The medical team will stay in the village to provide medical care. We trekkers will start on our mountain adventure.

Each of us experiences the inevitable highs and lows of embarking on a trek of this magnitude. The few cold, rainy, muddy nights are balanced with the consistently crisp and clear mornings, with the sun warming our spirits and the surrounding peaks. Breakfasts are hearty, with hot cereal, omelets, chapattis slathered with peanut butter and honey or jam, all washed down with tin cups of scalding tea. The trail in this backcountry is rough, some of it requiring scrambling over deadfall.

The final challenging climb of our hike is Gokyo Ri (5360 m), which promises an uninterrupted view of Everest and her consorts. Eight of our fourteen decide to attempt the climb. The five men move out ahead of us three women early in the ascent. The men have two Sherpas, we have one each. The ascent is steep, switching higher and upward. The lake recedes to a small ice-covered patch below. I am walking so slowly it feels like slow motion. We stop every 20 or 30 steps. My head is dizzy at times. I stumble. The oxygen just won't fill my heavy legs and feet. How does anyone climb Everest? We three, and our Sherpas, call it a day at 17,000 feet. We sit in the sun on the rocky path and all six of us share chocolate bars and water. We have our 17,000 feet party. We are exhilarated to have experienced this altitude. We swear never to do altitude again…until the next carrot appears. Later that morning, back in camp, we proudly applaud our hearty band of guys. They made the summit of Gokyo Ri!

At Lukla, our final camp, we are treated to a sleep in a teahouse. On our final night on trek, we build fine memories of dancing with the Sherpas, cake, and rum passed along and sipped from our tin cups. We dance to the Sherpas' music as the floor of the teahouse shakes and rocks.

But one more adventure is waiting for us in the morning. The Nepalese mountain runways are scraped out of the earth and built on slopes, the better to slow a plane on landing and accelerate a plane on takeoff. Lukla runway is paved but ends with a sheer drop into thousands of feet of thin air. We are a happy and carefree bunch as we pile into the Twin Otter. At the farthest point possible from the runway drop-off, the pilot revs the engine till I think the rivets will pop out of the wings. Suddenly the brake is released and we hurtle down that short, steeply sloped runway. The wheels lift moments before reaching the drop and relieved clapping erupts all around.

I watch the Kathmandu Valley slip by below, the tidy villages and farms using every available space. Spring crops are greening the valley walls. This has been a trip of a lifetime. Already I yearn to return.

Mount Everest

MARIE MELNICHUK

My most memorable hike was to view snow-capped Mount Everest in fall of 1987.

Arriving in Kathmandu, Nepal, in November, I spent a few days acclimatizing to altitude at 1360 metres, or about 5,000 feet, as well as the culture. I was in awe of the many Buddhist and Hindu temples. Friendly Nepalese people helped in arranging for a permit and purchasing a trekking map to Kala Pathar. This is a peak above Everest Base Camp that offers a 360-degree panoramic view of Mount Everest and its surrounding peaks. Mount Everest is not visible from Kathmandu Valley, but the valley is the jumping-off place for many treks in Nepal.

The Jiri Trail is the traditional way to journey to Kala Pathar. It is the route originally taken by Sir Edmund Hillary and his group when they went to Everest. It's a much easier trek now, with trekking lodges, sometimes called teahouses, for accommodation and meals available on the route. Early one morning, I clambered on a bus to Jiri, along with 60 to 80 other passengers, for a bone-jolting 14-hour ride, partly in the bus, partly on top of it. On the bus I met an Australian couple with their young nephew and a Sherpa guide. They invited me to travel with them the next day if I could find a porter-guide. As luck would have it, the nephew of owners of the teahouse or lodge, Prem, had come to the lodge looking for such an opportunity. Prem had hiked this trek once before and, although only 16, was mature and spoke some English. He was an asset on the trip, very helpful with other travellers and in communicating with owners of teahouses. Prem carried my small backpack and sleeping bag, as well as his own, while I just carried my daypack, water and camera and binoculars.

The six of us hiked together for the next nine days from Jiri (2150 m) to Namche Bazaar, the Sherpa capital (3440 m), taking our time to acclimatize to the increasing altitude. We entered Sagarmatha National Park (Sagarmatha is the Nepalese name for Mount Everest) before Namche Bazaar, where hikers were checked in. The vistas were incredible: snow-capped peaks, ice fields and glaciers, forests of rhododendrons, rivers fed by glacial waters, suspension bridges, wondrous blue skies — fantastic photographic opportunities, though these were the days before digital cameras. As we climbed over mountain passes, there was frost in the morning, and in the valleys, flowers bloomed.

One stopover, about midway to Namche Bazaar, was at Taksindhu Cheese Factory, near the Dudh Kosi River. This was a joint project with Switzerland, and we indulged ourselves with cheese raclette and apple brandy. Along the way, we saw Himalayan griffon vultures and the famed lammergeyer, as well as a variety of other birds, but no Yeti. Generally breakfast was chapatti, or porridge, toast, eggs, and salty butter tea or other tea. The water we would carry for the day was boiled with drops of iodine added so that it was safe to drink. Lunches and dinners were generally vegetarian — dal bhat (rice with lentils) and vegetables if available. Sometimes there was cheese, Sherpa stew, apples and tangerines. The higher we hiked, the less variety of food, as past a certain altitude, the food and fuel had to be carried up. We rested in Namche Bazaar for a day. It was critical to have certain "rest" days to help in acclimatizing to the increasing altitude.

From that point, Prem and I continued toward Kala Pathar, while the other four headed off to Goyko, another peak. Along the way, we stopped at Thyangboche monastery (3875 m), an imposing structure with excellent views of Mount Everest and Ama Dablam. The last Sherpa village, Pheriche (4243 m), had a medical clinic manned by a volunteer Canadian physician from Calgary. The clinic also had a compression chamber for use in the event of severe altitude sickness. Another rest day was scheduled in Pheriche.

We met many hikers and shared information. The scenery became more rugged and air thinner as we hiked on. After 4000 metres, the trees dwindled, with dwarf juniper and other alpine scrub up to about 5000 metres, then permanent snow. At Lobuche, 4930 metres, the highest altitude at which we spent a night, I experienced symptoms of altitude sickness — headaches, nausea and insomnia — even after medication. At this point, even Prem was suffering from some altitude sickness.

On December 5, Prem and I left Lobuche just after 7 AM with daypacks for the last part of our uphill climb. The trail led through ice pinnacles. We stopped at Gorak Shep (5160 m) for tea and reached Kala Pathar (5545 m) at about 2 PM. At that point, the air was very thin. I was taking three breaths for each step. It is difficult to express the emotions at reaching this peak. I had a 360-degree panorama. Mount Everest, at 8840 metres, loomed above us. Other peaks of over 8000 metres surrounded us. At my feet was a tiny common rose finch. I had immense feelings of joy and freedom. Perhaps I was light-headed from low oxygen. After an hour, and many photos, we started down.

This hike was over 20 years ago but remains in my mind, permanently, indelibly, my most memorable hike.

The Routeburn Track connects Mount Aspiring National Park with Fiordland National Park.

— Photograph by Martin Horsky

NEW ZEALAND

A Rainy Day on the Routeburn Track

JOHN McCULLAM

The year 2000 saw me and friend Tony, our packs full of clothing, raingear, sleeping bags and food, at the beginning of the Routeburn Track. The Track is on New Zealand's South Island. It had been sunny in Queenstown, but signs of a storm brewing were evident. We tramped for three hours along the Routeburn River, passing the remains of a massive January 1994 landslide and climbing up a very steep hill to the Routeburn Falls 48-bed hut, with its wonderful view of the lush Routeburn Valley. Dinner was pleasant — pasta with fresh vegetables and even wine.

The next day deluges of rain and gale-force winds imprisoned us in our hut until noon, when we went forth again. The path was engulfed in water that was cascading down from above as we climbed steadily over bare rock. After another steep ascent, we reached Lake Harris — serene and visible. The track along the edge of the lake had been blasted from rock. The incessant rain drove us to seek refuge in a shelter, where we could see steam rising from damp bodies and wet socks.

After a quick lunch, we headed out into the steady downpour and continued our climb over more bare rock. The mountain streams were full at this point and were mainly bridged. We were above the bush line, exposed to constant rain. I wore my Gore-Tex jacket and rain pants over my bathing suit, but they did not prevent me from being thoroughly drenched. Just as I began to feel cold and a little in despair, Lake Mackenzie came into view and I noticed tonight's hut in the distance. After a few switchbacks, we reached the warmth of shelter. Dinner was a social affair, reuniting with fellow hikers from the previous night, a mix of ages and nationalities. To bed early, and I dreamt often but actually slept well.

The next two days were mainly free of rain. On the final day, we actually walked over easy terrain in full sun with mountains as a backdrop. But as I was walking, my thoughts were on the challenge that nature had given us three days before. The rain and the rock had made me one with my surroundings. In the sun and on flat ground, I was a mere spectator.

Queen Charlotte Wilderness Park

RUTH NIELSEN

It was in 2004 that my sister Ardra and I took our self-planned trip to New Zealand. There were many opportunities to hike throughout the islands, but the one we chose was the Queen Charlotte Track, as it gave us a three-day break from our touring, and the place looked divine. It is located on a point of land on the northern tip of the South Island, reached by taking a boat out of Picton. We stayed at the lodge in the Queen Charlotte Wilderness Park. The lodge is privately owned and operated by Ron and Gerry Marriot, who state they are "in the business of saving their environment." The lodge was small, with only three rooms, and had the appearance of a Canadian cottage.

We were unable to go out the first day as it was raining rather hard, but instead we enjoyed reading and catching up in our journals. The second day came out, and off we went with a packed lunch prepared by the lodge "woofer" staff.

Young fiddlehead fern. — Photograph by Pyast

The trail to the point was in most part on the crest of the peninsula, with magnificent views out over the sound on the left and right, views of calm seawater and not-to-distant islands in the deep blue.

The plant life, the trees, the butterflies, the views were a treat to behold, but then we came to a clearing and, lo and behold, there were a few horses and some cattle. We had been told about them but did not expect to see them. Farming was unprofitable in the region, and these animals were living freely as the last survivors. Getting them off the point would be very difficult and considered too costly. On the Bruce Trail, we try to avoid being in the same field as animals, as no one can surmise their intentions.

I first saw the horses and whistled to attract their attention. Not a good idea, as this also attracted a bull, which I had not seen as it was on lower ground, thank goodness, and behind some shrubbery. He had a harem to protect, and our presence was not welcome. I give my sister many opportunities to laugh at me and my expressions on our trip, and this occasion was one of them. As mentioned, we were on higher ground, but to continue on our path would have brought us level with this big black bull, so our trek was cut short. We have pictures of this fellow and also of the trail that leads on to the point, which looked wonderful but will only be travelled in our imaginations, as who knows what this bull would have done had we got closer.

It was again a delightful hike back, with our gorgeous views now in the opposite direction. Our fellow guests had a few good laughs at our expense when told of our encounter with the "wildlife."

Hiking the Milford Track

NINA CARLISLE

Come with me to New Zealand, land of the long, white cloud, and travel to Fiordland, in the southwestern tip of the South Island, and from there to the Milford Track.

Fiordland is in the latitude of the Roaring Forties. High winds, snow and drenching rain can occur at any time of the year. Constant effort is needed to repair and rebuild bridges, boardwalks and huts after storm damage. However, as I was about to find out, there are days of idyllic weather.

The Track, 53.5 kilometres (33.5 miles) in length, was blazed by Quintin Mackinnon, accompanied by Ernest Mitchell, and was completed in 1888. It stretches from Glade House Wharf, at the head of Lake Te Anau, through the U-shaped valley of the Clinton River, over the 1154-metre saddle of the MacKinnon Pass, and down the valley of the Arthur River to Sandfly Point on Milford Sound. It follows closely along the route taken in the early days by the Maoris in their search for greenstone, or jade, as it is more commonly known.

By the end of the 1899 season, 100 people had completed the Track. That number has now grown to around 14,000 annually. During the booking season (October to April), numbers are strictly controlled, and the four-day walk may be undertaken in only one direction, from Glade House Wharf to Sandfly Point. At other times of the year, it may be travelled in either direction, but extreme weather conditions pose great hazards and avalanche risk is high. Fifty avalanche paths cross directly over the Track.

After a three-hour coach journey from Queenstown, we arrived at Te Anau Downs in time to board the motor launch for the one-hour trip across the lake to Glade House Wharf, where we disembarked and began our walk along the well-worn Track through mature beech woods to Glade House.

A warm welcome awaited us from the staff at Glade House. After introductions all around, nourishing food and a detailed briefing for Day 2, we retired early. Our bunkroom housed four people. I made a mental note to buy earplugs at the camp store before setting out next day. After breakfast, we posed for the customary group portrait and then were on our way.

A few metres from Glade House, the Track crosses the glacier-fed Clinton River via a swing bridge. Partway across, I looked down into the crystal-clear water and was startled to see a 6-foot-long black eel.

For the first few kilometres, the Track through the beech forest is flat, and then it begins a gentle climb into the west branch of the Clinton Valley. The U-shaped valley, with its with sheer rock walls rising up to 4,000 feet, was carved out by glaciers during the last ice age. Early pioneers referred to the place as the Valley of the Perpendicular.

At Hirere Falls shelter, about three hours from our starting point at Glade House, the guides had soup and hot drinks ready for lunch. And there we met Charlie the kea! Keas are wild parrots and are found only in the southwestern part of the South Island. They are intelligent, mischievous and destructive. They love to chew on windscreen wiper blades, undo zippers on backpacks, and steal sandwiches.

Shortly after returning to the Track, a clearing in the forest provided a view of the McKinnon Pass — our major challenge for Day 3.

By mid-afternoon I reached "the Prairies" — a flat, open stretch of land — only to find the Track underwater. I had built up a head of steam after lunch in an attempt to make a quick transit through areas warning of the dangers of avalanche and, apart from the brief lunch stop at Hirere lunch shelter, had not seen a guide or any member of our group on the track. The water was up to my knees, but the path

One hiker mused that travelling to New Zealand and missing the Milford Track is like travelling to Paris and missing the Eiffel Tower. — Photograph by mundoview

was firm underfoot and the yellow marker posts guided the way. I had no option but to continue on alone, eventually reaching higher ground at the "Bus Stop," a shelter in case of severe flooding.

Shortly afterwards, Pompolona Lodge came into view. Mutton-fat candles are listed among the ingredients in the recipe for the famous Pompolona scones, but they were not on the menu. That night, there were only two in our bunkroom, and I had my earplugs!

Shortly after daybreak, the lights came on, jolting us awake. This was the day to which all us had looked forward — up and over the MacKinnon Pass. Within an hour, we were on our way. For the third consecutive day, the weather was fine for the start of the walk.

From Pompolona Lodge, the Track climbs gradually over scrubland through the Clinton Canyon to Lake Mintaro. The St. Quintin Falls can be seen on the right and Mt. Balloon (1853 m) and Mt. Hart (1782 m), the sentinels of the pass, come into view. The Track again crosses the Clinton River via a swing bridge and at this point begins the ascent to the top of the MacKinnon Pass.

I started out from the valley floor at a steady pace and began the ascent on the nine zigzags, pausing frequently to rest and look back towards the Clinton Valley, where we had walked the previous two days.

The Mount Cook lilies were in bloom. These beautiful white flowers, actually the largest species of the buttercup family, covered the mountainsides.

As the Track climbed towards the top of the pass, the mists came down and the wind started to pick up. By the time I reached the cairn built in memory of Quintin MacKinnon, I was battling gale-force winds and driving rain. At the base of the cairn, one of the guides dispensed hot chocolate from Thermos flasks that she had carried from Pompolona Lodge. The hot, sweet drink gave the shot of energy needed for the half-hour walk to Pass Hut.

The history of the building, destruction and rebuilding of Pass Hut is a tale of the weather conditions experienced in this area. The hut was first built in 1927 as a lunch stop and shelter. It was blown down twice between 1928 and 1947. Ten years later, rebuilding began, and a new hut was finished in 1958. In 1969, the hut was again demolished by high winds and was replaced by an A-frame, which survived until 1982–83, when it was replaced by the present building.

I was beginning to flag when Pass Hut came into view through the low cloud. Nothing could have been more welcome than the hot soup the guides had prepared. It worked wonders to restore energy, and after a short rest I was on my way again.

From Pass Hut to Quintin Lodge, the Track descends 870 metres (2,854 ft) in under 6 kilometres (4 miles). It is by far the toughest part of the four-day walk. One stumble on the slippery rocks could cause serious injury.

For much of the way, the Track follows the course of the Roaring Burn stream. The river's torrential glacial-fed waters cascade through narrow gullies and create incredibly beautiful waterfalls and rapids. In the 1996–97 season, safety on the walkway was greatly improved by the construction of a series of metal stairways and lookout platforms.

At the end of the day's walk, the Track passes over the Roaring Burn on a swing bridge and leads on to Quintin Lodge.

As I entered the hut, I noticed a seriously distressed, obviously unplayable, upright piano. Many years ago, so the story goes, the custodian of the lodge bought the piano for his wife to ease her loneliness. The instrument was transported from Milford Sound on a set of moveable railway lines, 13.5 miles up the Arthur Valley to Quintin Lodge. Considering its dilapidated state, I wondered whether perhaps the piano had accidentally derailed a few times en route.

There was great elation that night. All of us had completed the toughest day and arrived unscathed.

In a guest book dating back some years, I was delighted to find the names of Eric and Sally Kennedy. Eric had served as president of the Bruce Trail Association during the 1970s.

Our gear had dried out overnight, and we set out early next morning in fine weather for the final stage of our journey. I was feeling the effects of the previous day's walk.

Shortly after leaving the lodge, the top two sections of the Sutherland Falls come into view. Discovered by Donald Sutherland in 1880, the falls descend in three stages totalling 580 metres (approx. 1,900 ft) and are the fifth highest in the world.

The Track follows the raging waters of the Arthur River down Gentle Annie, a misnomer at this point, and after two hours reaches the Boatshed Shelter — a stop for morning tea.

My memories of the next several miles are of rushing water and precarious swing bridges. I vaguely remember seeing MacKay Falls and the fabled Bell Rock. I am sure I paused beside beautiful Lake Ada. I know I hesitated before crossing the rickety swing bridge at Giant's Gate Falls and wondered whether the structure could withstand the weight of just one more walker. I was bone-weary, and the walk had become a slog.

It was not until I was making my way through the lush rainforest that grows in the lower Arthur Valley and was suddenly startled by the sound of a weka scuttling away from the Track and into the bush that I was brought back to an awareness of the beauty of my surroundings. Huge tree ferns grew beside the path, wild parrots circled overhead, and I could hear the call of wood pigeons.

I reached mile 33.5 at Sandfly Point by mid-afternoon. The official trail sign, decorated with boots in various stages of dilapidation, is the backdrop for thousands of photographs. I managed a weak smile for the official photographer.

The last part of the journey is a 20-minute crossing by motor launch from Sandfly Point to the boat terminal at Milford Sound.

A beautiful mural at the terminal bears a message in the language of the Maori people: *Toitu He Kainga: Whatungarongaro He Tangata*. In translation: Long after people have disappeared the land will remain!